Beefsteak Raid

Ghost Ship of the Confederacy
Sea Devil of the Confederacy

BEEFSTEAK RAID

Edward Boykin

FUNK & WAGNALLS COMPANY · NEW YORK

1

To a Soldier

SAMUEL VENABLE BOYKIN

27th Div. AEF 1917-1919
DSC
9th Air Force 1941-1945
BS

Contents

NOTES AND ACKNOWLEDGMENTS, BIBLIOGRAPHY, and INDEX will be found following page 286.

ROUTE OF HAMPTON'S BEEFSTEAK RAID

1. Sycamore Church, where Hampton's men struck the First District of Columbia Cavalry at dawn on September 16, 1864, and destroyed it.

2. Grant's great corral on the edge of the James River.

3. Ebenezer Church, where the Federals fought desperately to cut off Hampton's return with the cattle.

4. Cook's Bridge over the Blackwater. It had been destroyed by Federals, and Hampton had to rebuild it while en route to capture the cattle.

5. Here Hampton sent the captured herd further south, realizing that the Federals were speeding down the Jerusalem plank road to cut off his retreat.

6. From about this point on the Boydton plank road, Hampton's raiders set out before dawn on September 14, 1864.

7. City Point, at the junction of the James and Appomattox Rivers, where Grant established his vast base of operations against Petersburg and Richmond.

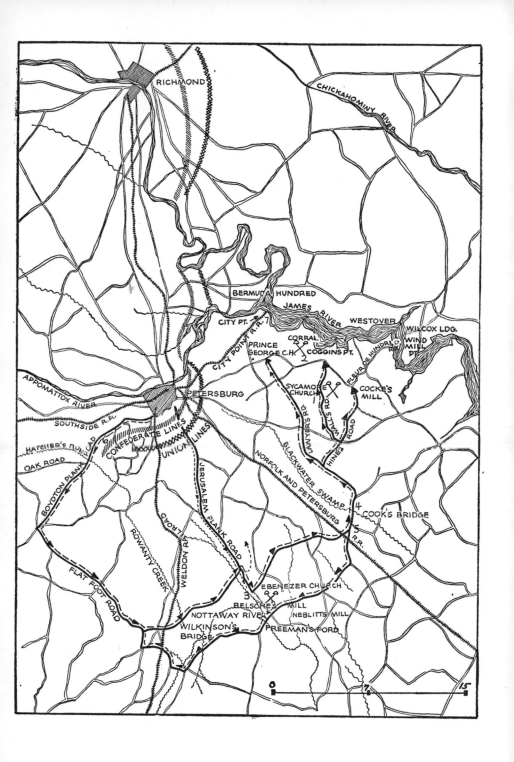

PART I

Backdrop

A Cow Named Mildred

The little old lady wore a calico dress a trifle too short for her. Her sleeves were rolled up; her sunbonnet was slightly battered. She had strolled over from her weather-beaten farmhouse near Quarles Mill on the North Anna River to have a chat with the generalissimo of the Union armies.

It was nearing sundown, May 25, 1864. Ulysses Grant was seated on a camp chair outside his headquarters tent, puffing a cigar and gazing across the Virginia countryside. Firing on the front had died down. Lee had intrenched his graybacks in an almost impregnable position south of the river. Grant was facing another stern roadblock in his bloody trek towards the James.

Brushing past several aides who sought to interpose, the chirpy visitor strutted boldly up to Grant. "Howdy do!" she began, her gray eyes twinkling.

Grant rose and bowed with some dignity. "Howdy, madam!"

"I believe you command all these Yankees that have come down here cavortin' all over the place."

"I have that honor," admitted Grant with a trace of a smile.

His visitor continued, "I'm powerful glad Gen'l Lee been licking you all. Now he's got you jest where he wants you."

Amused, Grant offered her a camp chair. Getting more neighborly she went on, "Afore long Lee'll be chasing you all back up through Pennsylvania. Was you up there last summer when he got after you all?"

Grant replied that he was elsewhere at the time. "I had business in another direction," he explained, though he failed to say he was somewhat occupied at Vicksburg. Staff Colonel Horace Porter said Grant had a hard time keeping his face straight but Porter left untold the rest of a good story.

"I hear you got some cattle with you," observed the lady, eyeing the general closely.

"I have a few," said Grant.

"How many you got?" she inquired sharply, squinting at him.

"Well, let's see. We started off with about five thousand. . . ."

"Five thousand!" she gasped. "Whew! How many of 'em are cows?"

"We don't have much use for cows."

"What do you do with all them he-cattle?"

Grant gazed directly at her. "We eat 'em."

"That's a powerful lot of beef."

"Yes, ma'am, it is, but I've got a powerful lot of boys to eat it," assured Grant.

"That you have. Looks like some of 'em done snook into my barn last night and stole my cow. Maybe they'll eat her, too. Her name's Mildred, best cow in Caroline County."

"She may have strayed," ventured Grant defensively.

"She ain't strayed," asserted the old lady. "Somebody stole her."

"Well, if we find her, madam, we'll send her back to you," said Grant, rising.

Horace Porter failed to state that the old lady's cow mysteriously eloped with the supreme commander's mess when Grant moved by the left flank towards Cold Harbor. Indeed, Mildred occupied the exalted status of milkbar for the general-in-chief's menage until she came to the bridge that Grant built. Then. . . .

The Bridge

At midnight June 14, 1864, Grant's *Grande Armée* in blue began crossing the James River on the longest pontoon bridge the world had seen since Xerxes threw his boatway across the Hellespont to invade Greece twenty-odd centuries ago.

Overhead the splendor of the moon transfigured Virginia's historic river into a broad mirror that reflected dimly the surge, the ceaseless flow of Grant's blue host. Tipped with moonlight, their thousands of gun-barrels gleamed like white jewels in the night. The grandeur of it all was spellbinding. If nothing else, it would leave a picture etched on the memories of those who saw it. The boys who walked on the silver river that night would remember it for the rest of their lives though for hundreds of foot-sloggers in the ranks the "rest" would not be long.

The impact of this narrow overpass on American history transcends the snatch of the Remagen Bridge over the Rhine in World War II, a feat Winston Churchill labeled "the greatest fortune of war that fell into our hands." For there was no bridge to fall into Grant's hands. He had no such blind luck. He had to build one. Had he not made his dramatic crossing of the James when he did (a river as wide and deep as the Danube at Vienna), or flirted with disaster while so doing, there might have been no United States of America to fight in this last global conflict.

Yet Grant's epic Operation James has been played down, possibly obscured by the appalling blood-letting that preceded it or by other aspects of his perilous, fifty-mile sneak-play around Lee's right. The goal was Petersburg, military gateway to Richmond and hub of the chief railroads that fed rebeldom's capital and Lee's army— and, at the moment, dangling defenseless as a ripe plum. Grant crossed this historic barrier within striking distance of an alert, aggressive enemy, Robert E. Lee, the greatest chance-taker in the business, who packed a knockout wallop in either hand.

Built in seven hours, the bridge was the logistic wonder of the war. Late in the afternoon of June 13, Grant's leading echelons began arriving at Wilcox Landing, bridgehead-soon-to-be, on the north bank of the James below Westover. They found swarms of pioneers hacking a corridor through a grove of cypress and sycamore across a broad marsh to the river's edge. By midnight thousands of soldiers had bivouacked on the fields overlooking the James and the meadows running back from it.

The blades of two hundred axemen flashed bright in the last rays of the sun. The forest kings had to be cut level with the morass, then sized into twenty-foot logs. All through the night the men labored under the flicker of lightwood knots and a milk-white moon. The humid darkness reeked with mosquitoes, while fireflies by thousands streaked through the gloom like tiny comets.

By dawn they had hewn five thousand logs, rafting three thousand of them half a mile across the river to Windmill Point where the south bridgehead was taking shape. Sun-up found them corduroying the north causeway to the river. From the scene, Assistant Secretary of War Charles A. Dana flashed his chief at Washington, "It is a pretty heavy job to corduroy a marsh which is fully half a mile wide and quite deep." All day under a sun that burned like a fiery furnace, the blue roadbuilders clung to their task, working knee-deep in the black muck, paving the way to the north bridgehead with logs.

Not until 4 P.M., June 14, did Henry Benham's engineer brigade actually begin building the bridge. Pontoon rafts, planking, lashings and hooks, towed up from Fort Monroe overnight, were waiting on barges anchored just off shore. The afternoon sun was gilding the waters when the blue pontoniers took over. Working from both ends, they had slapped the last plank in place by eleven that night. Twenty-one hundred feet long, thirteen wide, this boatway spanned a swift current eighty feet deep with a tidefall of four. The boards were lashed to one hundred and one pontoons that looked scarcely capable of supporting the weight of a single trooper and his mount. To give it greater stability three big schooners were double-anchored in midstream above the bridge with cables running to the midsection.

In the postwar dispensation of laurels, bridgeman Benham received scant praise though the Official Records, depicting the hour-by-hour scenes in this bold drama, bear witness to his zeal. Yet his name rings no bell for the average American. An able operator, Benham graduated first in his class at West Point in 1837. This had auto-

matically cast him with the Engineer Corps though he
began the war as a captain of infantry under McClellan
in West Virginia. There he had acquired luster as killer
of the first general officer slain in the war, Confederate
Robert Garnett, who fell skirmishing with Benham's
company at Carrick's Ford on the Cheat River. Switching
back to his native element he threw at least nine pontoon
bridges across the Rappahannock in Hooker's futile en-
deavors to outmaneuver Lee and Jackson.

Charged with bridging the James in a hurry Benham
had promised, "I shall not sleep till the bridge is laid."
Nor did he. His report had a classic quality:

> For the next forty hours a continuous stream of wag-
> ons passed over the bridge (from 4000 to 6000 wagons)
> —some said fifty miles of wagons—and nearly all the
> artillery of this army, and by far the greater portion of
> the infantry and all its cavalry present and even to its
> head of 5000 or more beef cattle (the most injurious of
> all) without accident to man or beast.
>
> My officers and men were scarcely allowed any sleep
> during these hours nor myself even as much as four
> hours; for it was in anxiety, not to say trembling, that I
> saw the destinies of this whole army of our country
> committed to this single frail foot bridge, with steamers
> and other vessels drifting against it, and with much of
> its planking previously worn almost entirely through.
>
> This bridge, besides some 200 feet of trestle work,
> was, for over 2000 feet on pontoons, and for the greater
> part of the distance in deep water—in some parts up to
> 85 feet, with a very strong current running; and it trans-
> ported nearly all the material, artillery and trains, with
> the greater portion of the men of this large army.
>
> You may be sure I was very well content and satisfied

and felt like "him that putteth off his armor" when it was over.

The broad waterway over which Grant's bluecoats tramped for hours on end flowed through a land splashed with the history of Virginia's heroic age. It reeked with legends of those who founded free government in America. Just above the bridge, Westover's lovely façade peered through its proscenium of spring greens. It was a show-place then, as it is now, home of the colonial grandee William Byrd. According to local legend, Byrd's daughter Evelyn, dead of a broken heart, rose nightly from her sleep in the garden to gaze imploringly downriver for the lover who had sailed away never to come back. McClellan had headquartered at Westover when he stormed up the peninsula in 1862 to the threshold of Richmond, only to be foiled by the man now swapping pawns with Grant in the deadliest chess game of all. Scars of Little Mac's occupancy were yet fresh.

Facing the wide waters of Harrison's Bar rose the plantation house, Berkeley, cradle of the Harrisons and ancestral backdrop of two presidents. Near Wilcox Landing, Grant's strawfoots ducked past Sherwood Forest, home of late ex-President Tyler. Upriver, beyond Berkeley, stood the Forest where Thomas Jefferson courted Martha Wayles with music and philosophy and bore her off to become the first mistress of Monticello.

Across the shining waters, in the upstream distance, was Jordan's Point, named for a member of the first free legislative assembly in America. Directly across from Wilcox Landing, near the south bridgehead on Windmill Point, was Fleur de Hundred, patented by Sir George Yeardley in 1619 and melodiously named for his wife.

Here he built the first windmill in America from which the point derived its name.

On beyond Jordan's Point, on a southside bluff jutting into the wide swirl where the James and Appomattox mingled their yellow flows, a riverside village, City Point, had suddenly awakened from reveries of the past to find itself logistic hub of a great civil war. Overnight it would be converted into a seaport with a mile of wharves, the vast bustling base of operations of the "Armies Operating against Richmond" and Petersburg eight miles away. Here, singularly enough, Grant would set up headquarters in the yard of the old Eppes house that bore a prophetic name, Appomattox. By the irony of war, around the first "curle" in the James after leaving City Point, stood Shirley, girlhood home of the mother of Grant's vigilant antagonist.

To General Meade's scientist aide, Theodore Lyman, the James brought pleasing reminders "of Narragansett Bay going to Newport" though Lyman had yet to glimpse the tortuous loops and "curles" of the stream from City Point up to the falls, thirty miles, where Richmond sat on her seven hills. As the crow flies it was half that far. Gray batteries swept downstream at every bend. By the way were sandbars and muddy islands that gurgled up and vanished with the turbid spring freshets. The river was fringed with swamps and bayous masked by massive tangles of wild vines. Towering above the morasses were monumental cypresses that were ancient when the English gained the first permanent foothold in the New World in 1607.

Over Benham's narrow bridge, in forty-eight hours, Grant passed his thousands of fighting men; his incredible impedimenta; his sixty-mile train of white-topped wagons laden with forage, dry rations and ammunition; his five thousand dogies that strung out nine miles from head to drag. A lone casualty marred Grant's passage of the James—the headquarters cow, Mildred, whose Confederate leanings may have led her to desert her new-found friends at this crucial juncture. Her departure inspired Grant to a bit of humor, "It seems as if the loss of animals at this moment falls most heavily on the headquarters mess."

But Grant's confidence was on the upswing. Gory Cold Harbor was receding like a bad, bloody dream. In record time after reaching Wilcox Landing, his field telegraph was hooked onto the flimsy wire that skirted the James down to Fort Monroe and thence, roundabout, up Virginia's Eastern Shore to Washington. Calling for his manifold order book he scribbled a hasty message to the Chief of Staff. His cipher operator, Samuel H. Beckwith, clicked it off to the capital on the spot.

> June 14, 1864—1:30 P.M.
> Our forces will commence crossing the James today. The enemy shows no sign yet of having brought troops to the south side of Richmond. I will have Petersburg secured, if possible, before they get there in force. Our movement from Cold Harbor to the James River has been made with great celerity and so far without loss or accident.

Lincoln himself replied. "Have just read your despatch of 1:30 yesterday. I begin to see it. You will succeed. God bless you all."

But it is doubtful if even Lincoln envisioned any such kaleidoscopic spectacle as that enacted on the watery amphitheater of the James. Nature herself had beautified

the setting in vivid spring greens. Sunrise June 15 revealed Grant's magnificent array like the unfolding of a
many-scened drama, "moving rapidly, swiftly over the
low, level floating bridge in grand procession and all
seemed to be, as it were, down on the very surface of the
water itself."

For two days a dazzling June sun glinted on the burn-
ished gunbarrels and bayonets of the serried ranks slogging across the planking—danced on teeming batteries of
brass cannon whose big iron-rimmed wheels pounded bru-
tally on the complaining boards, rumbling like distant
thunder. It flashed dully on the clanking sabers and
clinking spurs of a horde of horse soldiers who clattered
across the bridge like ten thousand snare drums beating
all at once. It glistened on an unending ribbon of white-
covered wagons each drawn by six or four mules straining
at their heavy burdens. It brightened up the once-gay colors
of hundreds of powder-stained, battle-scarred war-banners.

Posted at the bridgeheads, regimental bands blared out
sprightly airs and stirring quicksteps, and (of all things!)
"Dixie," too. But why not? That's where they were going
—deep into the heart of Dixie itself. The musicians of the
114th Pennsylvania Zouaves tootled "Nelly Bly" unceas-
ingly as if it were the only tune in their repertory.

From the north came sporadic obligatos—bursts of musketry, salvos of artillery. Warren's Fifth Corps, last to
pull out of the Cold Harbor lines, after masking the
movements of the rest of the army, was pushing for Wilcox Landing leaving Wilson's cavalry to beat off rebel
horsemen who turned their attentions to the ponderous
wagon train that cluttered the narrow roads south to the
river. Out of shadowy thickets these gray whippets would
dash along the line of wagons firing at teamsters, plugging
holes in squealing mules and horses or setting fire to wag-

ons whose canvas covers flamed like tinder. To pile terror
on confusion they would gallop off to take a crack at the
frightened cattle herd, or rustle out a few head of beef.
Once at an eerie hour before daybreak, they struck at the
vast park of the wagon trains while the bullwhackers were
still rubbing sleep out of their eyes. They fired huge heaps
of breakfast hay which the animals were munching and
generally played hell until blue cavalry drove them off.

The surface of the James resembled a naval jigsaw
puzzle. Yankee gunboats watchdogged above and below
the bridge. Several tough Confederate warships still hovered just below Richmond. Only one need sneak down to
convert Grant's pontoon promenade into a repetition of
Napoleon's crossing of the Beresina on his retreat from
Moscow.

Half a dozen double-ender New York ferries were shut-
tling back and forth, fetching Hancock's Second Corps
across to Windmill Point. Grant had ordered Hancock,
who had reached the landing late June 13, not to wait for
the bridge to be finished, but to cross his corps by boat and
drive for Petersburg as fast as heat and human feet would
permit.

Garnishing the stupendous pageant with a victory touch
was the former Confederate ironclad *Atlanta*, recently
captured near Savannah, dozing in midstream like a big
mud turtle. The whoops of Grant's unkempt, unshaven,
sweaty veterans vied with the cheers of the sailors in natty
whites that looked as if they'd never known what dust
was. To Grant's dust-caked legionnaires, the clean decks,
the white awnings gleaming in the sun, the spotless, holy-
stoned decks were tremendously inviting. Meade's staff-
man, Theodore Lyman, found it "funny to run against the
marine in this inland region, and to see the naval officers

all so smug and well brushed in their clean uniforms. How sailorlike they look, with their blue shirts and flat caps! And our poor infantry, artillery and cavalry! Why, the more they serve, the less they look like soldiers and the more they resemble day laborers who have bought second-hand military clothes. I have so come to associate good troops with dusty, faded suits that I look with suspicion on anyone who has a stray bit of lace or other martial finery."

Nor was Lyman alone in his sentiments. The men in the ranks were already chuckling raillery and ribald wise-cracks at their naval companions in arms: "Where'd you get them fancy duds?" "Don't let Grant catch you in them white things." Back came "Go to hell and get yourself a haircut!" and certain unprintable suggestions of which the naval boys had a bountiful supply.

But it was a day to be remembered for the rank and file. Here was the broad river flowing as placidly as if it were denying its role in the bloody game of you-kill-me or I'll-kill-you. Spirits zoomed at sight of it. Morale soared for many a battle-weary, bronzed fighter who had this morning trudged doggedly along the stifling road through pine and scrub oak, suddenly to emerge and find himself facing a majestic river whose high green banks were studded with plantation manors and ripe with harvests whence the harvesters had fled.

Cold Harbor had shaken the morale of these well-disciplined soldiers. They had hurled themselves against Lee's breastworks without a quiver until their valor was quenched in blood. Behind them, all the way back to the Rapidan stretched a swath of graves rudely marked by crackerbox "headstones" and shallow pits where brave men were shoveled under like so much carrion. From

Spottsylvania, Rufus Ingalls had written a friend in Washington, "The world never heard of war before." Fifth Corps Commander Gouveneur K. Warren pointed up the carnage more tragically, "For thirty days now it has been one funeral procession past me; and it is too much!"

But here was the river they had talked of by campfires and sunlight—the river that had haunted their dreams under the open sky. It seemed incredible that they had reached it. What if it meant the last long mile for thousands of them! Jubilation raced through the ranks. Far different from the crackdown on even a word two nights ago when they slid out of the Cold Harbor lines in unbelievable silence under the keen ears of Lee's tigerish fighters. For hundreds of unwashed veterans in sun-bleached uniforms it was something to hooray about—and they did—as they swung in an irresistible tide down the sloping corduroy to the bridge that swayed under their heavy tread.

An irrepressible wag with a Yankee twang bubbled over

> *Roll, Jordan, roll!*
> *I wanter go to heaven when I die*
> *Just to see old Jordan roll.*

But a color bearer protested, "It ain't the Jordan! It's the Jeems!"

Jeems or James, it was one wide river to cross to victory. What lay south of it they knew not, nor did they seem to care on this brilliant June day. Grant knew and that was enough. Perhaps he was sidling to Richmond. At least they were observing dead Phil Kearny's battle maxim: Go in gaily.

Picturesquely a slogger in the 13th New Hampshire In-

fantry described this "last grand review of the war for
many a poor fellow on the Union side":

All day long, and in the hours of the night, the
bridge, nearly half a mile in length, is full—an unceasing tramp, no break in the column; but steadily, speedily, the great host forges on, as if every organization in
it were a huge link in some immense drawing chain,
that the God of War was now sweeping irresistibly into
place as an impregnable cordon around the . . . Confederacy. Squadron after squadron, regiment after regiment, brigade after brigade, division after division,
battery after battery, train after train, corps after corps
—each with all the appliances, ensigns, flags, arms, paraphernalia and material of real and tremendous war:
all lines and files in perfect order, place and time, moving under the control of the master mind of that one
greatest of American men and captains—Lieut.-Gen.
Ulysses S. Grant. . . . Constantly, for hour upon hour,
appears this unbroken stream of men, bursting into full
and sudden view from an unseen source in the dense
woods on the northern shore, entering low down upon
the bridge, crossing with quick route-step the wide level
to the southern shore, ascending the river bank and instantly disappearing as they came, we cannot see
whither; apparently inexhaustible in numbers and in-
vincible in power. . . .

For two days men in blue flooded all roads leading to
the spot known as Wilcox Landing, suddenly projected
into the fierce limelight of war. Swinging past Sherwood
Forest, plantation home of late President John Tyler a
mile or so back from the landing, grimy, sunburned
Northern boys whooped out "Tippecanoe and Tyler too!"
as if the boisterous campaign slogan could arouse the dead

president sleeping in the garden with his old horse, the General, buried hard by his master.

Standing at the front gate, three of Tyler's teenage children retorted by waving southern flags and singing out "Dixie" and "The Bonnie Blue Flag." At first the soldiers replied with good-natured joshing, but this soon wore off to sullen silence and hard looks. Presently a Yankee officer reined his horse at the roadside to offer a bit of fatherly advice.

"Young folks, I admire your spirit, but I suggest you stop singing Dixie. Some of my men don't like it. I can't be responsible for what they might say or do. Why not sing 'The Battle Cry of Freedom'?"

But the Tylers said no. Piping "Dixie" at the top of their lungs they withdrew to the big mansion where John Tyler's lovely Northern-born widow, Julia Gardiner Tyler, sat wondering what fate awaited the home of a former President of the United States.

On this morning of June 15, Grant stood in profound silence on a hillock overlooking the north bridgehead, gazing raptly on the momentous spectacle directly below him. He had tossed his cigar aside. His hands were clasped behind him. His trousers were stuck in muddy, knee-high boots. On his head was the plain slouch hat he donned the day he mounted Cincinnatti and crossed the Rapidan at Germanna Ford. Two shoulder straps were the only visible symbols of his generalissimo rank.

Whatever his emotions, if any, there was no manifestation of them. His aide Horace Porter, standing nearby, wondered whether "his mind was occupied with the magnitude and success of what he saw." Or could he be thinking of the 54,926 dead, wounded and missing he had left behind? Had Grant possessed the emotional capacities of Napoleon he might have exclaimed, as did the French emperor watching his troops file past on the way to Waterloo, "Magnifique! Magnifique!"

Drawn irresistibly to the scene as to a circus parade, Confederate small fry came from miles around. Awestruck, these youngsters stood silently gazing at the man whom their elders were denouncing as a modern Attila. Presently, as Grant turned and called for his horse, his eye caught sight of the boys. A quick smile crossed his bearded face. Out came a cheery "Hello, boys!" That was all.

But the strawfoots had already sighted the lone figure on the hilltop.

"If that ain't old Grant himself! He ain't dressed up neither. And no segar!"

Word sped along the column that the man who had led them from the Rapidan to the James was watching them file down the causeway to the bridge. Wild cheers swept out over the river. Hundreds waved their sweaty caps or held their muskets aloft. It was an ovation like that by the men of the Second Corps the night Grant turned the army towards Spottsylvania. Grant, the undemonstrative, gave a single sign of recognition. His hand rose in a long salute.

Today Grant stood at the summit. He *was* the summit. In his hands he held greater military power than ever the nation had bestowed on any soldier. There were no Joint Chiefs of Staff to paw over, dissect and grudgingly consent to his plans. D-day on the Rapidan was his decision alone. And the same applied to S-day (S for slaughter) at Cold Harbor. Operation James took shape the night of June 6 when Grant secretly despatched two aides to select the best point for crossing the James. He took upon himself, without consulting higher-ups, the risky, fifty-mile sideswing to nip off Petersburg, the ripe plum. Beauregard was there, to be sure, but with hardly a corporal's guard to beat off a blue attack in force. If he could get there before Lee, the war might wind up in a quick flash.

Lincoln had said, "You have entire charge of the armies. I do not wish to know your plans." Grant felt that the "Potomac army had never been thoroughly fought." It was still a superb fighting machine. He would make it even better.

George Meade's resounding title "Major General, Commanding the Army of the Potomac" was empty as a gourd. Meade became an order-taker the day Grant took over. Washington gossipers put it this way, "The Army of the Potomac is directed by Grant, commanded by Meade and led by Hancock, Sedgwick and Warren." However, these three splendid corps commanders were to vanish from the scene—Sedgwick by a sharpshooter's bullet; Hancock by old wounds; Warren by failure at Five Forks. Meade would cling to his anomalous job until Appomattox.

"I've Got a Boss Named Grant"

Grant's vast wagon train was—to Charles A. Dana—the "wonder of wonders," a smash-hit moving picture that all but defied his vivid, accurate pen. From the north bridgehead he again wired Washington, "All goes like a miracle. Lee appears to have had no idea of our crossing the James River. The great wagon train will all be over the bridge by daylight tomorrow. I must say here that the unprecedented pontoon bridge, nearly 700 yards long, is of admirable solidity."

But Dana's prediction went awry by many hours. Now it was June 17, 1864. The humid afternoon dragged on. So did the trains. The fiery ball of the sun had dyed the river copper red before the last of the wagons—the interminable caravan that according to Grant would, if laid in a straight line, stretch from the Rapidan to Richmond and half way back again—lumbered across the corduroyed chute and onto the bridge. On the high verdant banks appeared masses of blue cavalry that had safeguarded the long zigzag haul to the river of the fighting man's dreams.

Genius itself had directed the wagon train in the person of Colonel Rufus Ingalls. Grant handed out bouquets sparingly, but for Ingalls, his West Point classmate and future QMG of the Armies Operating Against Richmond, Grant pulled out all the stops. "Nothing ever disturbed or excited him. He was ready for every emergency. He could move and feed a hundred thousand men without ruffling his temper. If the command of the Army of the Potomac had ever become vacant, I would have given it to Ingalls."

On the night before the Rapidan crossover—May 3, 1864—Ingalls sat with Grant for a final briefing in the farmhouse headquarters near Culpeper. Orderlies were galloping through the huge encampment with sealed packages—orders for the Army to move at one minute past midnight. Campfires flickered for miles along the river. There were no drumbeats, no bugle calls—only a quiet mustering of troops, a folding of tents and an unending column preparing to swing southwards for Germanna and Ely's Ford.

"I am ready," asserted Ingalls whose wagons crowded roads for miles back from the river. "The trains will move with the army well east of the fighting."

The saga of the hazardous journey of Grant's ponderous wagon trains from the Rapidan to the James lacks the glamor and glow of battle even though they were never beyond the sound of the guns and often, as at Cold Harbor, within the flash of them. The magnitude of Ingalls' achievement gleams through his summary of the wagon trains—"4300 wagons, 825 ambulances, 29,945 artillery, cavalry, ambulance and team horses, 4046 private horses, 22,538 mules, making an aggregate of 56,499 animals."

He failed to mention 5000 wild-eyed, rangy longhorns— the General Cattle Herd—bringing up the rear and ready to stampede at the drop of a hat. The beeves took pace from the trains. If the trains halted, or bushwhackers tried to shoot them up, or a balky mule sat down in the road refusing to budge, or an axle broke, or any of a myriad mishaps came to pass, there were five thousand cattle to keep amused.

This vast locker of beef on the hoof gave a whirlwind finish to Grant's amazing extravaganza on the James. For miles beeves packed and queued along the road. No cattle drive in the West was ever like it. Nor would the Chisholm Trail, yet to come, ever match it. On the James there could be no spread-out plodding along, as on the broad western cattle trails. If contrary animals eloped to munch tempting tufts of grass, they had to be coaxed back into the snaky line. These critters had to be close-hauled along narrow roads, often bottomless and sometimes merely two abandoned ruts that slunk through swamp and wilderness over brown, fever-ridden streams that oozed like dark glue. "Keep 'em moving" through shadowy second-growth pine and tangles of vine where the air was heavy with the smell of decaying leaves and stagnant water and where tornadoes of mosquitoes tormented man and beast.

For the ninety-odd buckaroos—"herders" Grant called them—who coddled the dogies along, grazed and watered them, stung them with bull-whips when they got ornery, bedded them down by night, sang to them when the guns thundered close by, life was hard and dangerous. Jaded but tough as hickory, these men had virtually lived in the saddle since leaving the Rapidan. If guerillas or gray cavalry failed to pick them off, the sharp points of the long-

horns were there to disembowel them in a twinkle. On
history's page they drew a blank. Nor were they called
cowboys in 1864. But label them what you will, that's
what they were. Cattle drivers, drovers, vaqueros, cow-
punchers, cowpokes—the breed was the same. The records
of their service are meager. They were hired hands, not
soldiers.

Recruited mostly beyond the Mississippi, these men
gave the nation its first Wild West show, lacking only the
Indians whose painted faces, blood-curdling yells and sudden swoops were replaced by gray ghosts and rebel raiders
far more adept and deadly in the art of attack and vanish,
whose bag of tricks would have made pale faces out of
redskins. These men out-westerned the "heroes" of the
synthetic Westerns that today flicker across the nation's
television screens with crackling 44's, thundering herds
and well-rehearsed Indians.

A lusty brawling lot, Grant's herders drank hard, cussed
harder and chewed tobacco even in their sleep. On their
highheeled boots they wore big spurs whose musical jingle
made the horse soldiers jealous. No blue jeans for them,
but leather pants instead, and Stetsons too. They brought
the West with them. They carried big Colt six shooters
furnished by the government. Grant's bad boys, they
raised holy hell around the Potomac rendezvous at Belle
Plain before the big drive got going; fought with the
provost guards; and harassed the nearby farmers' wives
and daughters until the grapevine brought threats of retaliation at the end of rope when and if captured.

Grant paid them fifty dollars a month and "board." Big
money, because back west they got only ten. The job had
one drawback: no wenching in Virginia. It was a hardship, but they liked working for Grant. They were living
high on the hock. Perhaps, when Grant got to Richmond

he'd find "gals" for them. But they could handle cattle and that's what Grant wanted them for.

By the time they reached the James they were singing,

> *I've got a boss named Grant*
> *Who drinks his liquor red,*
> *He's headin' on to Richmond*
> *With cannon and with lead.*

> *He ain't no hand at cattle*
> *Though his breeches is stuck in his boots,*
> *But he's got five thousand longhorns*
> *To feed his men who shoots.*

Grant took more than a passing interest in his cowboys and his cattle. He prided himself on his farming bent, feeling as much at home handling cattle as directing armies in the field. During a battle lull in the Wilderness he and two aides pulled their mounts off the road to watch a small drove of beeves being driven off to butchering. The herders were having trouble. Firing was still sharp. The cattle were jumpy. At each roll of musketry they threatened to scatter helter-skelter. Suddenly one of them darted off the road towards Grant and his aides.

"Hey, pardner!" yelled a cowpoke to Grant. "Head off that critter for me, will you?"

Dismounting hurriedly, Grant stepped off the road waving his arms, and shooed the recalcitrant back into the road. He knew the herder had not recognized him.

"I think I'll take up herding after the war," he opined as he swung into his saddle. "It's easier."

On his thunderous overland campaign Grant's legions had devoured beeves by hundreds. In pounds it ran into

baffling figures. Twice the General Cattle Herd was re-
plenished from barges lugged down the Chesapeake and
up to the White House base on York River. Fresh meat
was part of the integrated pattern of victory over Lee's
army. "Beef cattle were driven with the trains and butch-
ered as wanted," said Grant in his memoirs. There would
be no more "dried beef on the hoof" like what he found
when he took over Rosecrans' half-starved army at Chattanooga.

But now the first wave of the milling dogies was tramp-
ing nearer the bridge under a stifling, blinding cloud of
dust churned up by thousands of hooves. Whiffs of James
River water had reached the cattle's distended nostrils.
Their red-rimmed eyes were rolling and the road was
shaking under their stomping feet. On they trudged, bawling and moaning, flecked with foam, mad for water. The
hot dust stuck on their tongues only to drip from their lips
in streams of loose mud.

At the bridgehead orders and counter orders were flying. Couriers and staff officers romped about madly.
Bridgeman Benham himself doubted the wisdom of trust-
ing the cattle to the bridge, or rather, the bridge to the
cattle, "I fear they will not only greatly delay the trains,
but may break the bridge down if allowed to cross." Commissary Captain John Woodward, heading up the General Cattle Herd, dashed up on a lathered horse with in-
sistent orders from General Meade, "The pontoon bridge
is under no circumstances to be used for crossing the cattle." They'll cut the bridge to pieces! Swim them over!
What if five hundred drown? They'll leap into the river
anyway and drown themselves. The western plains are
swarming and the commissaries are buying them by
thousands. Benham took a chance. Let 'em cross the bridge.

Presently they came in sight, a steamy torrent of beef:

longhorns, red cattle, yellow and brown, cattle of every hue nature permits, rounded up in the west or wherever the commissaries could buy them and shipped east by rail and canal. They moved in a tumultuous bedlam of dust, noise, heat, pushing, shoving, rattle of horns, clack-clack of hocks and yi-hoos of cowboys spurring their mustangs to head truants and contrary mossbacks back into line. Just here anything might happen with water on the wind and almost in sight. If the leaders broke and bolted for the high banks in a panic to get to water, God only knew what would happen.

In the van of the turbulent, bellowing stream, paced by the lead steers, rode trail-boss Tom Gentry, as good a cattleman as ever bossed an outfit back in Kansas. "Keep 'em in line! Keep 'em in line!" That's what his boys were doing, darting here, there, dodging horns longer and deadlier than Confederate bayonets. Riding at intervals alongside the restless column were others swinging short-handled bull-whips whose long lashes crackled like pistol shots and stung the soft underbellies like branding irons. If they scattered now, it would take a division of cavalry to round them up. There were nine miles of them and they were picking up speed.

Patiently, as if working a herd into a corral, the punchers wangled the first arrivals down the narrow causeway to the bridge. Frightened by the clatter of their own hooves on the pontoon planking, the leaders balked at the waterside, braced their front legs like pistons only to be swept along by the pressure of the unstoppable, close-packed masses of meat surging from behind. It was move on or be trampled to death by the oncoming thousands. Instinct must have warned them of it. The bell-ox rattled his tocsin and the leaders fell in docilely. It was as simple as that. In five minutes the bridge was alive with them,

their sharp, flinty hooves chopping and gouging the planking like cold chisels. But they were afloat on the swaying
bridge, moving southwards. Three million pounds of beef
on the hoof to feed Grant's boys in blue—and tantalize
the boys in gray!

What now for the bridge, the "engineer's nightmare,"
as some called it? Ungraceful, ungainly, for five days it
had swayed and bobbled under the rock and roll of
Grant's huge war paraphernalia that ground its boards
to splinters. Five days only it served. Then Grant
"burned" his bridge behind him. It was taken up. Averred
a distinguished Southern soldier, "The Confederacy was
lost when Grant crossed the James."

4

"The Yankees Are Coming!"

A frail old man, with long, uncut white locks that brushed his shoulders, sat at a desk. As he wrote, the pen scrawled wearily across the page of his diary. It was May 1865. The Confederacy lay in ashes around him. The blue invader ruled the land. The patriarch's words emerged like poison from the fangs of a dying rattler. He wrote on. His once-gentle eyes burned with bitterness. He closed.

And now with my latest writing and utterance, and what will be soon my latest breath, I hereby repeat and would willingly proclaim my unmitigated hatred to Yankee rule, to all political, social and business connections with Yankees and the perfidious, malignant and vile Yankee race.

The ink was hardly dry on the page before he opened a desk drawer and took out a derringer. He examined it to make sure it was capped and charged. Cocking the weapon, he slowly raised it. A single shot, and Edmund Ruffin, arch-secessionist, prince of haters, was gone. Edmund Ruffin, who fired the first cannon at Fort Sumter and reveled in it—"I was highly gratified by the compliment and delighted to perform the service." Rabid Edmund Ruffin, who had preached secession with a passion as intense as the love and care he lavished on the gently rolling fields and meadows at Beechwood, his home on the James, forty miles below Richmond.

Set on high ground at Coggin's Point, a protrusion from the south shore opposite Westover, Beechwood was no baronial mansion, but a comfortable, compact farmhouse, with lofty ceilings and tall windows that gave glimpses of the rolling river. Terraced walks edged by flowering shrubs and exotic plants ran down to the waterside. Here, in a pastoral paradise of his own nurturing, lived Edmund Ruffin amid his well-tilled acres.

An agricultural magician, Ruffin's fame had spanned two continents. His treatises on agronomy were read by thousands who lived on the soil. Visitors came from afar to marvel at his genius. Fertilizing impoverished fields with powdered shell marl, he had induced the land to flower like the vale of Eden. It was something new. Marl! And it worked. Yonder stretched his broad, lush pastures girdled by live fences of mock-orange and cedar or spliced by split rails into huge corrals where his cattle grazed and fattened on sweeps of blue grass and clover.

But Edmund Ruffin had long since fled Beechwood. In 1862 when McClellan hammered up the peninsula to the outskirts of Richmond, Beechwood, just across the river from the invader's track, got its first dosing of Northern vengeance. Ruffin's name was a goad even to the man in the ranks. Bluecoats had crossed the river to wreak havoc on the place, defacing its walls with tobacco juice and filth. Wrote one across the library mantle, "This house belongs to a Ruffin-ly sonofabitch." Gunners on Yankee warships mousing up the river took potshots at Beechwood, ventilating it with gaping shell holes. Deserted now, the lawns were untrimmed. June roses in the unkempt garden wasted their beauty on the summer airs. Yet war left unscorched the rich fields. When McClellan's blue tide ebbed under Lee's hammer blows Ruffin came home to take a look. Some day, he promised himself, he would begin anew, repair the wounds of war. Meanwhile his fields of clover and blue grass would seed and reseed themselves. By then the Confederacy would have won her fight and he would be living in a free South—or so he thought.

2

Now again Beechwood lay at the mercy of the blue intruders. Had Edmund Ruffin been home this June 15 he might have gazed downriver and seen Grant's hosts pouring across the pontoon bridge four miles below his riverside pastures. Hourly the number of Federal troops reaching the south bank was increasing. By midnight June 16 ninety thousand had crossed.

Streaming off Benham's bridge at Windmill Point, the bluecoats pressed along the Fleur de Hundred road until it struck the old Stage Road where they fanned westward under stifling billows of dust. Twenty miles up ahead lay Petersburg, waiting to be snatched. A faraway booming like distant summer thunder announced that the Eighteenth Corps was already assaulting the eastern redoubts of the Dimmock Line, the so-called impregnable stop-all that crumbled quickly under the first Union blows.

Capture loomed for the principal outwork, such it was, and bulwark of the rebel capital. In the van strode Hancock's Second Corps, twenty-eight thousand men, who had been ferried across. Hancock, the Superb, rode in an ambulance. His old Gettysburg wound had opened afresh but he was hurrying his men through the afternoon inferno. Orders were strict. No leaving ranks to strip red ripe cherry trees. Not much pausing to fill canteens. The road wound past small farms and fields gone to sedge, past weather-stained houses that hadn't felt paint for years, through thickets of sassafras and wild plum. The wind had died. Heat settled down like a hot blanket.

Grant and his staff had commandeered a gunboat at Wilcox Landing to run him up the river to City Point, eight miles from Petersburg where he could speed the attack if it lagged.

The twenty miles to Petersburg, or rather to the outer rim of its vast earthwork defenses, was inundated by infantry, cannon, wagons. At route step—flags cased—the columns marched relentlessly, bearded, dirty, their faded blue powdered with gray dust.

The landscape had a stripped-to-the-bone, hungry look. An air of desolation overhung it. Barn doors gaped, smoke houses stared vacantly, chicken coops stood ajar. On farmhouse porches sat silent graybeards and old women in sunbonnets, many with babies in their arms. Subdued, filled with anxious forebodings, numbed to speechlessness, they stared at the blue deluge as if doubting what their eyes gazed on.

Younger women kept out of sight, peering through closed blinds and slightly open doors. Pinch-faced, frightened children in faded calico shrank closer to their grandsires, gazing wistfully at the procession but smiling no response to the cheery, "Hi, sis!" or "Hello, little girl!" that beamed from the blue passers-by.

Young men were not to be seen save an occasional figure in faded gray minus an arm or a leg, his fighting days over. The conscript dragnet had swept up everything from sixteen to sixty except those who hid in the swamps, but most of the young able-bodied were following Lee. Hardly a family hereabouts that had not felt heartbreak, a son or a husband dead on a battlefield they'd never heard of.

When Grant's hosts suddenly debouched out of the woods on the north bank to leapfrog across the James, a wave of terror swept the southshore countryside. Cows, horses, mules vanished as if by magic, spirited off to hide-outs deep in the swamps. Into big willow baskets went squalling roosters and hens, ducks and turkeys, if they had them, and off to the swamp. Pigs too were quickly bundled away to hidden stys. Household silver, such as they had, was doused into the well or buried hastily. Jars of preserves and vegetables vanished from well-ordered shelves. Kitchens were denuded and became as bare as Mother Hubbard's cupboard. Proprietors of small road-side stores had hurriedly stripped their shelves of their meager wares and carted them off to caches deep in the stub pine thickets. Rickety wagons were piled high with cherished, wornout chattels ready to rattle off to a refuge somewhere. But where? The blue was everywhere. Virginia was being overrun from the mountains to the sea. Even the Valley was being scorched.

The Yankees are coming! Grant, the Butcher, with his blue killers! Lurid, terrifying tales of Yankee ravages below the Rapidan had raced ahead of him. Looting was on the rampage. Foraging they called it. Visions of rapine, burned homes and plundering rose before the eyes of these farmfolks as they watched the blue columns hiking along through clouds of opaque dust.

Circling in the hot caldron of the sky overhead were buzzards by the hundreds. They had followed the army's stinking swath, feasting on dead men and animals. Never before was such a repast spread for them. Now they, too, had crossed the James.

Even the "houn' dawgs," so much a part of life in this land of possum and rabbit, slunk under porches, refusing to come out as if afraid of a nameless something.

But where was Lee's army? If Grant was so cut to pieces at Cold Harbor that his men stumbled over their own dead, as Richmond claimed, why was he now crashing the capital's backdoor? It didn't make sense. What did make sense were the interminable blue columns, numerous as sands of the sea, powerful enough to conquer the world, or so it seemed.

But for small, barefooted rebels who clustered at every hamlet it was de luxe excitement. To their delight, sweaty Yankee bandsmen would occasionally unlimber their pieces and strike up a few bars of a lively march, winding up with a flourish of "Dixie" that struck an immediate, irresistible chord. Too tempting likewise for these urchins were the bits of sutler's candy tossed them by men who, for all their blue coats, most likely had children of their own up North, or in the West, or somewhere.

3

Noon, June 17, 1864. At the south bridgehead on Windmill Point, Captain John Woodward stood beside his horse impatiently waiting for the last wagons to get out of the way and go creaking down the Fleur de Hundred

Road. They had been passing for hours on end. Endless it seemed to young Woodward, drunk with fatigue. Weary, dirty, he could have slept on a bed of nails. As near as he could figure it, the wagon train would need four more hours to finish crossing. Stumbling into a field he tied his horse to a sapling. With his saddle for a pillow he slept for an hour. When he awoke wagons were still rolling over the river.

The officer bore a resounding title: "Commissary of Subsistence in Charge of the General Cattle Herd." His job description was accurate, but for the captain it was a goddamned thankless chore and that was exactly the way he felt about it at the moment. Besides, his rump was sore and he'd had a bellyache for two weeks.

Just because he had worked in a warehouse back home in Elmira, New York, he felt hardly qualified to direct the handout of tons of Yankee food or to babysit for a lot of ornery cattle. If he had to be killed in this war, he'd far rather be plugged by Confederate lead than gutted by a longhorn. Woodward had volunteered in the 23rd New York Infantry and upped to a captaincy in the Subsistence Corps. He had asked for the switch from the doughfoots.

All the way from the Rapidan he'd ridden with the trains or rather with the cavalry convoy strung alongside the cattle as they moseyed southwards. To Woodward the long waits were nightmares. If a wagon bogged down in a roadside quagmire everything behind it must halt while teamsters filled the muddy pitfall with brush and saplings or pried the wheels out of the mire with heavy oak poles. It was a pitiful sight to see six horses or mules suddenly plunge into bottomless muck and thrash about frantically for solid footing.

Before leaving the Rapidan QMG, Ingalls had issued specific instructions for feeding the animals. Cattle got ten pounds of hay apiece daily from forage carried by the wagon trains, unless good grazing could be found en route. It was a big "unless," finding good grazing for five thousand cattle. Feeding that many beeves meant fifty thousand pounds of hay twice a day and every bale of it hauled on the wagons except a smattering filched from wayside barns or haystacks. Horses and mules got more, and grain to boot. They did the hauling. They couldn't be grazed and there were over fifty thousand of them. QMG had allotted fourteen pounds of hay per draft animal, twice a day.

Woodward also kept count of the herd. The boss herder checked them every two days. On the hazardous trek to the James, bushwhackers had killed a dozen; another dozen had strayed; heat had killed off a score. Heaven only knew how many the army had eaten. The record was good, and Woodward was resigned to his job. Grant's big push might even sweep Petersburg into the Yankee catch-all and end the war just like that.

He had inquired patiently of a knot of the local gentry who had gathered near the south bridgehead, "Where's Beechwood?" He got only headshakings and vague "I don't knows." These bastards, he thought, were as uncommunicative as so many sphinxes. They knew all right but they weren't telling the Yankees. His predicament was relieved by a Negro teamster who "borrowed" a stogie from him.

"Cap'n," said the bullwhacker as he bit off the end of the stogie, "I thought we was going to Richmond."

"We are," smiled Woodward, "some day."

"But this ain't the way to Richmond."

"Grant must think it is," observed Woodward.

"It's the Petersburg road, cap'n. Maybe Gen'l Grant's

done changed the road like he's changing everything else. Is you going to Richmond, cap'n?"

"Not just yet. I'm looking for a place called Beech-wood."

"Old man Ruffin's place?"

"That's it, I guess." Woodward fished out a paper and glanced at it. "Yep, Ruffin's the name."

"That's a good place, cap'n. Lots of grass for cattle to eat. That's how it uster be when I lived down here."

Woodward perked up. "How far is it?"

" 'Bout five miles down this road. Maybe a little more. You jest follow the road tell jest before you comes to Merchant's Hope Church. You can't miss it. Turn right and you'll soon be there."

Back in the saddle Woodward joined the migration, threading his way cautiously along the flank of the crawling trains that churned up suffocating tornadoes of dust. He had never conceived of such dust. It seeped into his nostrils, his eyes, his mouth, even his pores. It coated his sweaty body like glue.

A sweltering hour brought him to the church where provost guards with bayonets and sulphurous oaths were yanking stragglers off wagons and needling them ahead to their outfits. Skulkers and deadbeats got no shrift at all. Sharp prods brought bursts of profanity. Nor were tempers improved by heat and hard marching.

Outside the ancient church stood a country parson amidst his flock which had no doubt sought sanctuary from the expected fury of the invaders inside the church. Built of tapestry brick, the old structure caught Woodward's eye. Old as Virginia herself, he thought—and, at that, he was only fifty years off. If he'd guessed 1657, he'd have hit it on the head. He wondered how it got its name, Merchant's Hope. He'd have to find that out some day. But he was looking for Beechwood, not the nomenclature of colonial churches. He consulted the provost sergeant, a tough hombre, who knew his business.

"Captain, you've come a little too far. Go back about a mile the way you came and turn left."

Damn, thought Woodward, and damn again. A mile of bucking a tide of wagons, mules, horses and fogs of dust.

Added the provost sergeant, "Captain, you'd better keep a pretty sharp eye. These sonsabitches ain't saying much, but they're taking it awful hard. We'll be here all night. If you need help, fire your pistol. We'll hear it."

"I've found that out already," agreed Woodward. "Talkative as so many goddamned clams."

Presently, reining to the left on a side road, he gave his horse his head. It was refreshing to get away from the everlasting tramp-tramp and rumble. Jogging along at a mincing gait he soon emerged from a patch of woods that topped a rise in the road. Ahead of him lay Beechwood, home of "Secession" Ruffin, set well back from the river. Between the blue visitor and the house stretched a vista of well-ordered fields and lush meadows. Beyond the house gleamed the James. He could see the far shore. As for grass, there were oceans of it, knee-deep. He longed to throw himself on it and sleep for a century. What a place to fatten cattle! Here they could pick up the weight they had sweated off on the stifling Virginia roads.

The road wound through an avenue of oaks and sycamores and on past outbuildings: a greenhouse, its panes smashed; stables, barns, whitewashed slave cabins now vacant. Next the smithy, carpenter shop, smoke house and outkitchen close by the big house. Over a neglected flower garden hovered an air of desolation made more poignant

by a handful of roses that lifted their heads above the
weeds seeking to despoil them.

Dismounting at the hitching post Woodward unloos-
ened his holster. He was curious, but cautious. With meas-
ured step he approached the house. The front door dangled mournfully by a single hinge. Gunboats had riddled
the place. Good shooting, thought Woodward. Shells
had gored holes in the white clapboard walls big enough
to crawl through. The house was roofless. Set afire by a
shell it had burned just enough to leave two gaunt, naked
chimneys protruding through charred roof beams. Warily
the officer ventured inside. His boots echoed hollowly.
Here was desolation pure and unadulterated. Dirt and
degradation blotched the floors and walls. The carpet,
specially woven for Ruffin and adorned with colorful pat-
terns of fruits and flowers, was sprinkled with human of-
fal.

The library shelves were empty, Ruffin's volumes
strewn and disheveled on the floor amid chunks of plaster.
His tall secretary, reaching almost to the ceiling, was
bashed in. Doors were torn from their frames, and the high
peer-mirrors in the parlor shattered into thousands of
pieces. The fine walnut balustrade leading upstairs was
hacked and gashed.

Littering the hall were hundreds of soiled tracts. He
picked up one that bore the title, "The Political Economy
of Slavery," only to drop it as he would a leper scab. Ruffin had printed them by thousands, mailed them to every
corner of the thirty-four states and the territories. This
one crackled with the ideas that had obsessed him: it laid
on the North's industrial back the blame for the economic
poverty, the life of endless toil, of the Northern farmer,
whereas—and Ruffin's passion glowed between the lines
—under slavery's system a farmer could become a gentle-

man if he wished. Thought Woodward: Ruffin had
wanted war. He had foreseen victory for the South, quick
and sure. Well, this was war, a carnival of mass extermina-
tion of man and his dwelling places. Ruffin had gotten
what he wanted, but with a grim vengeance on which he
had little recked.

But this was no time for philosophical reflection on
Ruffin's doctrines. Stepping outside, Woodward sucked in
lungfuls of fresh air, hot but gratifying. The Commissary
Captain had not come to inspect the wreckage of a fine
old home. He had seen scores of them since leaving the
Rapidan, many reduced to bare, fire-blackened chimneys
keeping vigil over cold ashes. He had found what he was
looking for—grass, pasturage. The herders could encamp
under the big oaks. Barges could come up the river and
unload at the Ruffin wharf. The setup was ideal. Union
cavalry would picket the Stage Road and the place would
be reasonably immune to marauding guerillas and bands
of gray raiders.

Taking the road again through the hot, sizzling dust he
reached the bridgehead to see the lead cattle halfway
across the river and trail-boss Gentry wondering what the
hell to do with them, where to graze them and bed them
down for the night. The afternoon was waning.

"Straight down this road," said Woodward. "I'll ride
along ahead of you."

What sweet revenge, thought the officer: Yankee cattle
fattening on Beechwood's blue grass and clover to feed the
bellies of Yankees now storming the last ramparts of the
Confederacy. What crowning desecration for the home of
Edmund Ruffin, secessionist de luxe!

5

The Fed and the Cornfed

On the day Grant's thousands of beeves clattered across the James and headed for Beechwood Confederate Commissary, General Northrup was warning War Secretary Seddon of a further reduction in the daily meat ration of Lee's army. Beef had vanished from the grayback's menu at the outbreak of the bloody tussle in the Wilderness. The daily handout was "Nassau bacon" that had run the blockade and hardly enough to grease the palate of a hungry fighting man. The impending cut would reduce it to one-third of a pound per man during actual combat and to one-fourth while the men eased up in camp or behind breastworks waiting for Grant's next fiery onslaught.

Filling out the daily bill of fare of the man in Lee's ranks was a pint of cornmeal (often unsalted) which, many insisted, was ground with the cob on it, inspiring the grim, apropos description of the opposing armies as the "Fed and Cornfed."

In depicting the hunger—"the hardest hardship to bear"—that assailed Lee's men, cannoneer William Dame of the Richmond Howitzers cited the gruesome fate of a cow that strayed between the lines at the Bloody Angle only to be cut down by a hurricane of fire. Two nights later, learning that the dead cow was still "available," Dame and several batterymates crept onto no man's land in search of the gastronomic windfall though fearful others had got there first.

"It was a hideous place to go for a beefsteak," related Dame. "The ground was covered with dead Federal soldiers, many in an advanced stage of decay. On our front many dead lay unburied until the odor of them was so dreadful we could hardly stay in our works. The carcass of that cow was touching five dead bodies. But we got our beef all the same. We were the first to get to the cow and we cut out hunks of the flesh as best we could and got back to our guns. We were always hungry. We never got a square meal. Some days we had bread and no meat; some days there was meat and no bread. For two days we had neither bread nor meat."

Going the rounds of the army at this critical phase of the struggle was the humorous story of a soldier who went to the surgeon with a pain in his stomach. The sawbones prodded the boy's abdomen until he felt a hard lump that didn't belong there. Reconnoitering further he discovered more hard lumps. Mystified by so many projections on the man's insides he came up with the solution: he was actually feeling the young fellow's backbone right through his stomach! The story reached Lee who was not amused.

From Colonel Venable, Lee's aide, came the tale of a small package delivered at GHQ near Orange Courthouse shortly before the opening of the bloody spring campaign.

The package contained an anonymous letter wrapped around a sandwich made of a slice of raw fat pork between two oak chips. The letter writer observed that it was his daily ration of meat. Then, disconsolately, he added that he found it impossible to exist on such scant fare and, though a gentleman, he was reduced by the pangs of hunger to stealing from his fellows. It was a shocker for Lee.

Spring 1864 brought a welcome sprouting of wild vegetation on the meadows along the roads leading south to Richmond. Between bursts of gunfire Lee's men often crawled about on hands and knees picking dandelions, sheep sorrel, or digging wild onions and other green shoots with their bayonets. "Confederate salad," as they dubbed it, added a much needed and craved dash of "greens" to the unbroken diet of salt meat, but it couldn't put an ounce of flesh on the rattly frames of men who had almost forgotten what a square meal looked like. Beef itself was only a memory, and it was what they yearned for most.

Yet while Lee's lean and hungry men were battling Grant's well-fed hosts on a third of a pound of bacon a day, the Texas ranges swarmed with longhorns. Herds ran wild, multiplying like rabbits. Three million head of cattle glutted the state, but there was no way to get them to market, that is, across the Mississippi to fill the empty bellies of Southern armies. Texas had furnished beef to the Confederacy up to 1863 when her meat lockers were slammed tight. After Vicksburg's fall, Union gunboats controlled the Mississippi from the Ohio down while the blockade sealed off the Gulf ports. A few hardy, daring cattlemen drove herds cross country to the Mississippi, dodging Federal vedettes picketing the roads and even the swamps, to swim the dogies across the river, but it didn't pay off. Half the herds were sucked under by the swift current. What the cattlemen got for the balance was a bundle of Confederate money, so watered down by now, that it hardly paid for the grub the cowpokes had eaten on the way.

The Civil War role of the lowly beef critter is still untold. Over three million of him and his brothers were bought by Federal commissaries during the four year struggle and slaughtered to feed the armies in the field. The Confederate figures were a scant fraction of this. The dogie was fought over and fought for; killed by enemy bullets as well as the knives of the butchers; captured and often recaptured; driven over high mountains and through deep waters, always bringing up the rear of a marching army. Yet, in a sense, he was as vital to Union victory as gunpowder itself.

In June 1864, while Grant's guns thundered barely eight miles from Richmond Confederate Commissary, General Northrup was issuing grandiloquent broadsides. The army, he proclaimed, "must bear the brunt of hunger as well as of arms." This incompetent martinet, West Point, 1831, was an intimate of President Davis, who, for reasons yet unrevealed, shielded him against the bitter clamor for his removal until the Confederacy was toppling under the North's all-out assault. It was Lee's hard-tried veterans who bore the real burden of Northrup's shortcomings.

2

For all his grandiose shortcomings "Blond God" Jo Hooker, during his brief sojourn as commander of the Army of the Potomac, had at least revolutionized the army's housekeeping department with a new idea: a man fights best on a full stomach. Grant shared this idea fully. His instructions were brief and pointed. Federal commissaries were ordered to buy only topgrade steers for his army. He no doubt felt about it as the Constable of France felt about his adversaries on the eve of Agincourt: "Give them great meals of beef, and iron and steel, and they will eat like wolves and fight like devils."

That was, perhaps, why ten days after the General Cattle Herd bedded down on Edmund Ruffin's fine pastures at Coggin's Point, Grant threw a heavier cordon of crack cavalry around the "great meals of beef" grazing behind his army along the James. The herd now numbered over four thousand. Three or more million pounds of red meat was too tempting a target for graybacks craving the sight of even a single ounce. As their belts grew tighter so would their desperation.

6

Beast Butler Strides Up the James

In the spring of 1864 Ulysses Grant came out of the West to take supreme command of the Northern armies. On March 8 he had his first look at the city of Washington. No fanfare, no delegations, no flourish of trumpets greeted him as he stepped off the train. Hiring a hack he drove unostentatiously to the old Willard Hotel. The lobby was crowded with army contractors, job seekers, politicians and war nondescripts. No one recognized the travel-worn soldier in the weather-beaten uniform as he approached the desk and quietly asked for a room. The clerk sized up the new arrival as just another major general.

Said the clerk, "I have nothing but a room on the top floor."

"That will do," said Grant, deadpan, making his historic entry on the hotel register, "U. S. Grant and son, Galena, Ills."

Next day, at the White House, President Lincoln

handed him a three-star commission as generalissimo of the Union fighting forces.

Grant had the knack of winning battles that McClellan, Pope, Burnside and Meade had lacked. Out West he had racked up a string of victories as long as his arm. At his wits' end to find a general who could chisel out ultimate victory, Lincoln found his prayers answered by Grant. They said he hit the bottle too often. What difference did it make, as long as he won battles? Lincoln made that plain as he handed him absolute military power. It looked suspiciously as if the right man was at last in the saddle.

In an unpretentious farmhouse near Culpeper, Virginia, where the Army of the Potomac sprawled for miles along the north bank of the Rapidan, Grant drafted his blueprint to end the war. His grand strategy was starkly, bloodily simple. The rebel armies would be herded into a vast corral, from the Red River to the Atlantic, from the Potomac to the Gulf, rounded up towards a common center and rubbed out remorselessly. "The thing has been seesawing too long," said Grant, planning this Cannae battle of annihilation. There would be no let-up. He'd give the rebels no rest night or day. He'd smash at them wherever they made a stand. Blood and plenty would flow in this slugfest.

Until now, the North with all her preponderance of weapons, men and money had lacked the priceless ingredient of combat leadership. This Grant brought with him out of the West. Northern armies had fought independently, as if the generals owned them and were jealous of the other fellow's success. "Without concert"— averred Grant—"like a balky team, no two of them ever pulling together." Grant would package Northern armed might and hammer at the Confederacy until by mere attrition, if in no other way, the South was brought low. Her back was already to the wall, her people's morale sinking, her resources failing. But no general seemed able to deliver the knockout punch. The Southern muster rolls revealed nigh half a million men though less than fifty percent of these were actually under arms. Yet these underfed, ragged fighters were the unkillables and the killers, tried by fire, who would exact Northern blood and death for every foot of ground they gave up. Guerillas, homeguards and bushwhackers probably padded the South's total with another twenty thousand. Whatever it was, Grant would whip them to a standstill and shoot them down to the last man. Although he had a two-to-one handicap to start with—twice as many Unions as Rebels—how could he lose? Widows and mothers would plead at Lincoln's doorstep in mourning weeds, but never mind, let 'em plead. Chain smoker Grant reduced ten boxes of cigars to ashes while planning the fanciest bloodletting the American continent had ever dreamed of.

Once Northern armies had penetrated the hollow shell of the South, they would gut the land, destroy the means of making war, sweep it bare as Grant's hand. Of railroads only roadbeds and twisted rails would be left. Ashes would replace war factories. If civilians got hurt, women raped, it was just too bad.

On May 1, 1864, two days before the North's D-day, the field returns, that is, the number of men Grant could absolutely put on the battle lines, numbered 533,347 "present for duty equipped." His paper army ran the figure up to 662,345. In all there were twenty-one army corps. Grant had few illusions. He was not addicted to vain thinking. His armies would strike simultaneously, and to make certain of this he announced, "I will direct the date of their departure, the points at which they will strike." Grant took no chances.

Grant's concerted drive involved eight armies, three major operations and five corollary movements. The combined armies of the Cumberland, Tennessee and Ohio, 100,000 men under Sherman, would strike at Johnston's force in northwest Georgia, sweep down on Atlanta and cut the heart out of Georgia. Beyond the Mississippi, Banks was to move up the Red River and capture Shreveport. Hustling back to New Orleans he would ship his army to Mobile and move north through Alabama to threaten Johnston in the rear while Sherman was piling down from Chattanooga.

The Valley of Virginia, Granary of the Confederacy, was to get red carpet treatment with fire and sword. Command of this Department of West Virginia (as it was called) was assigned to the German émigré, General Franz Sigel, who had commanded the "German Corps" in the Army of the Potomac. This appointment of the German revolutionary was a mistake. Grant knew this. The choice of Sigel to blacken the golden fields of the Valley had political implications. It would help swing the German vote Lincoln's way. Enlistees were chanting a catch phrase, "I goes to fit mit Sigel."

Ambrose Burnside, weighed in the balance at Fredericksburg and found wanting as an army commander, was to move his Ninth Corps, 30,000 men, along the Potomac and screen the railroads running south, then join up with the Army of the Potomac.

Deadliest of the Confederate forces was Lee's army now grimly barring the way into the Wilderness south of the Rapidan, ready to waylay the Army of the Potomac the moment it stepped over the river. Lee had taken the measure of this army too often. On Virginia soil Lee had crumpled Grant's predecessors in apple pie order—McClellan, Pope, Burnside, Hooker, Meade. Since taking command before Richmond in 1862 Lee had not lost a battle in his native state. His prestige with his men ran sky high. With Marse Robert leading them they were unbeatable. So they thought and so it looked. The South's ablest commander, the gray high command would sacrifice all else to sustain his army. To defeat the South, Lee's army must be snuffed out. Destroy Lee and the whole Confederate caboodle, Richmond and everything else, would collapse. Actually, Grant expected Lee to dispute the Rapidan river crossing. He never dreamed Lee would let him pass into the Wilderness before turning hell loose on him.

Commanding the Army of the Potomac was George Meade, a good, conscientious soldier whose chief glory was checking Lee's army at Gettysburg though he failed to reap the fruits of it. Were he the aggressive type he might have destroyed Lee's broken forces while they floundered, bleeding, back across the Potomac. Rumor had it Grant intended displacing Meade for a more even-tempered, less irascible commander. Yet under Meade this army had fought the turning point battle of the war.

Meade was a patriot. To the incoming general-in-chief he said, "The emergency of the country is above all other considerations. Remove me at once if it suits your plans."

"I see no reason for displacing you," was Grant's quiet reply.

On taking command Grant announced his intention not of directing but of making his supreme headquarters with the Army of the Potomac. He tried, so he said, "to make General Meade's position as nearly as possible what it would have if I had been in Washington or any other

place away from his command." It didn't pan out too
well. Grant was to lead the Army of the Potomac. Meade
was really not the man to take on Lee in the Wilderness.
He was never inducted into the inner circle of the Grant-
Sherman-Sheridan clique. In the end it broke his heart.
"His gorgeous headquarters tent" was nothing more than
a clearing house for Grant's orders to the battle lines.
Over this tent near Brandy Station floated a beautiful
silken flag which reminded Grant, who abhorred showi-
ness, of the magnificence of the conquerors of imperial
Rome.

The Army of the Potomac was a splendid fighting machine whose fortunes had ebbed low too often. Since
Gettysburg it had not struck a blow. These hardy, veteran
fighters had never known a truly inspiring leader unless it
be George McClellan, who took too much counsel of his
fears. In March 1864 their tents and huts whitened the
hillsides and valleys for miles along the north bank of
the Rapidan. Only the stream separated the two armies.
Pickets, blue and gray, drew water from it. From Clark's
Mountain, overlooking the plains where the two great
armies were encamped, Confederate signal officers could
sweep the horizon for ten miles and report every movement to Lee. Obviously Grant was going to cross the
Rapidan. Would he come by Lee's right flank or his left?

But Grant's new broom swept clean. His coming had
cheered the men. They felt they had a winner. Meade
was not too popular. Meade put too much store by his
rank. His two stars were something to bow down to. He
dressed many an officer down mercilessly for not observing proper respect for the constellation on his shoulders.
The long letdown in morale of the Army of the Potomac
ended with Grant. The men had gone from doubt to be-

wilderment to despondency. These were the men, or
rather their dead comrades, who paid the butcher's bill
for inept commanders.

On May 1, 1864, Lee's "effective total" was 61,953 men
and 224 guns. Grant effectives ran to 4409 officers and
114,360 enlisted men. Properly disposed for battle Grant's
men would have covered a front of 21 miles, two ranks
deep, with one-third of them held in reserve. Lee's army
similarly disposed would cover only 12 miles.

With power to do as he saw fit Grant began lopping off
heads. The incompetents, the battle broken, were ousted
by scores. Corps and division commanders were assayed
and ushered out, or upped, as the need might be.

Up to 1863 Federal cavalry had acquired little luster
as a fighting arm. For two years of war it operated in
driblets. Hooker, despite his deficiencies as a leader, had
unified the horse soldiers into one corps and ordered it
to prove its mettle by ringing his army with a screen of
pickets. This would at least keep tabs on the gray infiltra-
tors who were constantly crossing his lines, stealing the
secrets of what he was cooking up in his tent at Falmouth
Heights. To lacklustre George Stoneman, Hooker gave
the Chief of Cavalry job. Possessing little battle ardor
Stoneman just couldn't cope with Jeb Stuart's light-heeled
riders, who poked no end of fun at the awkward Union
Cavalry. "The people of the North just don't know how
to ride horses." Maybe not, but they were learning the
hard way, pounding after Stuart who rode rings around
the Union armies.

In a sense Southerners were born in the saddle. Much
of the South was "horse" country. These youngsters had
bred, broken, trained and lived horses. They rode like
Bedouins, stuck on a horse's back as if nailed there. They
knew horseflesh and how to take care of it, which was half

the battle. It's safe to say that no cavalry was ever better mounted than the first regiments that followed Stuart, clopclopping along the hard Virginia roads by day, by night, by starlight and moon, with a song that ran, "If you want to have a good time, Jine the caval-ree!"

The Confederate government never supplied mounts for its cavalry as did the Federals. You had to have a horse if you "jined" the horse soldiers. If your horse got killed, the government paid you what it thought he was worth and gave you time off to buy another.

It was reasonable to assume that born and bred horsemen would make better troopers than the Federals, but little cavalry fights, raids on Union depots and pickets killed men just as dead as big battles. In time the gray firstlings and their horses went over the hill.

Contractors for the Federal Quartermaster General bought horses for quantity rather than quality. A horse was a horse whether his destiny was dragging cannon, or wagons, or joining the swift right arm of the armies. They bought them with every disease known to horseflesh. Over 600,000 horses gave their lives for the Union.

In planning his big offensive Grant gave a new role to cavalry. It would screen his flanks, protect his vast trains, but it would do far more. Raids deep in enemy country, sweeps behind Lee's lines, quick thrusts that would destroy supply lines and demoralize the people were added to cavalry's portfolio.

Meade's Chief of Cavalry, Alfred Pleasanton, got the ax pronto. A swanking, foppish fellow he tried hard but he, too, was no match for rollicking, fast flying Jeb Stuart.

"I want an officer of fire and nerve to command my cavalry," said Grant to "Old Brains" Halleck, Chief of Staff.

Halleck came up with "How would Sheridan do?"

"Just the man," agreed Grant, who then and there put the finger on the pint-sized 115-pound infantryman whose divisions he had watched sweeping up Missionary Ridge. So Sheridan hurried east to take over Grant's thirteen thousand horsemen now armed with new rebel-killers, Spencer repeating carbines of which a trooper of the Ninth Virginia, who marveled at their firepower, said, "Them guns can shoot all day without reloading."

2

The final, but not the least important, cog in Grant's war machine was the Army of the James, some 40,000 men lolling about their encampment near Fort Monroe at the mouth of the river whose name they bore. When the Army of the Potomac brushed past Lee's pickets and crunched into the Wilderness, the Army of the James was to embark up the James, a river no less important to the Confederacy than the Mississippi. Moving upriver it would seize a beachhead on the south bank as far up and as near to Richmond as possible. This toehold would isolate Petersburg, slice the rail lines leading south, and wedge a sizable force between the rebel capital and Petersburg.

In effect, the Army of the James would be the lower jaw of a huge nutcracker, of which the Army of the Potomac was the upper grinders. Grant would keep Lee so bloodily engaged he would be unable to spare a regiment to beat off the Army of the James. Richmond might fall of its own weight. If Lee fell back into Richmond, he would put himself right between the jaws of the two armies.

A fine strategic conception, with but a single flaw, or rather, a character known to history as "Beast" Butler, who at the moment was Major General Benjamin F. Butler, commanding the Army of the James. His record was unsavory. He had acquired his two stars before Grant came on the scene. Mystery still beclouds his mesmeric sway over Lincoln. Grant was aware of Butler's character and incompetence, but there wasn't much he could do about it. Obviously, he must have discussed Butler with Lincoln, who had once opined that Butler was as full of poison as a dead dog. Not a glowing opinion to be sure. Grant's failure to expunge Butler was a costly mistake. All the same Butler could have wangled Lincoln's eye teeth out of his mouth had he so desired.

Arrogant, conceited, this political misfit from Massachusetts refused to be expunged from the bloody *corrida* coming up. He intended to take the field in person. He might even wind up with Richmond dangling at his paunchy belt, a feat that could make him president. It raised the suspicion that Grant was afraid of Butler. Had Grant been a free agent he would have ousted him as he did hundreds of proven incompetence.

Lincoln and the politicians tried to shoo Butler off by offering him second place on the Lincoln ticket for re-election in November 1864. Butler slyly agreed to accept, if Lincoln "would give him a bond with sureties in the full sum of his four years salary that he will die or resign within three months after his inauguration." Actually, Butler threw away the presidency. Lincoln was dead six months after the election.

Butler expected and got high command in the grand spring campaign that started off the first week in May just as the lilacs and trilliums began blooming in the Wilderness.

Saddled with the droop-eyed politician-general Grant issued precise instructions. "When you are notified to move take City Point with as much force as possible.

Fortify, or rather intrench at once and concentrate all your troops for the field *there* as rapidly as you can. Operate on the south side of the James, Richmond being your objective point." Grant then went awry by adding, "All the minor details of your advance are left entirely to your direction." Butler was about as fitted to direct these operations as a drummer boy. Probably less so.

To minimize the handicap Grant assigned two able, professional soldiers to command Butler's two corps, Quincy A. Gillmore and William F. "Baldy" Smith.

One minute past midnight, May 4, was shove-off hour for the Army of the James. In the Wilderness, Grant's Army of the Potomac slept fitfully on their guns sensing the slaughter that would come with the morrow. Grant had crossed the Rapidan.

Lights dimmed, Butler's motley armada of transports, coasters, schooners, tugs, barges and even canal boats headed up the James from Fort Monroe. A flotilla of gunboats and monitors convoyed the forty transports each carrying 500 men. In the van, on the bridge of the *Greyhound,* stood Admiral-General Butler, who poohpoohed Admiral Lee's warning of torpedoes in the river and masked batteries among the willows and foliage that fringed the banks. By noon Fort Powhatan, Confederate stronghold, loomed dead ahead. Squatting on a bluff where the river made a sharp bend the fort's guns frowned in two directions. Butler expected a last ditch fight. The monitors moved up. Gunners stood at quarters ready to deluge the earthwork with big navy shells. Landing parties shouldered their gear. Then, without ado, without firing a shot, the feeble garrison decamped. With whoops and cheers a marine detachment dashed ashore to hoist the Union flag over the "captured" stronghold. Nor could Butler resist speeding a despatch boat to Fort Monroe

with a message to be flashed to Washington, "Fort Powhatan is ours."

Rounding Windmill Point, where five weeks hence
Grant's pontoniers would anchor the south end of their
bridge, Butler sailed onto the broad waters of Harrison's
Bar. Off to port, Coggins Point jutted into the roadstead.
Ruffin's Beechwood rose amid the trees. Some suggested
giving "the old bastard's place a dousing." But Butler said
no.

In the distance City Point loomed, a rebel flag flying
over the bluff. Grant had ordered, "Take City Point and
fortify it." At four o'clock the *Manano* warped alongside
the wharf below the bluff. First to leap ashore with a few
riflemen was Colonel Thomas Livermore, aide to "Baldy"
Smith, commanding the Eighteenth Corps. "Without waiting to look at surroundings much, I jumped ashore with
an axe in one hand with which to cut down the rebel
flag. In company with our headquarters guards I ran up
the bluff. Above us we saw rebels putting their rifles out
of the window of a little house, but they retreated as we
climbed toward them, and with the aid of my companions, I soon had the flag. Our guard pursued the few rebels
who were there and captured most of them."

3

News that Beast Butler and his army were coming up the
James raced ahead like red plague. At noon a courier
galloped in hot haste up to the war office on Main Street
in Richmond with a message wigwagged from a Confederate lookout on Swans Point opposite Jamestown Island.
Wild alarm swept the city. Church bells began tolling.
The old bell in Capitol Square joined the clanging
chorus. Richmond had known panicky hours before. In

1862 when McClellan's blue host pounded to her very threshold, Lee had come to the rescue and delivered the city from the invaders. Now Lee was embattled in a life and death grapple with Grant in the Wilderness sixty miles away with not a man to spare. Richmond had been stripped of troops to reinforce him. Catastrophe loomed. The armory was opened and muskets passed out to any man who could shoulder a gun and pull a trigger. War clerks, messengers, old men, school boys joined the exodus to man the works below the city. Between Richmond and calamity stood only Fort Darling at Drewry's Bluff seven miles below the city. The day passed in feverish tension. Business houses shut their doors. Averred War Clerk Jones, "There is now some excitement and trepidation among the shopkeepers and extortioners who are compelled by State law to shoulder muskets for the defense of the city."

The sun was still high when a shocking message chattered over the telegraph from Petersburg, "There are two single turreted monitors, one double turreted, three gunboats and about forty transports coming up the James. Two gunboats have gone up the Appomattox. Each transport will average five hundred men. Some have horses on board. White and negro troops are in the expedition. They are landing at City Point and have hauled down the Confederate flag and raised the Yankee flag."

At nine that night even more dismaying news pattered in. Butler had landed his army at Bermuda Hundred, fourteen miles below the city. He was knocking at the gates. He need only push out three miles to cut the Richmond-Petersburg railroad and the telegraph, and isolate the capital.

Consternation struck Petersburg, too. Butler at City Point, eight miles away! The Cockade City of the Union, as James Monroe had christened it, breathed hard. For days in 1862 McClellan might have taken it for the asking. Not until Little Mac's disastrous repulse did the Confederacy hierarchy concede its strategic importance. Thereupon a skilled engineer, Captain Charles H. Dimmock, West Point, 1821, projected an arc of breastworks and gun embrasures, ten miles around, anchored on the Appomattox below and above the city. On May 5, the Dimmock Line's presumed impregnability had an allaying effect on the fears of Petersburgers. But the line had two serious defects: there were no troops to man it and it gave little protection northwards.

Richmond spent a throbbing anxious night. Through the dark hours her citizenry slept little, straining their ears for Butler's guns. Lights burned all night in the war office where Secretary Seddon flooded the wires with appeals for succor. Down the coast winged his outcries, "We are in the very crisis of our fortunes and want every man. The city is in hot danger." To *beau ideal* Pierre G. T. Beauregard, overall commander of the Virginias south of the James and Appomattox, with headquarters at Weldon, North Carolina, went "There is not an hour to lose." At Wilmington, Beauregard loaded Hagood's veteran brigade onto three trains of flat and cattle cars and hurried them north to the rescue of the capital city.

At four o'clock this bright May 5 afternoon, capture of strategic Petersburg was a pushover. Between Butler—if he came—and the old town stood a puny force of six hundred commanded by George Pickett, he of the flowing locks the ladies loved and the famous, abortive charge at Gettysburg. It was a set-up operation even for a lame duck like Butler. Any moment as the afternoon hours waned Pickett expected to see solid blue columns swinging along the City Point road to crack through the thin-

held Dimmock Line. To Richmond he wired, "Enemy
have possession of City Point. I have but one regiment
here. Troops arriving from the South, Hagood's Brigade
and others. Can I detain them?" Richmond wired back a
flat no. Send them on to Richmond. But Pickett faced an
even worse situation north of the city. He had less than a
thousand men to protect the south half of the Richmond-
Petersburg railroad.

Long after dark Pickett wired again, "The enemy has
landed at Bermuda Hundred. They will cut the railroad
today, advancing from Bermuda Hundred." That was of
course what a trained military mind like Pickett's would
have expected. After all, Pickett was a good soldier. He
had his shortcomings and he was to go out in a blaze of
anything but glory. Today he was calling the shots as he
saw them.

Had Butler occupied the high ground at City Point in
force, fortified it, as Grant had ordered, and speared a fast
column at Petersburg, he could have bagged the town by
night and changed the course of history. But he didn't.
Only the Almighty knows why.

Instead, in disregard of Grant's orders, he landed an un-
tried, poorly disciplined division of colored troops at City
Point and chugged on up the river to disembark into a
huge trap of his own contriving. Stealth played no part in
Butler's approach to the rebel capital; yet, as luck would
have it, he caught the city napping and unprepared. Had
Butler proclaimed his coming with a chime of ship's bells
he could not have advertised it better. Still, so unexpected
was his arrival that the Confederate officer in the signal
tower at Bermuda Hundred was fishing in the James
when Butler's armada hove round the bend. Dropping his
line and catch he galloped off to spread the alarm. Butler's mess sergeant took over the string of river perch. It

was a laugh. The Confederates had even caught a fish dinner for him.

By sunset Butler's transports had warped alongside the river bank and the Army of the James poured ashore. Bands played gaily. The whole affair seemed too good to be true. Butler had "stormed," as he called it, up the river to within fourteen miles of Richmond and he hadn't fired a gun. He took up a position of great natural strength on the narrow neck of Bermuda Hundred peninsula on which he had landed. His left rested on the Appomattox at Walthall Landing, his right on the James four miles below Drewry's Bluff bastion. The neck was less than four miles across. Three miles west of the neck ran the Richmond-Petersburg railroad, turnpike, and telegraph lines, almost within shooting distance. Instead of throwing out a force to seize the railroad, rip up the tracks and barricade themselves along the roadbed he ordered his men to snug down for the night. If Butler's men were tired, it was from leaning on the rail watching the sleepy shores slide by. Hundreds had snoozed on deck in the warm May sunshine all day. They had hardly stretched their legs.

Next morning Butler threw out a brigade to cut the railroad. Confederate pickets hastily ran off while the bluecoats proceeded to wreck six miles of track. They were having a field day, tearing up rails, heating them over big fires and twisting them into neckties when three trains came puffing slowly up to the southern terminus of their destruction. Hagood's graybacks had arrived from North Carolina. They hopped off the cars like hornets out of a nest, rifles crackling as they came.

Two days later Butler plunged head on against Fort Darling and its outworks around Drewry's Bluff, a fiasco that backfired with 3500 dead and wounded. Butler's Richmond drive had blown up in disaster. Strengthening the entrenchments across the neck Butler retired into the bottle-shaped peninsula, thus neutralizing his army. The Confederates promptly paralleled his entrenched line with one of their own requiring few men to hold it. Grant spotlighted Butler's plight with the sardonic comment, "His army was as completely shut off from further operations directly against Richmond as if it had been in a bottle strongly corked."

Thus was Richmond relieved, Petersburg uncaptured and the might-have-been's compounded. Butler's days as a commanding officer were numbered but he would ride high for awhile, strut about his camp like a mogul, quarrel with his corps commanders and make himself generally unuseful until Grant, in extremis, finally stripped him down. On the bright side of the ledger, City Point was in Federal hands. Grant would shortly convert it into an impregnable base of operations against Richmond and Petersburg.

7

Enter the Horse Soldiers

On May 5—while the Army of the James was chugging up the river to grab a beachhead, as Grant had ordered, "as far up on the south side as you can"—Butler's cavalry division trotted out of its encampment behind Portsmouth and headed up the east side of the Blackwater River.

It was the division's shakedown march. The men were eager to get going. They were on the move at last and that was the big thing. Picketing stumps of burned bridges, sporadic sniping across the river at their gray opposites, was hellish tiresome, and it killed men for no good reason that cavalry could see.

Bugles that stabbed right into the brains of sleeping cavalrymen blew reveille at 12:01 A.M. An hour later the column shuffled out with a burst of cheers while the division band, which was to follow by transport, struck up "The Girl I Left Behind Me." The column, a long dark blur, merged into the hush and shadows of the river road.

Strung out for nearly three miles, with advance well ahead, the division scooped up its pickets as it jogged along. Four regiments of horse (two brigades) there were, 3000 sabers, jingling westward, firing Parthian shots at rebel outposts through the early morning haze that shrouded the river. By dawn they were well on their way and the men braced themselves for hours in the saddle. In the middle of the column rolled four guns of a Wisconsin Battery.

Five days rations for man and beast dangled over the horses' rumps. Carbines snugged in the saddle boots, Colt pistols were belted at the troopers' waists, sabers hung from the saddles. Fifty rounds of ammunition per trooper completed their lethal armament. The rest of their gear—blankets rolled in oil cloth, lariats, feed bags, tobacco and God only knows what else—was cinched by rope and strap to their saddles. Quite an array of trappings, not forgetting those imperative prerequisites: dice and decks of greasy cards to help share the wealth on payday when it came, always late.

Riding with the lead regiment was the man Grant himself had tabbed to command the division, August Valentine Kautz. Cigar in his teeth, shiny new stars on his shoulders, a big black horse between his legs, he looked just what he was, a hard-grained, bluff cavalryman, who began soldiering as a shavetail lieutenant in Grant's old 4th Infantry. Like Grant's, and Sheridan's, Kautz's fancy ran to black horseflesh. His was a beauty, dark as midnight.

Kautz took command at Fort Monroe on April 21. Using magic as well as a lot of cussing, he had in a fortnight whipped four loose-jointed regiments into a ragged, workable outfit, if for no other reason than that the men welcomed a man who promised to end their boredom and inaction. Waiting was often harder than fighting and no one

knew it better than a horse soldier. Kautz had a knack of
kneading raw stuff into worthwhile soldiers. His "Cus-
toms of the Service," a small compendium of do's and
don't's for noncoms and privates, could be found in the
saddlebags of almost every trooper, and officer too, in the
column. Kautz saw to that soon after he reached Fort
Monroe and made it damned tough if they didn't read
it. He had a habit of occasionally spurring alongside a
slouchy, sleepy trooper and firing a what-to-do-when question at him. God help the man who failed to come up with
some sort of answer.

This was Kautz's first independent command and, as he
put it, he "damned well" intended to make it work out.
He had reported to General Butler at Fort Monroe to find
himself cast for a vital role as Chief of Cavalry of the
Army of the James in the big drive coming up. His first
mission was important: lending a hand in the slow stran-
gulation of Lee's army. He was to raid the Petersburg
and Weldon Railroad, Lee's vital and as yet unscathed
supply line from the south, burn the Stony Creek and
Nottoway River bridges south of Petersburg and perpe-
trate any other feasible feats of skulduggery not outlawed
by the rules of "civilized warfare," that permitted anything from rape to arson. Snipping Lee's supply line
would halt reinforcements speeding north to Petersburg
at the same time that Butler was consolidating his lodg-
ment on the James and perhaps snatching the town.

Until the coming of Kautz the Blackwater bore a sinister connotation as an uncrossable barrier. No Yankee force
had been able to cross it and stay there. Deep, swift, dark-
colored, it roughly paralleled the James as it meandered
southeast from Petersburg, spreading out every few miles
in stinking, bottomless festers called swamps. The Confederates had fortified the Blackwater early in the game,

soon after the Yankees recaptured Norfolk and lopped off
Suffolk. It had been more of a threat than a front, though
it kept blood flowing rather freely. In planning his expedition Kautz proposed to skirt the Blackwater and slash
across it nearer its source where the rebels least expected
it. He ruled out Butler's idea of breaching it lower down
where the Yankees had been kicked in the face so often. It
meant building a bridge under fire, to Kautz "a very uncertain performance for which cavalry had no particular
qualification." What Butler didn't know about cavalry
would fill a set of books but this time he didn't try to air
what he didn't know. He accepted Kautz's counter-idea
flat down. The new Chief of Cavalry would presently con-
fide to his diary, "In my service under his command I always found General Butler reasonable and our relations
were always of the most agreeable nature." The fact was
that Butler had infinitely more confidence in Kautz whom
he'd never seen before than in his two crack infantry corps
commanders, Gillmore and "Baldy" Smith.

This settled, Kautz called in his colonels and majors
and laid it on the line. They were marching deep into
rebel territory, he expected to cross the Blackwater come
hell or high water and raise pluperfect hell with the rebel
railroad. What he wanted was performance, not alibis.
They had to make good or they wouldn't be his colonels
and majors long. He looked straight at them. The officers
swallowed hard, but they liked straight talk.

These men—without exception—had reached colo-
nelcy on their combat records. One, Samuel P. Spear,
commanding the 11th Pennsylvania Cavalry, might have
stepped right out of the pages of knight errantry. Onetime
sergeant in the 2nd Dragoons he had charged Mexican
batteries at Buena Vista as if they were toy guns. He had

one fault: fighting up front with his men. His body bore enough scars for four men.

Kautz's men—most of them—had learned fighting the hard, merciless way, scurrying after Confederate hotrod Jeb Stuart, cutting and thrusting with his light-footed riders. To them, war was no longer an exciting, patriotic adventure but a damned hard chore that had to be done, with a fifty-fifty chance of getting killed before it was over. Kautz's four regiments were 1st District of Columbia Cavalry, 11th Pennsylvania Cavalry, 5th Pennsylvania Cavalry and 3rd New York Cavalry, all volunteers. Kautz weeded out the obvious incompetents, physically unfit, and sour bellies. He spent two tireless days eyeing each man up and down with an X-ray ability to look at and through him and size up his capabilities. On the whole Kautz had good men who'd fight like hell if given the right leadership. One schism disturbed him. The 1st District of Columbia was a split-tail outfit. Half of them were Maine men, grousing eternally at being suddenly—because of lack of volunteers in Washington—regimented with the 1st District, an outfit better known as "Baker's Mounted Rangers," whose job was to keep order in and around the nation's capital. It was organized by the sinister chief of War Department detectives, Lafayette C. Baker, but now, in the field, commanded by Major J. Stannard Baker, no relative of the organizer.

Kautz set a much faster clip for the division this first day than the three miles per hour pace decreed by cavalry regulations, and this allowed for brief rests every two hours and stops to water the horses. He was a hard driver. He wanted to get where he was going and get there fast. Hell could break loose with Butler on the prowl up the James. Twelve thousand well-shod hooves drumming a dirt road could, and did, churn up clouds of dust. It was like riding in a fog much of the time. Kautz cantered up and down the long column twice. He had suggestions. Tie handkerchiefs over your mouths. It'll keep out the dust— some of it. Hundreds did, making them look like a horde of masked bandits. His men's and horses' wellbeing was a prime motivation with him. Keeping a cavalry outfit on the go was unending drudgery. Just keeping the column closed up was a constant chore, for straggling was a chronic cavalry custom. Feeding and watering horses was a hostler's job that had to be done. No water, no horse. Three thousand horses could drink a small creek dry at one filling. And horses like to take their time eating. You just can't cram oats down a horse's throat and say "Let's go."

Kautz was proud of his command. He liked spit and polish though there was precious little of that in a crackling war. His men, newly accoutered, looked downright smart in their tight-fitting, natty jackets, kepis shaped somewhat like flattened tincans and boots wrinkled as they should (or would) be. After all there was romance about cavalry, color and dash, though the realities of cavalry fighting were a far cry from the popular conception of horsemen spurring to a gallop on the instant and charging full tilt at an enemy *a mile away*. There was companionship, too. Man and horse. They shared the dangers, hardships and the grumbling. Horses are sensitive to the feelings of their masters, perhaps more so in war. Many the trooper who wept over his mount slain in battle as over a dead devoted friend.

By sunset Kautz had covered forty miles, threatening the principal crossings, but making no effort to do so other than trading shots across the Blackwater, without spreading alarm or exposing his design to head the stream. Bivouacking at Andrews Corners he rousted the outfit up at midnight and resumed the march, pressing on another fifty miles to Cypress Swamp where he blasted his way across the river and demolished the gray outpost taken completely by surprise by his dawn debut. He encamped on the well-wrecked Norfolk and Petersburg Railroad near Wakefield. Next morning he opened the ball. At Littleton his advance guard overran four Confederate commissary wagons which he burned for a starter. Traveling fast he struck the Petersburg and Weldon Railroad at Stony Creek before noon. This was his goal or rather one of them. Here was the railroad. Now to cut it up in fine pieces.

But the rebel bridgeguard, two companies of the 59th Virginia, had something to say about it. They began flipping bullets the moment Kautz came in sight. Dismounting two squadrons of the 3rd New York Kautz ordered them to clean out the rebel nest whose slugs were slapping by like angry bees. Kautz stuck an unlighted cigar in his teeth and began chewing on it as he watched the operation.

"Them galoots can sure shoot!" blurted a New York sergeant, dodging a ball that sizzled by too close for comfort.

"Don't duck, sergeant," said Kautz. "Have a cigar."

It was an old habit with him. He'd been known to hand out a dozen cigars a day to men in the ranks. A strange morale builder. A cigar from the general.

Outflanking the small barricade the New Yorkers smothered it with gunfire. A white handkerchief on a gunbarrel said the grays had had enough. A quick job, thought Kautz, well pleased, but not too happy over a dead lieutenant he'd grown to like and several troopers to

be buried on the spot. He bagged forty-odd rebels. Fifty
others had fled precipitately, shucking off their muskets as
they vacated the place.

"Now, get busy, boys!" said Kautz, who had rehearsed
his officers in the fine points of destroying a railroad.

The orgy began, first of many. Spreading out along the
tracks Kautz's wreckers began ripping rails from their
sleepers. The ties were piled up and fired. Then rails
were laid across the pyres. When red hot in the middle
they were lifted off, twisted around trees and left to cool
like iron boa constrictors, monuments to the Yankees' fury.

"The goddam rebels won't ride these rails any time
soon," cracked a New York boy, squirting a stream of
brown juice. He could massacre a plug of tobacco like a
hungry horse a bale of hay.

Now for the 110 foot wooden bridge over Stony Creek.
Dry as a bone, oily, it burned to the water's edge. To keep
it company, up in flames went depot, watertank, three
freight cars loaded with lumber and even a locomotive
turnpit.

Kautz had one regret. From prisoners he learned that
shortly before he arrived three trains of flatcars had rattled north with graybacks hanging on like monkeys. Re-
enforcements for Beauregard at Petersburg. Five more
trains were due about dusk. Avowed Kautz, "Had they arrived they could have saved the Nottoway River bridge"
to which he next turned his hot ministrations. Before bivouacking that night he sent Colonel Spear and the 11th
Pennsylvania down to apply a torch to the Nottoway
bridge, but this was no pink tea and with night coming on
Spear decided to wait till daylight before taking it on.

The Nottoway bridge was the longest (210 feet) and
highest bridge on the Weldon road between Petersburg
and North Carolina. Protecting it was a sizable redoubt

near the north bridgehead. Behind this earthwork huddled several companies of the 59th Virginia commanded by a spitting dragon, Colonel William B. Tabb. Tabb was not one to give up easily, but he made the mistake of venturing out of his strongpost to attack Spear's troopers who at dawn began ripping up track at Jarrett's a mile or so below the bridge. Hearing the firing, Kautz trotted down with the 3rd New York. Dismounting his men, Kautz sized up the terrain, then scratched off and white-flagged a note to Colonel Tabb demanding surrender or else. Tabb's reply was not nice. And insolent to boot. "Come and take it, you blue bastard!"

Tabb had suggested what Kautz immediately tried. Unlimbering two of his cannon on the roadbed he began plastering the redoubt across the river with canister. At the same time his carbineers drove the graybacks along the track and across the bridge so fast that the reserve in the redoubt were afraid to fire on the invaders lest they hit their own men. It was the 1st District's tryout of their new Henry sixteen shooters and they made the most of it. They sounded like packages of huge firecrackers exploding all at once. Being on the receiving end of these all-day shooters, as the trigger boys called them, was a new experience. Bloody too. Meanwhile Spear's men torched off the 210-foot bridge. In twenty minutes the strategic trestle was reduced to ashes. Lee himself was to bemoan its destruction.

Stingaree Tabb had taken this toll: 15 dead Yankees, 35 wounded. Kautz admitted, "had the rebel commander remained in the redoubt it would have been very difficult for us to have burned the bridge without serious loss." But his mission was to expunge the bridge, and that was accomplished. Quite a feather in his cap at that. Tabb and his men still held the redoubt, keeping up a fiendish

racket. Slugs of lead were still zipping unpleasantly close
when Kautz decided to call it a day. His report was naive,
"I reluctantly left Colonel Tabb to guard where the
bridge had been."

Now to bury his dead and get going. An unshaven sergeant picked out a grave digging detail and told them to
get busy: wrap the bodies in their blankets and shovel
them under as fast as possible. The regiment had to move
on. Just like that. A dead man was no good any more.

Kautz took counsel of his fears as his diary would later
reveal. "I was embarrassed with 130 prisoners and 30
wounded. Beauregard might arrive in force any time from
the South and I did not know what might be in our way to
prevent me from reaching City Point. There was no place
I could reasonably expect to attack with much success and
nothing left for me to do except make my way back to the
Army of the James."

Destruction of the bridges would at least block troop
movements north for days though these rebels were ingen-
ious devils and adept as beavers at rebuilding. Something
else Kautz thought about: Jeb Stuart and his squadrons no
doubt had a full-time job protecting Lee's flanks in the
Wilderness and keeping tabs on Sheridan, the new Federal Chief of Cavalry. There was little fear of Jeb's cutting loose and cracking down on the raiders. Traps would
of course be set for Kautz. Homeguards would lay for him.
The telegraph had flicked the news of his raid far and
wide though his men had pulled down miles of wire. Yet
up to now there was no indication of pursuit.

He bivouacked near Sussex Courthouse. His camp resembled a picnic ground, and his men were on top of the
world. They had pillaged to their heart's content while
their officers were powerless to stop them. Saddlebags

were stuffed with loot; haversacks bulged with booty, including even trinkets dragooned from farm folk tasting the first bitterness of Yankee greed. Smoke houses were ransacked—first come, first served. Stolen hams and sides of bacon were roped to almost every saddle. It was banditry pure and simple.

Before leaving Fort Monroe Kautz had promised "summary execution of men caught in the act" of plundering. Had he carried out his threat he would have shot three-fourths of his command. What was euphemistically designated as "foraging" was cavalry's ancient prerogative. Napoleon himself had laid down the "forager's maxim" for his army in Italy—"Soldiers! You need everything! The enemy has everything!"

At daylight the column moved off. By sunrise the advance struck the Jerusalem plank road. Not a gray picket in sight though Kautz took no chances and sped troopers off to scour the road up and down, probe the underbrush, flush out graycoats hiding in hope of potshots.

Lighting a fresh cigar and leaning on his saddle pommel Kautz puffed thoughtfully while his men beat the bushes. May had clothed the countryside in loveliest tints of green—dogwood whitened in every copse—ringlets of wild violets and trilliums bedecked the roadside—the day itself sparkled like a clear jewel. Kautz called up his colonels and put it squarely up to them. What should he do? He *might* jog boldly up the plank road and crash his way into Petersburg—and on to glory. Otherwise he could work his way eastward to City Point. By now Kautz's men would have followed him anywhere, even to Petersburg at this moment hanging on the ropes. They had taken a fancy to this tough horse soldier with a cigar stuck in his mouth and a habit of passing them out to the men in the

ranks. He had led them into the heart of rebel country
and showed them how to raid the most important railroad
in the Confederacy and get away with it.

"Sergeant" Spear (he preferred this distinction to
"colonel") spoke up. "Let's take a crack at Petersburg.
Butler may even be there by now."

"How far is it?" asked Kautz.

"Less than twenty miles. If Butler isn't there, he's at
City Point. One thing certain: the rebels are scared stiff
with Butler a few miles away on the James. We could
probably take the town in a walk."

Kautz caucused his other colonels. They didn't share
Spear's confidence. Reinforcements had passed north before they struck the bridge at Stony Creek.

Kautz settled it. "We'll go on to City Point. Keep the
column closed up."

Marching north on the Jerusalem Plank Road they
turned east ten miles below Petersburg and headed for
Zion Church. Next morning, riding somewhat pridefully
ahead of his men, Kautz trotted into City Point to find
that Butler had seized the place and moved up the river to
disembark at Bermuda Hundred. Among the choicer bits
of plunder he brought with him was a once-luxurious
hackney coach whose faded satin-upholstered interior and
silver-mounted harness bespoke its past grandeur. Kautz
had used it as an ambulance and filled it with wounded
who couldn't walk. Two troopers of the 11th Pennsylvania
had laid claim to this vintage piece. Kautz rendered a
Solomon-like verdict in the dispute, "You can both have it
at the end of the war."

The limelight beamed on Kautz. Plaudits poured in.
"I dined with the general (Butler)," he wrote in his
diary. Lee himself supplied the accolade: admission that

the breaks in the Weldon road would necessitate further tightening of belts already tight, days of shorter rations for men and horses until the gaps were repaired.

Immensely pleased, Butler promptly ordered Kautz to give a dose of the same hot medicine to the Richmond-Danville and Southside railroads. On May 12 while Butler was bloodying his nose against Drewry's Bluff up the James, Kautz led his command westward through the Bermuda Hundred neck. *A la* Jeb Stuart, who this day lay dying at Richmond with a Yankee slug in his liver, Kautz began a sweep around Petersburg. He struck the Danville road at a point twelve miles below Richmond where his track busters and firemen got busy, ripping up three miles of rails and burning everything they got their hands on.

Hopscotching from one station to another Kautz torched off depots, watertanks, anything that fire could consume. Switching his operations to the Southside railroad he hit the jackpot. Lady luck came chugging along with a trainload of bacon, flour and forage en route to Petersburg—just in time for Kautz's men to seize and fire it. The glare could be seen as far as Petersburg. Ranging south Kautz wasted no more time on well-guarded bridgeheads. Picking up his trail of the week before, he crossed the Weldon road at Jarratt's to find that the watertank he had burned was replaced, a new bridge halfway across the Nottoway and the gap in the rails well on the way to closing. Colonel Tabb was still on the job so Kautz decided not to molest this wildcat a second time. On this swing-around Kautz met sporadic resistance that augured ominously. Homeguards with squirrel guns and irregulars who stayed out of sight blazed at the column from thickets and sped away. Kautz admitted, "The column was several times cut by small parties charging through it while on

the march." He reached Bermuda Hundred to find that
Butler had entrenched across the neck and retreated into
the bottle-shaped peninsula.

But Kautz had a complaint, "The Petersburg and Richmond papers were full of reports of our work but they had
not learned that I was the commander. Colonel Spear was
accredited with blame for all the damage done."

It stung his ego though the injustice was quickly recti-
fied. "The raids had been sufficiently notorious to bring
my name before the country in the papers, and not mis-
spelled either, as it had been the year before in Kentucky.
I received many congratulatory letters. My brother, a lieutenant in the Navy, had noticed my promotion in the
papers and wrote from Panama congratulating me and
stated that my photographs must now be worth ten cents
each."

At the tag end of Kautz's report of his operations he
spoke out: "I deplore a disposition to pillage and plunder
on the part of the men and a want of proper officering on
the part of some of the officers to check this tendency.
There seems to be a looseness of sentiment (not unusual
to cavalry) in this respect in the command that is to be
regretted as it adds no luster to our cause, but rather mars
the splendor of their military achievements." He might as
well have tried to dam Niagara Falls with words as to
deny cavalry its "Civil War rights."

Kautz was a disciplinarian but he was fair. Cavalry had
to be kept in line, particularly volunteers, who liked to run
wild. Ninety percent of his troopers came by that route.
But even good men raised hell sometimes. If they didn't,
there was something wrong with them. Kautz made due
allowances. In a fight his men could be depended on to do
what they were told—and die in the doing if need be.
After all, that was what cavalry was for.

The court-martial records of Kautz's men are revealing. Verdicts came in due course to him for confirmation. He weighed the man against the "crime." Take hardrock Sergeant John Scott, 1st District of Columbia Cavalry. You can still read the court's verdict and Kautz's approval. It seems that Scott had straggled on the march. Ordered by his lieutenant to get back in the column unruly Scott declined with "I'll be damned if I do." The lieutenant repeated the order. Scott protested with "Kiss my ———," fitting his words to the proper (or improper) gesture. The lieutenant tried a third time. Whereupon Scott challenged the officer to personal combat, "I'm as good a man as you. I can lick the hell out of you. Get out of my way, goddamn you!"

Court martial ensued. Charge: Insubordination. Verdict: To stand on the head of an upright barrel for six hours a day for a month. In confirming the verdict, Kautz endorsed it, "Approved, AVK. Should have been stiffer."

Yet in a fight Scott was as tough as they come, and dependable.

2

August Kautz was a dedicated soldier. As much so as any man in the Union armies. As a professional fighting man he was popular with his subordinates and the men in the ranks; not so much with the higher-ups.

An Ohio farmboy (born in Germany on the eve of his parents' emigration to America) he was just out of his teens when he volunteered for the Mexican War. Wounded at Buena Vista, he brought home a scar to show for it. It won him an appointment to West Point after he was mustered out in 1848, and he entered the Academy that same year.

Graduating in 1852 the stocky, brown-eyed lieutenant was ordered to Fort Steilacoom in Washington Territory and assigned to Company I, 4th Infantry, whose captain was a bibulous officer named Ulysses Grant. It was a welcome duty. The Grants and the Kautzes were neighbors back in Ohio.

On the far west frontier Kautz was twice clipped by redskin bullets, at the White River and Rogue River fights. He spent five years in "unbearable little posts on frontier, many nights sleeping out in the wet and cold in pursuit of Indians," but he said he preferred "this life of adventure, full of excitement and the Indian trail" to the "social life of a crowded city and the comforts of civilization."

Ordered east in 1859 he left behind a towering, unique monument to himself in what today is Mount Rainier National Park. This white, glistening memorial, the Kautz Glacier, was fashioned by nature and named in 1857 when, with an Indian and an enlisted man, Kautz scaled the second highest peak of the mountain, the first white man ever to reach this ice-clad summit. Endowed with the constitution of an ox and the physique of a gladiator, he was eminently equipped for hunting, mountain climbing, camping and the rugged game of war.

Five brevets adorned Kautz's Civil War record. Entering the struggle as a captain in the 6th United States Cavalry, he won two brevets on McClellan's bloody trek up the Peninsula in 1862. In 1863 he could be found chasing elusive John Morgan in Kentucky though he was never to break lances with Jeb Stuart.

Kautz lacked the flair and color of his blue running mates, but in a stand-up fight he had guts, and plenty of them. James Wilson did Kautz an uncalled-for disservice when he accused him of folding up when the chips were down on Wilson's raid south of Lee's army in late June

1864. It is likely Wilson would have fared far worse had Kautz not been there.

One serious defect flawed his record as a cavalryman. He was too orthodox, too much of a fighter by the book for the quick-change touch and go of the horse soldiers. Excessively methodical, a stickler for doing things as they were supposed to be done, he failed to reach the summit for just those reasons. He was never a match for the man with whom he crossed sabers most often, Wade Hampton.

In 1864 Grant put a star on him. Kautz finished off the war as a Major General of Volunteers. It is not clear why he was appointed a member of the Military Tribunal that tried and condemned the Lincoln conspirators.

Kautz played out his hand in the bloody *petite guerre* behind Grant's fortified lines at Petersburg. On the day Richmond fell Kautz and his cavalry led the blue invaders into the stricken, burning city.

8

Thermopylae at Petersburg

June 9, 1864, was a day of shine and shadow. Under the great white flotillas of clouds winging across the blue skies, August Kautz made his biggest bid for fame. Basking in the sun, Petersburg lay at his feet to be taken for the asking. Kautz's near-capture is gratefully inscribed on a rugged granite marker on the Jerusalem plank road (now Route 301) on the outskirts of the town a mile below the Crater battlefield.

This stone marks the spot where the old men and boys of Petersburg under Gen. R. E. Colston and Colonel F. M. Archer, 125 strong, on June 9, 1864 distinguished themselves in a fight with 1300 Federal cavalry under General Kautz, gaining time for the defeat of the expedition.

That's why June 9 is Petersburg's Memorial Day and why even now the name of Kautz still tastes bitter on the palates of its citizens.

On this day in 1864 Grant was licking his wounds at Cold Harbor before swinging the Army of the Potomac east across the James to pool forces with General Butler and his 40,000 men sweating it out ingloriously in his "bottle" at Bermuda Hundred.

Now, belatedly, Butler bestirred himself to pinch off the town before Grant got there. He mapped out an air-tight squeeze-play that would wrap it up in a hurry. A deserter had informed Butler that the town was thinly held by a single regiment and a force of poorly-trained, second-class militia. To clinch the deserter's story, Elizabeth Van Lew, "Crazy Bet," his secret agent in Richmond, snaked out a message giving the strength and location of Petersburg's defenders. A quick dash would turn the trick. For years after the war it was current—though never confirmed—that Miss Van Lew suggested to Butler the idea of blitzing the town with cavalry from the south while feinting with infantry from the east.

Three A.M., June 9. Kautz, with 1500 horse and two cannon, rode out of his Bermuda Hundred camp and crossed the short pontoon bridge over the Appomattox at Point of Rocks five miles east of the town. Apparently little effort was made to deaden the trampling of the horsemen on the pontoon planking though the competent Kautz issued strict orders that sabers were to be strapped tight to prevent telltale clinking against stirrup irons. The Confederates had keen ears. They could translate sounds into coming events like the seers of ancient Persia. Kautz's men rode light. No blanket rolls, one day's forage and rations. They'd find what they needed in Petersburg. The town should be in their hands by noon. Word was passed down the ranks that Petersburg was a pushover. "We were given to understand that the town was at our mercy," said a trooper of the 3rd New York Cavalry, "and that we had only to march into it." Added attraction was the town it-self, a forager's paradise. Good pickings. Grand old homes stuffed with toothsome food and desirable valuables.

Swinging south with the 11th Pennsylvania Cavalry in the lead, Kautz detoured through Prince George County to strike the Jerusalem plank road five miles below Pe-tersburg. The head of his column reached the plank road two hours behind Butler's timetable, but this couldn't be helped. A stubborn Georgia cavalry outpost gave him a running fight near Lee's Mill, blazing at the column from every thicket. Kautz finally spread-eagled the road, with flankers out wide right and left. Scooping up a hundred Georgians, he sent them back to City Point. Leaving a dozen others dead he galloped off to slam his way into the town.

Meanwhile the upper jaw of Butler's princers—4500 of his "best troops" white and colored, under General Quincy A. Gillmore—straggled over the pontoons behind Kautz to move directly on the town. The chain of mis-takes was initiated by Butler himself who gave command of this half of the operation to Gillmore rather than the more vigorous "Baldy" Smith, his other corps com-mander. Gillmore began by fouling up the timing. He was ordered to move out ahead of Kautz. Butler's orders were explicit, "This is not to be artillery work, but a quick decisive push." Gillmore's mission was not a diver-sion. He was to crack the feebly manned rebel works on the east, storm ahead and join forces with Kautz breaking through from the south. If Gillmore penetrated the town before Kautz, he was to destroy all public buildings, pub-lic stores, the bridge across the Appomattox, depots, freight cars and anything else he thought destroyable. Off the record Butler said, burn the town if it seemed desirable, meaning it would be. With some élan Gillmore's men drove in the gray pickets; yet instead of a walloping assault he made a pitiful gesture. Approaching Battery Five, a huge earthwork on the eastern sector, he pirouetted his men before it as if on parade. Awed by its size he decided it was too strongly held and pulled his men back without trying, and, even more exasperating to the hopeful Butler, without waiting to hear Kautz firing at the south portal. Inside the fortification the Confederates were staging a resounding bluff. General Wise had three Negro bands marching up and down, waving flags, blaring patriotic airs as if a dozen regiments were arriving, come in the nick of time. It was a threadbare ruse but Gillmore took a good long look at the flags, listened to the musical commotion and promptly decamped. By nine o'clock he had withdrawn five miles where he sat down and twiddled his thumbs.

But the town was alerted. The bell in the courthouse tower tolled ominously. The enemy was at the gates and the city well nigh defenseless. Beauregard's veterans were holding the lines north of the Appomattox. To combat the twin-drive—Gillmore from the east, Kautz from the south—Petersburg's guardians amounted to about fifteen hundred, six hundred of them seasoned troops, the rest, as Butler described them, "old men and boys, the grave and the cradle being robbed in equal proportions."

Panoplied in choking dust Kautz's column plowed doggedly up the Jerusalem plank road. Gray pickets scuttled ahead of him as he drew near his goal. At about 10:30 Kautz's bluecoats halted, out of range, before a crude earthwork barricade with fence rails stuck in it like a big pincushion. It lay athwart the plank road where it inter-

sected the perimeter of unmanned breastworks about Petersburg. Today it was the tollgate to the town.

Lying low behind this roadblock was a band of "second
class" militia (just as Butler had said), 125 old men and
boys from the town and adjacent countryside, teenagers,
over-agers, and even silverheads. They did not even have
uniforms. One, Francis Major, seventy-odd, could at least
pull a trigger. This homeguard had been on watch ever
since Butler came up the James and began his threatening
probes. Hearing Gillmore's sporadic firing to the northeast they had manned their barricade, only to wait hours
before two frantic vedettes came tearing up the road
shouting that blue cavalry, "Miles of it," was right around
the bend.

Commanding this outpost was Major Fletcher A. Archer,
Mexican War veteran, who, like

> *Sempronius Atratrius*
> *Was left in charge at home,*
> *With boys and with gray-headed men*
> *To keep the gates of Rome.*

Archer had disposed his little band along the work judi-
ciously. It overlapped to the right and left. Walking along
the line Archer gave them a calm, unemotional pep talk
that stressed the home and fireside angle. Paraphrasing
words uttered on Lexington Green ninety years before, he
said, "Don't fire until I give the command." A wise pre-
caution. The youngsters were getting jumpy. Martial
ardor was beating high. Here, at last, were live Yankees to
shoot at. They'd been hankering for the chance. Off yonder, three hundred yards down the road, the blue horse
had halted to reconnoiter but apparently were lining up
to move ahead again. Strung out along their barricade the

defenders were already poking their firelocks over the parapet and taking aim at their intended victims. Their gunbarrels were crammed with anything shootable, even buck and birdshot.

From a young "Petersburg Rifleman," Anthony M. Keiley, who stood behind the barricade with his townsmen, came a nearly contemporary account of what happened. He said, "Our venerable muskets were not worth a tinker's imprecation at longer range than one hundred yards and were compelled *per force* to watch the preparations for our capture or slaughter, much after the fashion that a rational turtle may be presumed to contemplate the preliminaries of a civic dinner in London."

Without waiting for Kautz to ride up from the middle of the column, Colonel Spear ordered the lead squadron of the 11th Pennsylvania to charge the obstruction with sabers drawn. There was little delay. Spear was a rough-and-tumble, let's-get-going cavalryman. Placing himself abreast of the squadron he turned to his bugler, "Give 'em a Charge! Make it a good one!" The bugler complied piercingly. Then, bellowing "Come on, boys!" they were off. It began at a rapid walk. At two hundred yards they spurred to a faster gait. Not a shot had been fired. Their long blades glittered in the sunlight. Their steeds caught the excitement. Upping their pace and yelling like demons they racked up the road at a thundering gallop.

For the raw, amateur riflemen behind the obstruction it was a thrilling, awe-inspiring sight. "Here they come!" spat from mouth to mouth. "Hundreds of 'em! Great God!" But they stood their ground. It looked as if the very impetus of the blue avalanche would override the barrier and pile up on top of them.

"Steady, boys! Steady!" It was Archer's calming voice. He waited. It was a hard wait for the boys whose fingers

chafed at the triggers. At about seventy-five yards (effective execution range of the vintage firearms) the lead
horseman's big yellow chevrons stood out like sign boards.
Just then Major Archer gave the magic word, "Fire!" The
parapet erupted in jets of red. The blue frontrunners
caught the blast in midair. It staggered their onrush and
it hurt. Sabers flew through the air describing bright or-
bits. A trooper pitched from his saddle like a bluebird off
a rail to sprawl in the dust face down. His wounded horse
went screaming off into Timothy Rives' cornfield. Enveloped in dust and smoke, horses and riders milled about
in a confused mêlée.

The gunsmoke cleared. Behind the barrier Major Archer
spoke again. "Load!" It wasn't necessary. The boys were
already at it. The oldsters too. "Ready!" The fowling
pieces rattled on the parapet. "Fire!" Into the disorgan-
ized jam-up on the road went another volley. It was
aimed too high. Old men, young men were quivering
with excitement. Had this burst been fired straight like
the first the execution would have been murderous. As it
was, one dead and five wounded lay in the road. Riderless
horses dashed wildly into the fields. The first wave was
broken. In his second report of the action Colonel Spear
said, "Had the enemy reserved this fire for a few minutes
longer the most fearful result to my command would have
ensued."

Keiley described it, "A little of that military coquetry
called reconnaissance determined our enemy to feel us
first with a small portion of his command and on came at
a sweeping gallop a gallant company of troopers, with as
confident an air as though all that was necessary was that
they should 'come' and 'see' in order to 'conquer.' Every-
one could see that this was a party we could easily manage
and we possessed, therefore, our souls in great patience

till we could see the chevron on the arm of the non-commissioned officer who led them—a brave fellow—and then there broke forth (from such amiable muskets as could be induced to go off) a discharge that scattered the cavaliers like chaff."

Hastily picking up his casualties Spear wheeled his squadron and dusted back out of gunshot to re-form for a second try, when Kautz cantered up. But success was too intoxicating for the boys. One bantling youngster, overcome by zeal, leaped on the parapet to wave his blanket at the retreating bluecoats and shout, "Come on back, you bastards! Try it again!"

This, Kautz was preparing to do, but he went at it as if he had all day. First he plied his binoculars, eyeing everything in sight. He studied the redoubt as if it were an abstruse problem in higher mathematics. The moment called for a fast round-the-flanks play. No waiting. Kautz had actually surprised the redoubt. Butler had assured him the defenders would take to their heels like a bunch of scared yokels at a show of force. Kautz had convinced himself of it. Instinctively he sized them up as "green-apples" (he said as much) who would melt away under gunfire like butter in the June sun. But he took his time getting ready to smash 'em up and gallop into the town. Every few minutes he'd cup his ears hoping to hear Gillmore banging away at the northeast portal.

His other colonels rode up for a huddle.

"General, we'd better move in on these bastards in a hurry." It was "Sergeant" Spear and he knew what he was talking about.

Kautz took out his watch. "Let's get well set before we try again. We should wait till we hear Gillmore's firing. I thought he'd be there now."

"Maybe he can't get there," argued Spear.

"We don't have enough men to go in by ourselves," said Kautz, chucking away a dead cigar and lighting a fresh one.

"We do if we move at once," replied Spear with some impatience. "We don't need Gillmore. These bums are homeguards. We can clean them out in fifteen minutes. Look at this." He picked a lead pellet out of his neck. "They're shooting birdshot at us."

Spear was a good soldier. His disgust was obvious but discipline and obedience were ingrained.

Kautz decided it. He'd make hash of these brash upstarts in short order. Fine words, only it wasn't short. Kautz frittered away precious minutes deploying his men. Every saber (or so it seemed) had to be in just the right place, every piece of gear just as the book said. Even the men in the ranks grumbled. They knew it would go harder with them the longer they waited. Gillmore's falsetto poke at Battery Five was even in Kautz's favor. The Confederates couldn't spare a drummer boy from that sector to reinforce the plank road. Gillmore might snap out of it and plunge back in earnest. Time was of the essence, and that too was in Kautz's favor *at this moment*.

Dismounting two squadrons of the 1st District carbineers he fanned them out in two waves of skirmishers on both sides of the road to slide round the flanks, take the redoubt in rear and give the "insiders" a dose of sixteen-shooter medicine. On a second line, at right angles to the road, he strung out Pennsylvania horse, 300 of them. They were to boot up to the embankment, dismount, leap on the parapet and get busy with their Colts. Kautz's dispositions were good. He'd overwhelm the redoubt by sheer power of fire and numbers. But what should have taken twenty-five minutes was piddled away to almost an hour.

At eleven-thirty (there were four variants of the exact

time) bugles again crowed the Charge and the bluecoats moved out for the kill. Running wide, the 1st District men curvetted round the flanks. Their carbines spat out a galling fire that dropped the homeguards like partridges in a covey. The Pennsylvanians charged up to the parapet, took a volley in their stride, dismounted and clambered up like Roman wall-scalers. Their Colts poured it on. In minutes the old men and boys were being shot at from three sides, and falling fast.

Continued Keiley: "Now came the serious attack. The enemy advanced, outnumbering us five to one, and armed with the six shooting rifle, thus increasing over fifty fold their actual superiority—and there we fought them till we were so surrounded that the two men nearest me were shot in the back while facing the line of original approach; till our camp in rear of the work was full of the foe; till the noblest blood of our city stained the clay of the breastworks as they gave out their lives, gun in hand and faces forward, on the spot where their officers had placed them.

"One by one they fell around me—Bellingham, the last—and as I turned and stooped to change his position to one of greater comfort at his request, the enemy swooped over the earthwork behind me, the foremost presenting his loaded carbine, demanded my surrender with unrepeatable violence of language that suggested bloodshed. All avenue of escape being cut off I yielded with what grace I could to my fate, captive to a hatchet-faced member of the 1st District of Columbia cavalry."

The assault, said Kautz, "so demoralized the raw troops that little damage was done to our side. The enemy lost heavily in dead and wounded. We took forty-two prisoners and one cannon." This last, incidentally, was no help to the defenders. They had round shot only, no canister.

Surrounded, swept by sheets of rapid fire, the little garrison was about to be annihilated when Major Archer ordered a quick retreat. Otherwise his last man, and himself, would have been killed or captured. They retired—
what was left of them—in reasonably good order, leaving
behind a bloody mess. Near Blandford Cemetery they
turned into the New Road that sloped down into the
town. Here they met the "patients and the penitents,"
convalescent soldiers from the Confederate hospital who
could at least pull a trigger, and jailbirds whose clamor to
be released to fight was gratified on the spot.

Kautz's bugler blew Halt though it was surely no time
to halt. Off to the left the spires of Petersburg rose against
the blue sky. Kautz actually stood at the city limits, on the
crest Grant would reach for in vain seven weeks hence in
a bloody squash of 5000 dead and wounded boys in blue.

But where was Gillmore? Kautz wondered. Retrospec-
tively, he was to say, "Could I have had Gillmore at hand
we could have held Petersburg and the long historic siege
that followed would have taken place elsewhere if at all."
But he could have gone it alone even at this late moment.
The fates, or whoever shuffles the cards in the game of war,
had stacked them for him. What he needed at this moment was drive from within. But Kautz didn't drive. More
time was frittered away. The bulk of his men had hardly
fired a shot. Keeping up pressure on the routed homeguards he could have hammered on and taken the town.

Meanwhile General Beauregard, importuned for help,
was notifying Richmond he might have to abandon the
town, "Have sent all the troops I can spare from my lines."
Drawing off Graham's Battery, Petersburg's Own, and
General Jimmy Dearing's regiment of cavalry, he sped
them off to the rescue. Lashing their mounts they came on

the run, but they had seven miles to cover and Kautz stood at the city's edge.

Again the bugles sang Forward. Kautz turned into the New Road that led down a ravine and up a hill into the town. Off to the right Kautz's field glasses revealed the city reservoir which he apparently mistook for a fortified stockade that momentarily might burst into fire. His glasses may also have revealed numbers of women and children who, with sinking hearts, lined the opposite hill-top to watch the approach of the invaders.

On reaching Petersburg, Dearing saw the hopelessness of the situation and promptly telegraphed Beauregard, "If the city is to be saved, send reinforcements at once. Enemy has taken entrenchments and is advancing and in possession of part of the defensive works around Peters-burg."

But Kautz was advancing too cautiously, killing time, consulting his apprehensions. It was the old McClellan bugaboo when he stood in sight of the roof tops of Rich-mond in 1862. Kautz was wasting tremendous, imponder-able minutes in which the war might have been shortened by months. Undying fame awaited him if only he would slam ahead, take his losses and seize the town.

At the bottom of the ravine Kautz halted his column again because, as he said, "The enemy suddenly opened fire from the other side of the ravine with four pieces of artillery and several hundred muskets. The advance was so much below the enemy that little if any damage was done as the balls passed over our heads. Before a second volley could be delivered we fell back under cover."

Graham's Battery had crossed Pocahontas Bridge over the Appomattox on the gallop. Tanned, sweat-stained, the artillery boys bent forward in their saddles like jockeys, lashing the mounts to more speed. They turned corners with the outside wheels of cannon-carriages spinning in the air, sped over rough streets that might well have exploded the jolting caissons. Unlimbering two guns on the crest of the hill they began splattering canister at Kautz's men at the bottom of the ravine though the Official Reports said pointedly that their fire didn't wound a man.

"An examination of the situation"—again Kautz talking to his diary—"convinced me that whilst I could meet and overcome the force confronting me I should be delayed so long that reinforcements from the main line would be in my rear and cut me off, for there was no evidence that General Gillmore was occupying the enemy in the direction of the Jordan Point Road along which he had advanced. As we retired by the way we had come the enemy opened upon us with one piece of artillery and some musketry."

Kautz's retreat was precipitate. His losses were trifling, four killed, twenty wounded. He still had nearly 1500 battle-wise horse soldiers who could have wrapped up the town and by this time be resting their mounts under the big elms and maples along Sycamore Street. But the grandsires and boys had at least won a reprieve for the town, saving it for bigger and redder battles to come and a ten months siege. Confederate Brigadier General R. E. Colston, commanding the Petersburg defenses on the right, admitted, "Had they (the homeguards) retreated five or ten minutes sooner the artillery, which was the first check to Kautz's advance, instead of meeting them at the south side of the city, would have been intercepted before they could cross the bridge, and the city probably remained in enemy hands."

Kautz was apparently licked before he started. His

diary reveals it, "I had little confidence in the attack for I had no faith in the cavalry or the colored troops." He had carried out his orders to the letter. He broke through though he failed to cash in on it and tossed away the opportunity of a career. Butler blamed Gillmore for failure to take Petersburg and cashiered him on the spot. The Petersburg slip-through-the-fingers, in part, induced the bad blood between Kautz and young General James Wilson, who once assailed Kautz with prolonging the war. In his memoirs Wilson went further, "Kautz was an infantryman who was never a success as a cavalry commander." Yet Wilson poured out the same vitriol on Sheridan. Kautz was at least in good company. His fault was lack of the *sine qua non* of horse fighting, the element of recklessness, to take a chance and crowd it, plus the inability to do the unorthodox and do it fast. Petersburg would have been his had he done so.

2

At eight o'clock that night Kautz swung from his horse and stumbled stiffly into General Butler's oversize tent at Bermuda Hundred. He had been in the saddle twenty hours.

Entering the stuffy, dimly lit tent he found the squint-eyed commander of the Army of the James on the rampage, blueing the air with oaths and ire. Butler's audience, two of Grant's staff colonels, sat on camp stools in discreet silence. Butler paused to introduce able Horace Porter and Cyrus Ballou Compton, young West Pointer, to whose judgment at the moment Grant paid greater heed than that of any other man on his staff save perhaps Rawlins. Presumably, it was Compton's reiterated demand for head on, smash-'em-up assaults on Lee's army that had strewn Northern corpses and reddened the landscape from the Rapidan to Cold Harbor.

Resuming his flow of invective Butler motioned Kautz to a seat and zoomed off on another flight. He was livid. His "stout, shapeless body" shook with rage. Between outbursts he ambled back and forth over the tent floor "on a set of legs that looked as if made for somebody else, and hastily glued to him by mistake." Object of his outcries was Gillmore, whose miserable showing (as Butler believed) had produced the day's military abortion. Presently Kautz managed to explain why he had not fought his way into Petersburg. It sounded plausible. GHQ would later assay his near-capture though no official strictures were ever directed at him. Just now his prestige was on the rise. His two successful rail-twisting raids had showered him with éclat. The howls of the Confederates over the damage to their lifeline railroads was enough in itself to glaze over his miscarriage before Petersburg.

Presently Butler read aloud from a despatch he intended telegraphing the Secretary of War, "General Kautz charged the enemy works at Petersburg and carried them, penetrating the town, but not being supported by General Gillmore, who had withdrawn his forces without a conflict, he was obliged to withdraw without further effect. General Kautz captured 40 prisoners and 1 piece of artillery. It is a misfortune that Gillmore did not support him."

Butler then turned to Kautz, "General, I am satisfied with what you've done. Now to something else."

Thereupon Kautz was inducted into the top secret. Grant was about to move his army by the left flank from Cold Harbor, cross the James, seize Petersburg and strike at Lee's army through its underbelly. He had despatched the two colonels to Bermuda Hundred (roundabout) to reconnoiter down the James and "select the best point on the river for crossing and the safest from attack while crossing." They had made a choice and were that night embarking on their hazardous return journey to Grant's headquarters.

Porter spoke up. "General Kautz, we've selected two bridgeheads, Wilcox Landing on the north bank, and Windmill Point on the south. The river is narrowest between these two points. Moreover, it offers the best protection for our huge wagon trains. We also have about five thousand beef cattle to get across. We've thought of swimming them."

"You'd drown half of them, Colonel," advised Kautz. "They'd be washed up on the shore for miles down the river. The place you've selected is half a mile wide. The current is too swift for cattle to swim."

Butler cut in. "Them West Point engineers can decide how to get 'em across." Apparently, it mattered little to Butler that Colonel Compton was one of "them West Point engineers," or that Compton had graduated number one in his Class, 1855. Butler's distaste for West Point and all it stood for amounted to positive genius. "They know more'n anybody else. What we need is a safe place to graze 'em. That's a lot of beefsteak."

Kautz agreed that it was. His thoroughness produced a suggestion. On taking command of Butler's cavalry division he had memorized every crude road map available. He already knew Prince George County along the James below City Point by heart.

"There's Secession Ruffin's place, Beechwood," he ventured.

"That old sonofabitch!" exploded Butler. "No, we ain't thought of his place."

"Exactly where is it, general?" inquired Compton.

"On Coggin's Point up the river several miles from Windmill Point. Almost directly opposite Westover. Good grass and pastures a mile long."

Butler turned to the two colonels. "Sounds like it's made to order. You'll report it to General Grant."

Kautz added, "We're already picketing the Stage Road from Fort Powhatan to City Point. It passes a mile from Beechwood. That would give the cattle some protection."

"They'll need it," observed Butler. "Them rebel bastards are getting hungrier every day. After all Lincoln ain't a bull. He can't make cattle like he makes generals. Secession Ruffin! Won't he have fits when he hears about it."

Butler reached for his decanter. "Commissary rotgut's better than nothing," he commented sourly as he poured out four stiff drinks. "To your safe return, gentlemen!"

9

Grant Has General Troubles

Grant had reason to boast. "I think it is pretty well to get across a great river and come up here and attack Lee in his rear before he is ready for us." Seated on the edge of his field cot in his temporary headquarters at City Point, clad in his undershirt and drawers, Grant was indulging in a rare bit of braggadocio. An aide had just brought him a late report from the front. It was a deep, hot night June 16, 1864.

Grant had won the Petersburg sweepstakes, but the town was not yet his. The wide open chance to pocket this strategic plum was at the very instant slipping through the fingers of his overcautious, slumbering generals. Two tries had failed. With the town dangling by a hair, Grant's nine to one odds were fading with the minutes. The firing of the second try had died down to sporadic outbursts.

The official records are crammed with unprecise, hesitating orders. Hardly a line bears the crackling ring of authority and urgency which the moment demanded. Into the records creep recrimination and vacillation by the men who could make or break the race for Petersburg. Grant's whole army was south of the James. Thousands of them were banging at Petersburg's eastern portal. Lee's main forces had not yet crossed the river.

The instant called for a fast powerplay, *now*, not tomorrow, with everything he could throw in. Grant had that day ordered, "I want an assault made at 6 o'clock in the evening," though his words have a casualness hardly understandable.

Yet more amazing was the blunder of the day before. Able "Baldy" Smith's Eighteenth Corps, 16,000 men, had cracked the eastern rim of Petersburg's vaunted Dimmock Line and snatched half a mile of it, swamping its meager defenders. But the timing was awful. Staffwork collapsed. Coordination between artillery and foot soldiers was tragic. Even so, Petersburg was Smith's for the taking, so meager was the gray line Smith attacked with clouds of skirmishers rather than in column. He personally reconnoitered and decided the earthworks were a gigantic delusion. By nine o'clock his bluecoats had swept over the gray entrenchments, capturing men and guns. When General Hinks urged driving on into Petersburg Smith vetoed it. A quick decisive jab now would finish the matter and Grant could ride Cincinnatti into the town with a band playing "Hail the Conquering Hero Comes," if he so desired. Smith believed the town lay at his mercy. He was right. In a field wire to Ben Butler he boasted, "I hold the key to Petersburg."

To clinch it, out of the night came Hancock's Second Corps swinging off the dusty ridges of the City Point Road. They resembled gray ghosts under coatings of dust. Weary, grimy, they were full of fight and ready to go

in. But Smith had already decided on the next move. He
would bivouac for the night. He asked of Hancock only
that he relieve the men in the trenches who had stormed
the rebel positions. Petersburg was his and tomorrow just
round the corner. So two generals and forty thousand men
called it a night and went to sleep while the Confederates pitched in like beavers. Retiring nearer the city they
dug new trenches with everything that would turn even a
spoonful of protective dirt. For them it was a tense, ex-
hausting night.

Meade's aide, Theodore Lyman, bemoaned bitterly to
his diary, "Oh! that they had attacked at once. Petersburg
would have gone like a rotten branch. In war there is a
critical instant—a night—perhaps only a half hour
when everything culminates. He is the military genius
who recognizes this instant and acts upon it, neither pre-
cipitating nor postponing the critical moment. There is
thus good reason why great soldiers should be so rare that
generations pass without producing a single one."

On the scene at Petersburg was Beauregard. Addicted to
vanity and (so 'twas claimed) tinting his locks, the little
Creole was nonetheless a good soldier. Few could have
met the crisis more ably than he. Manning his lines
against the Union shock were 2200 effectives and a handful of cavalry. One man to every four and a half yards of
the works. For two days he had kept a staff officer hot-
footing between critical Petersburg and Lee north of the
James, begging for reinforcements.

Beauregard would later admit, "Petersburg was clearly
at the mercy of the Federal commander who had all but
captured it. Strange to say General Smith contented himself with breaking into our lines and attempted nothing
further that night." But Beauregard forgot to mention
Gracie's Alabamians who rushed to a gap in the line vow-

ing the Yankees would never enter the town but over the dead bodies of their last man. Their stand closed the break temporarily enabling Beauregard to withdraw his feeble forces to a new line unpleasantly nearer the town.

A private in the ranks of the Second Corps that had dusted through the long June day to reach Petersburg recalled, "Every man in the II Army Corps knew that not many miles away Lee's army was marching furiously to save Petersburg and Richmond and the Confederacy. We could almost see those veteran troops lean, squalid and hungry and battle-torn, with jaws set and anxious looking eyes, striding rapidly through the dust, pouring over bridges, crowding through the streets of villages and hurrying to face us, and we knew that once they got behind the works in our front we could not drive them out."

But this night of June 15 nothing "culminated," and the next day things lagged until 6 P.M. Then Meade and his staff rode out to mastermind the attack Grant had so lackadaisically (it seemed) ordered and watch the bluecoats go forward. Taking a stand behind his batteries thundering away at the freshly dug rebel trenches across a little valley he witnessed "a most striking sight," framed against a backdrop of the town's church spires and the sullen red sunset. The blue guns were blasting spitefully. Shells blue and gray whizzed overhead, musketry rolled heavily. "The air, hazy with dust, gave a copper red color to the declining sun, which was soon heightened by the powder smoke that rose from the batteries. The scene reminded me of one of those stiff but faithful engravings of Napoleon's battles that one sees in European collections."

Night came on. A second day of indecision had failed to take Petersburg. By midnight Grant had ninety thousand men facing Beauregard's pitiful barrier. June 17 was to be victory day. Petersburg would be dragooned out of Con-

federate hands. For Beauregard "the last had arrived."
He had managed, by robbing Peter to pay Paul in stripping his Bermuda Hundred neck lines, to get ten thousand men along the Petersburg east front. Grant's odds
were dwindling. The day was ill-starred, indecisive, red.
Victory still withheld her accolade.

June 18 saw the Union high command's last chance to
destroy their weak antagonist before Lee's whole army
arrived. At dawn Lee's iron veterans began streaming into
the Petersburg lines though Lee himself "was not yet
satisfied as to General Grant's movements." But now to
finish the job. Three Federal corps, masses of blue,
hurled themselves against the Petersburg works in a cruel,
brutal affair that bade fair to repeat the slaughter of Cold
Harbor. Valiantly Grant's men died by hundreds. Lee's
veterans knew their business only too well. Dealing out
death and agony had become an art for them.

While Lee groped, mystified, refusing to believe Grant
had vacated his shallow trenches at Cold Harbor and
crossed the James, Grant's generals had thrown away portentous opportunity against the feeble Petersburg lines.
But Lee had tossed away equally momentous hours. Expert artilleryman, Porter Alexander, sized it up succinctly:
"During these three days June 15, 16 and 17 Grant's
whole army was arriving at and attacking Petersburg
which was defended at first by about 2500 men. Lee, with
Longstreet's and Hill's corps, for the same three days lay
idle in the woods on the north bank only replacing some
of Beauregard's troops taken to Petersburg from in front
of Butler. But for this Longstreet's corps might have
manned the entrenchments of Petersburg when Grant's
troops first appeared before them, and it is not too much
to claim that his defeat would have been not less bloody
and disastrous than was the one at Cold Harbor. Thus,

the last and best chance of Confederate success, was not lost in the repulse at Gettysburg, nor in any combat of arms. They were lost during the three days of lying idle in camp, believing that Grant was hemmed in by the broad part of the James below City Point and had nowhere to go but to come and attack us."

One night before bridging the James, Grant called fire-eating Brigadier General James H. Wilson (West Point 1860) to his tent. Grant had taken a fancy to the flashy young officer in the West and given him command of a cavalry division for the big shove south from the Rapidan. Wilson called the shots as he saw them. He was one of the "Grant Men."

This night Grant appeared strained, worried. Bluntly he asked, "Wilson, what is the matter with this army?"

Wilson replied frankly, "There is a great deal the matter with it, but I can tell you much more easily how to cure it."

"How?" asked Grant.

"Send for Parker, the Indian chief, and, after giving him a tomahawk, a scalping knife, and a gallon of the worst whiskey the Commissary Department can supply, send him out with orders to bring in the scalps of major generals."

Grant smiled. "Whose?" The "chief" was one of Grant's staff, Colonel Ely Parker, full blooded Iroquois, black haired and dark visaged.

"Oh, the first he comes to, and so on in succession till he gets at least a dozen."

Nor was Grant ever to read the tragic words his gallant brigadier, Emory Upton, wrote his sister:

I am disgusted with the generalship displayed. Our men have, in many instances, been foolishly and wantonly sacrificed. Assault after assault has been ordered upon the enemy entrenchments when they knew nothing about the strength or position of the enemy. Thousands of lives might have been spared by the exercise of a little skill; but, as it is, the courage of the poor men is expected to obviate all difficulties. Some of our corps commanders are not fit to be corporals. Lazy and indolent, they will not even ride along their lines; yet, without hesitancy, they will order us to attack the enemy, no matter what their position or numbers. Twenty thousand of our killed and wounded should today be in our ranks.

This from Emory Upton during the shambles on the way to the James.

2

Historians have equipped Grant with a "basilisk gaze." If he had a "basilisk gaze," this humid June afternoon it was no doubt fixed on a mental image of what was happening to his grand campaign to end all campaigns. The costly overland drive had not as yet panned out as successfully as he had hoped. The whole shebang was behind the Culpeper timetable. Not yet had Sherman scooped up Atlanta. Nor had Grant himself cornered Lee as he believed he would. Before the Rapidan jump-off, Grant, explaining his strategy to his staff, went to a map on the wall and put his finger on Petersburg, remarking, "When my troops are there Richmond is mine. Lee must retreat or surrender."

Now Grant was "there," or right at it. Lee, stubbornly, naturally, refused to come out of his trenches into the open where Grant's multitudinous bluecoats and cannon could wipe out his army in one big bloodstain. Mathematically, Lee was correct. But Lee himself had said that when Grant reached the James, "It will become a siege and then it will be a mere question of time."

Sorest spot on the military vista was the Shenandoah Valley where General Franz Sigel had fiascoed miserably, verifying Chief of Staff Halleck's estimate of the German peacock: "If you expect anything from him you will be mistaken. He will do nothing but run. He never did anything else."

Actually Sigel possessed about as much military skill as a strutting rooster. He was sincere enough, but sincerity doesn't always win battles. He affected a warlike decor that rattled like a pedler with a load of frying pans. But Sigel's men liked his jangling get-up and got a thrill out of his pep talk the day before the Army of the Shenandoah took off down the Valley, a day ahead of Grant's passage of the Rapidan.

His objective was Staunton, vital supply and shipping station where the Virginia Central came over the Blue Ridge into the Valley though, of course, his actual target lay all around him on the sweet, uncharred vale of the Shenandoah, the Confederacy's granary, now carpeted with green, soon to be golden, fields of grain. Sigel vowed to reduce it to a bed of black embers before the grain ripened.

But disaster overtook him on May 15 at New Market where he encountered John C. Breckinridge, former U.S. Senator from Kentucky and now able general, charged with stopping the Federal drive up the Valley. Concentrating his small command at New Market and calling for help on the "seedcorn battalion" of two hundred and fifty cadets of the Virginia Military Institute, Breckinridge gave Sigel a terrific beating. At a crucial moment the "rock-a-bye-babies" from the Institute swept over the luckless Sigel's lines, bayoneting cannoneers, taking their losses and consigning Sigel to the limbo where he belonged.

In a masterly piece of euphemism Sigel telegraphed Grant of his helter-skelter rout and retreat from New Market, describing his defeat as a "retrograde movement affected in good order." The bad news reached Grant during the savage hand to hand struggle at the Bloody Angle. Grant took the tidings imperturbably. His unassailable calm was unruffled. Only once did he ever cry over spilt milk, or blood, as it was in this case, and that came long after. Like Edison, he had the custom when a cow kicked over the bucket to pick it up and go after another cow. His way to retrieve disaster was to redouble his effort and wipe out the past by success.

Out went Sigel. In shuttled David Hunter, oldest West Pointer wearing a star. Like his predecessor he was no great shakes as a leader. Sixty-two years old, he was considered handsome by Washington standards. His combination handlebar-waterfall mustache gave him a fierce, up-and-at-'em look that charmed the ladies. It differed from the run of the mill Civil War facial crabgrass. He personified the adage "Old soldiers never die" though sometimes they fumble. Of Hunter, Grant asked that his "troops eat out Virginia clear and clean as far as they go so that crows flying over it for the balance of the season will have to carry their own provender."

On May 26 Hunter's army rolled up the Valley. Destination: Lynchburg, where the Confederacy had storehouses, foundries, factories, railroads waiting to be torched off. This done he was to move back to Staunton, turn east over the Blue Ridge, destroying the Virginia Central as he went, and hook up with Sheridan at Charlottesville. But Hunter was not to win laurels on the battlefield. His chief éclat arose from presiding over the trial of the slayers of Abraham Lincoln.

In his brief stay in the lovely Shenandoah Hunter acquired a reputation for infamy which the passage of a century has not erased. He brought wanton, calculated pillage, and plunder. Upon reaching Lexington, he avenged Sigel's defeat at New Market by burning the buildings of the Virginia Military Institute. Up in flames went handsome private homes, including that of Virginia's Governor Letcher. It was dress rehearsal for the entry of the hottest torch-bearer of all, Phil Sheridan, soon to come on stage.

But a knight errant sped over the Blue Ridge to challenge the blue dragon scorching the Valley, "Old Jubilee" Early, a cussing, tobacco-chewing, grizzled West Point classmate of Jo Hooker and John Sedgwick. A picturesque soldier and a handy man in a fight. To meet Hunter's threat Lee ordered Early to withdraw his veteran II Corps from the lines east of Richmond and force-march to the Valley. By foot and rail Early's men hustled over the mountains to Lynchburg where the grayjackets hopped off their flatcars and caught the house-burner redhanded. Suddenly Hunter became the hunted. He fled northward, strewing his retreat with a second trail of incendiarism. Faking a shortage of ammunition he took his army completely out of the Valley, running over the Alleghenies into what had become West Virginia. His "bold march" came to a quick end. So did Hunter. Grant's Valley strategy had fizzled badly.

Having scotched Hunter, Early streaked up the Valley to give Yankeedom's capital the scare of its life. The Valley was open and wheat was being harvested. As if Stonewall Jackson's Foot Cavalry was on the march again,

Early's men drove hard, across the Potomac to the outskirts of Washington while the Federal high command went into panicky handsprings. President Lincoln called on the populace: "Let us be vigilant and keep cool." It was mid-July and hot as hell, and Early was at the gates of the city. Grant had to pull his veteran VI Corps out of the Petersburg lines and despatch it to the capital. By July 15 Early had played out his hand and the capital breathed easier.

Thus did Grant's frustrations mount with the heat of the summer while down at Coggin's Point three thousand or more beef cattle fattened on the lush green pastures around Beechwood.

Down from Washington came Lincoln's pep-up telegram, "Hold on with a bull-dog grip, and chew and choke, as much as possible." Grant was doing exactly that.

3

On June 7 Grant had hopefully despatched his new cavalry chief, Phil Sheridan, with two trooper divisions, to keep a rendezvous at Charlottesville with Hunter, who after desecrating the Valley, was to cross the Blue Ridge and pool forces with Sheridan. Together they would sweep down the Virginia Central railroad (now the C & O) and destroy it and the James River Canal completely down as near Richmond as they could drive. Sheridan still basked in the glory of slaying fabulous Jeb Stuart at Yellow Tavern.

On this barnstorming trip Sheridan carried a galaxy of daring horse officers—David Gregg, Wesley Merritt, George A. Custer and A. T. Torbert. These tough young leaders knew their business. So did their blue troopers whose firepower (new Spencer six-shot carbines) gave them a fifty percent handicap over the Confederate single-shot muzzleloaders.

But Grant had overlooked a slight consideration: rebel cavalry might have something to say about Sheridan's movements. Commanding the gray horse in Stuart's stead was a remarkable fighter, Wade Hampton, as fine a combat officer as the South had produced, a horse soldier who wielded a twelve-pound sword and wielded it well and often. Twice it had cleft adversaries' skulls down to the neck. Riding without let-up Hampton caught up with Sheridan near Trevillians, a way station on the Virginia Central. In a two-day, pure cavalry duel, with losses running high, Hampton punished Sheridan severely. The blue units were badly cut up. Blue and gray both claimed victory.

Punch-drunk, Sheridan hotfooted back for the Union lines as fast as exhausted horses could carry him. En route his men shot over two thousand of their own horses who couldn't keep pace with the retreat. On June 25 his command straggled down to Wilcox Landing on the James where the gray riders gave him such a blazing farewell that Grant despatched infantry to bail him out, "Sheridan has been attacked this evening and with great difficulty and heavy loss of men has saved his trains so far."

Sheridan's apologia spoke for itself in his report to Grant, "I regret my inability to carry out your instructions."

While Sheridan was limping back circuitously from Trevillians, Grant had sped a daring young man in blue, James Harrison Wilson, to raid westward, then circle south round Petersburg and cut the Southside and Weldon lines feeding Lee's army. If Grant could cut Lee's communication, and *keep them cut,* starvation, more deadly than Miniés, grape and canister, would do the rest. To help with the destruction Grant ordered Kautz and his division to accompany Wilson. It was to be a repeat of Kautz's fire-throwing act on a far grander scale.

With the parting blessing of Abraham Lincoln, and after visiting Grant's headquarters, the raiders set off with high hopes. Meeting little resistance, they struck at will, gapping the Southside railroad westward for twenty-five miles. Turning their attention to the Richmond & Danville they rode hard to destroy the Staunton River bridge, only to be repulsed by a small band under Captain L. T. Farinholt whose defense of the bridge still glorifies his name. Swinging east to rip up the Weldon Road, Wilson and Kautz were trapped by Wade Hampton near Reams Station south of Petersburg. Their commands were all but annihilated. The depredations of Wilson's men had verged on the fanatic. In Wilson's own captured headquarters wagon, Hampton's men found a silver communion service seized from St. John's Church in Lunenberg County.

But Wilson and Kautz had struck a body blow at Lee's vital supply lines, leaving breaks it would take weeks to repair. Said Grant, "I regret the disaster, but the work done by Wilson and his cavalry is of great importance."

10

Beleaguered City

By mid-June Grant had massed one hundred thousand men against the defenses of Petersburg. The long, bitter siege was on. Lee was pinned down at last as Grant had hoped for. So was Grant. Between him and the town rose a lethal, flaming barrier that might hold out forever unless he could crack or outflank it.

So near was Petersburg that Grant's gunners on the heights could set their watches by the clock in the courthouse tower that miraculously breasted unscratched the hurricanes of shells hurtling past it.

Repulsed bloodily in his headlong assault on Lee's lines at Cold Harbor, foiled of capturing Petersburg by the disputations and ineptness of his generals, Grant philosophically observed, "Now we will rest the men and use the spade for their protection until a new vein can be struck."

But there was no rest. Under the broiling sun, stripped to the buff, sweaty Northern boys fell to with ax, pick and shovel hacking the zigzag yellow gash that would

elongate itself into a sixty-mile double arc of fortified entrenchments. Yet, with all the vast panoply of war, the
prodigality of food, clothing and death-dealing imple-
ments, one essential item for the comfort and sustenance
of boys in blue was overlooked. No one had thought of
providing summer uniforms for these fighters. They had
to sweat it out in wool.

Lee's brilliant artillery chief, Porter Alexander, described the Confederate defenses at Petersburg as a "long
intrenched citadel." The same applied to the blue's. Warfare had never seen more elaborate labyrinths of trenches,
involutions, approaches, traverses, covered ways, rifle pits,
shelters, redoubts, signal towers and square earth-log forts.
Designed with keen engineering acumen, every hillock became a miniature fortress whose guns could sweep
the slashed-bare open space around it like death in a
chariot. Great stretches of the lines were buttressed by
miles of bristling *chevaux de frises*, sharpened stakes that
could impale a charging soldier, and abattis, felled trees,
ends sharpened and pointed towards the enemy. These
were the barbed wire entanglements of the day.

Between the two armies stretched a no man's land that
in places narrowed down to less than one hundred yards
though diverging to half a mile at its southwest terminus.
Across the narrow sector, eagle-eyed sharpshooters plied
their deadly business of picking off lives day and night.
Mounted on firesteps, their long-range rifles poking
through cunningly concealed firing slits, they watched for
the least enemy movement, even a face at a firing slot. So
expert were they that a moment's exposure could bring
certain death or serious wounding. Many a battered old
hat on a ramrod was lifted above the parapet—to draw
fire—and withdrawn looking like a sieve. It was one way
of revealing sharpshooters' hideaways.

Meade's aide, Theodore Lyman, wrote his wife, "The lines are very close. Every finger, or cap, or point of a gun that shows above the works, is instantly shot at." But Confederate Brigadier John Bratton, reporting his losses for June 1864, sounded a more doleful note, "The sharpshooting was incessant and active. Our daily loss was small but the sum total for the month loomed up heavily, ay, and wearily, sadly. Many of my noblest veterans whose kindling eyes had flashed out their staunch hearts' enthusiasm on so many glorious fields of battle, were stricken from our rolls, as it were, by the stealthy hand of the assassin. There is the chill of murder about the casualties this month and sad, sad is the regret when death thus strikes the brave."

Frontal assault on Lee's lines was abandoned. Taking Petersburg by storm, even with overwhelming numbers, was asking slaughter that would make Cold Harbor look like pingpong. As the hot months droned by, Grant's bluecoats inched their lines westward, stabbing, feinting at Lee's ramparts for a weak spot where they could drive an entering wedge, clawing relentlessly towards the two railroad lines that kept Lee's army alive and firing.

At the same time Yankee cavalry began wide swings west and south of the town, ripping up miles of these arterial rail lines as well as the plank roads that supplanted them. Time, death and blood were the essence of Grant's task. In time, and not too much of that, Lee's lines would thin out to a breaking point and crumble. The blue steamroller would crush the remnants like paper soldiers.

The battlefront—twenty six miles from head to toe as the crow flew—ran, wriggled and twisted from Lee's cavalry outpost on White Oak Swamp east of Richmond to the south where, on the north bank of the James, gray artillery with a plunging fire warned Yankee gunboats to keep their distance. Leaping the river, the lines crossed Bermuda Neck down to "the pleasant river Appomattuck," as Captain John Smith described it three centuries ago. From a point on the Appomattox, about a mile east of Petersburg, the entrenchments ribboned south over hill, hollow and stream to the Jerusalem plank road where it bent southwest to double-anchor on the rebel outwork, Fort Mahone, named for Petersburg's Billy Mahone, one of Lee's most daring division commanders, and Fort Sedgwick, its Yankee vis-à-vis, named for General John Sedgwick, who at Spottsylvania braved gray sharpshooters once too often. Blue and gray quickly and appropriately dubbed these works Fort Hell and Fort Damnation. In time the lines would push on beyond them to the west.

In the cramped trenches men died of bullets, shells and sunstroke. Bodies blackened in an hour under the beating, brassy sun. Adding to the tortures of the men crouched in the yellow, baking hot ditches were flies, mosquitoes and the stink of latrines and rotting bodies. The thermometer chased up to one hundred and hung there. For forty-six days the skies shed not a raindrop. Dust was ankle deep. Northern boys from the upper tiers of States, accustomed to the cooling, compensating night breezes after the heat of the day, never dreamed of such sticky, oppressive heat. It felled them indiscriminately. Sunstroke was as much dreaded as gunfire. The nearby low grounds of the James and Appomattox were hotbeds of malaria. Hundreds sickened and Federal medics suddenly faced a scourge they had not counted on. History might have told them this pestilence had decimated and almost obliterated the first colony to pitch camp on swampy Jamestown Island in 1607.

But siege meant bombardment and the rigors of it fell
not only on the rebel lines but on the beleaguered town
beyond. The gray firing was hot but hardly a match for
the Niagara of gunfire poured out by Grant's batteries
that often bellowed round the clock. His gunners soon got
the range of pretty much everything in town, including
Lee's headquarters across the Appomattox. To a Southern
clergyman who visited Grant's headquarters and asked
why his men fired at residential districts, Grant replied,
"They shot at the lines, but the gunners sometimes fired
too high and thus it happened that residences were
struck." This was hardly true. General Butler even proposed the use of incendiary shells to fire the whole town.

Public buildings and many private ones were sand-
bagged. Families dug backyard shelters six feet or more
deep, covered with heavy timbers and banked over with
earth. Hundreds fled, though many returned on hearing
of the low casualty rate. Flattering, or better flattening,
attention was paid to the railroad depot. Hits there could
impede troop movements and supply trains. The famed
Old Market nearby was ripped to pieces. The gas works
were struck sixty-five times. Also well blitzed was the
business section and over eight hundred shell hits were
scored on residential areas. Historic Center Hill, ancestral
home of the Bollings, was struck repeatedly. Here it was
that President Lincoln perpetrated his grim pun. The
matter of rent for so large a home for the general commanding the Petersburg district was under consideration.
Pointing to shell holes in the mansion, Lincoln observed,
"It seems to me that Grant's cannoneers have attended
sufficiently to the matter of rent."

Special target for Grant's gunners was the Petersburg
ironworks. They gave it the full treatment, thanks to
Petersburg's "Judas," old Bob Davis, who deserted to the

Yankee lines and disclosed the exact location of the foundry that was casting ball and shell for Lee's guns. This information brought a hail of fire on the ironworks that miraculously kept pouring metal amid waves of destruction. Not until the final overwhelming of Lee's lines did the foundry shut down.

Pride of the Federal batterymen was a squat, 13-inch mortar, weighing nine tons, that hurled a two-hundred pound projectile. Nicknamed Dictator by the bluecoats, Petersburgers knew the weapon as Long Tom and identified it by its peculiarly deep boom. Long Tom left many a scar on the town.

Nightly the curtain rose on a fiery drama, a smash hit to be sure if ever there was one. When darkness deepened, the front came aglow with the flash of the big siege guns. Arching high in the sky on their parabolic trajectory, huge mortar shells screamed like rockets while their sizzling fuses gave off trails of red fire.

Petersburg's outlying farms along the battle line even today yield harvests other than peanuts and garden truck. An estimated three million projectiles were exchanged by Yankee and Rebel during the town's nine-month investment. Minićs were uncountable. Farmers still plough up these cannon balls and occasionally unexploded shells. In many a farmyard you can see these relics piled in neat pyramids, mute, rusty reminders of the storms of death and destruction that swept the now peaceful countryside.

Eight miles behind the fiery drama Grant established the control panel of his massive offensive. Overnight the drowsy riverside hamlet on the sunbaked promontory at City Point spread-eagled into a vast base of operations where the North rendezvoused its incalculable military might and syphoned it off to the battle lines. Up the James to City Point's commodious anchorage plowed a never-

ending procession of supply ships, transports, sailing vessels, tugs with long barge-tows laden with everything the
mind of man could conceive of to destroy his fellow man.
One day an eyewitness counted two score steamboats, seventy-five sailing vessels and one hundred barges, anchored
in the roadstead, or moored at wharves that lined the
waterfront for a mile. City Point is today the thriving town
of Hopewell.

Young Morris Schaff, ordnance officer fresh out of
West Point, said City Point reminded him of the continuous range of levees at New Orleans with its network
of railroad tracks running to the jetties out in the stream.

Biggest attention-getter at City Point was the huge hospital. Covering two hundred acres it had beds enough
for ten thousand bluecoats. Overflows of munitions and
foods packed huge warehouses for quartermaster, ordnance
and commissary departments. By Grant's orders, this mass
of materiel was systematized and accounted for to the
last paper of pins. Quartermaster General Meigs boasted
that City Point could victual and supply half a million
fighting men if it became necessary.

In a single artillery park a visitor counted eight hundred
cannon and limbers waiting to replace those worn out by the
ceaseless bombardment of Lee's lines. City Point boasted
barracks for soldiers; housing for civilian employees; a
blacksmith shop where fifty horses could be shod at a
time; a bullpen where malefactors and prisoners were
herded, a "horrid Place" averred Septima Collins, army
wife who lived most comfortably in a "cosy farmhouse" at
City Point. "In this pigpen, I call it, in rain and snow and
frost I have seen hundreds perhaps thousands of men huddled together without a particle of shelter or protection
from the elements—perhaps there was no help for it. At
all events its horror and odor sicken me to think of." There

was also a gallows where deserters got their deserts and a palisade where spies were shot with hardly a semblance of trial the day they were caught.

This war emporium boasted a hotel run by an enterprising Philadelphia tavern keeper whose cuisine flaunted turtle, fish, oysters, seafood delicacies and fine wines. Sutlers' stores, caterers' markets and even a saloon or two mushroomed like everything else. There were bakeries that ran round the clock turning out thousands of fresh loaves to be rushed to the men at the front.

Episcopal Bishop Henry C. Lay of Arkansas, traveling on a pass visaed at Atlanta by General Sherman, visited City Point at its high tide. What he saw baffled his imagination; "not merely profusion, but extravagance, wagons, tents, artillery, *ad libitum*. Soldiers provided with everything, comforts of all sorts."

Had the Bishop visited the Yankee front lines he might have sniffed the inviting aroma of huge kettles in which company cooks were brewing stew made with fresh beef. Or he might have been treated to a steaming cup of coffee trundled right up to the front in huge urns by night and filled with the hot black liquid soldiers of modern wars crave so dearly. Possibly he might have read the crude pencilled "menu" gotten up by the cook of a New York regiment, with roast beef heading the list. Surely, though, it must have made him think of the graylegs crouched behind their parapets a hundred yards away, famishing for a real meal and no hope of getting it.

To funnel materiel, food, and forage, and rush reinforcements to his fighting lines Grant built a military railroad behind his entrenchments. It was the first in the history of war. Nor was it much of a road though its roadbed is still traceable. It was hooked onto what was left of the Petersburg-City Point line that in antebellum times connected the town with the James. By today's standards it was a Lilliputian affair. It even had a roundhouse. Ungraded, track ties were laid on the ground, up hill and down dale. Its engines chugged and whistled as it roller-coasted merrily along, belching smoke and flame from its bulbous smokestacks, providing the bluecoats with endless amusement. Horace Porter averred "its undulations were so marked that a train moving along it looked in the distance like a fly crawling on a corrugated washboard." For the president's visit to the front they made up a "Lincoln Special." As he mounted the platform of the dinky car he inquired with a smile, "Has this railroad got a lawyer?" Most likely he was reminded of his days as a railroad lawyer back in Illinois.

Through the hot months Grant ran his big show from a hospital tent that became overnight main office of the nation's biggest business. Camp chairs and a rustic bench comprised his office equipment. The telegraph line running down the James to Washington kept him in instant contact with the Union armies engaged in gutting the South. Shorter wires connected him with the front line at Petersburg. From headquarters a wooden stairway ran down the bluff to the official steamboat landing. On the day this wharf was completed and planked Grant walked down to look it over. Hands thrust in his pockets, cigar in his mouth, he failed to realize he was violating strict instructions he had just issued. He had not gone far before being challenged by a sentry, "It's against orders to come on this wharf with a lighted cigar." Throwing his Havana into the river he said, "I don't like to lose my smoke, but the sentinel's right. He evidently isn't going to let me violate my own instructions."

With the headquarters tent as its nucleus a war city

rapidly developed, laid off in streets of cottages for officers and important civil employees. City Point even boasted a water sprinkling system to lay the hot, thick dust. It was fed by a pumping station on the edge of the river.

Around him at HAUS (Headquarters of the Army of the United States) Grant assembled officers who possessed the knowledge of supply and transportation. On two of them he leaned more heavily than on all the others: Rufus Igalls, Quartermaster General of the Armies Operating Against Richmond, and Michael R. Morgan, Commissary General of Subsistence of the same operation. They became masters of logistics. Morgan was a brilliant officer sidetracked into the gastronomic service of the war. Only once did the limelight play on him. At Appomattox when Lee asked rations to feed the remnants of his starving army Grant turned to Morgan and ordered him to comply with Lee's request.

Defense of the widespread cantonment was vital. Across the City Point neck of land Grant's engineers ran fortified lines, implemented by well-gunned redoubts. Lining the south bank of the James were batteries emplaced to enfilade three peninsulas that became extensions of the City Point base—Jordan's, Indian and Coggin's Points. Lofty lookout towers sprouted along the shore manned by hawk-eyed signalmen whose field glasses searched the terrain round the clock. The cavalry trains were parked on Indian Point. At Jordan's a remount station was established. Here mountains of forage and grain were landed. At Coggin's Point, ten miles by crowflight from City Point, the General Cattle herd was already grazing on Ruffin's fine meadows. Corrals were built. The cowboys pitched camp under the spreading live oaks. Down the Chesapeake and up the James came bargeloads of cattle to replenish the herd. Weekly small droves of beeves were cut out and driven off to be parceled out to the regimental butchers behind the front lines.

Coggin's Point had acquired a brief war luster. Mc-Clellan, falling back from Richmond under Lee's blows, had based his defeated army at Harrison's Landing, near the great plantation mansion, Berkeley. He took refuge behind powerful field fortifications erected on the high ground behind the landing. It was directly across the river from Coggin's Point where Confederate General D. H. Hill quietly mounted several batteries. At midnight July 31, 1862, these guns opened fire on McClellan's encampment. Over one thousand rounds arched across the half mile of river to splatter iron fragments and panic on the sleeping bluecoats. At daylight they swarmed across the stream. Without waiting for them to land the gray batteries limbered up and vanished. Afterward—until the coming of Grant's cattle—Coggin's Point was only a target for potshots fired at Beechwood by Yankee gunboats plying up and down the river.

PART II

Premonitions

11

Petite Guerre in Blackwater Swamp

The afternoon was stifling when a dusty officer rode up to Grant's headquarters and dismounted. It was Colonel Michael R. Morgan, soon to be upped to star rank and hardly recognizable under a glaze of fine, gray dust. Grant was taking it easy under his tentfly, cigar cocked in the corner of his mouth, blouse unbuttoned at his throat.

"How are you, colonel?" said Grant as the officer strode up and saluted. "Sit down and cool off, if you can."

"I'm just back from Coggin's Point, general," began Morgan. "We've had trouble down there. Last night two wagons of forage were attacked on the Stage Road by bushwhackers. They killed the teamsters, fired the wagons and stole the mules."

"Guerillas," observed Grant dryly. "We shot 'em in the west. Isn't the road picketed?"

"Yes, but the nearest picket was half a mile away. He heard two shots. When he got there it was all over. A de-

tachment of the 3rd New York rounded up a single prisoner. Colonel Sharpe has him in hand now. Two days ago a
herder was found dead with a bullet in his back on the
road near Coggin's Point. He'd been dragged off his horse
and shot on the spot."

"These herders are a rough lot," said Grant. "That fellow might have been shot in a drunken brawl. Burning
wagons and killing the drivers is unfortunately a part of
this business. You'll have to expect some of it."

Morgan went on. "You know the telegraph line has
been cut a dozen times since we got here."

"I know," said Grant. "There're two things to do:
strengthen the picket line and shoot the rascals when we
catch them. Where are you grazing the cattle now? Maybe
we ought to move them closer to City Point."

"I've thought of that. Pasturage is poor all along the
river. The drought has dried it up. We've moved them
twice already. The best we can find is on the Ruffin and
Harrison farms near Coggin's Point."

"Colonel, you probably realize that putting beef cattle
down there on the river is like dangling a piece of meat
before a starving lion. He'll kill you to get it. Lee's men
don't have enough to eat. You see the condition of the
prisoners we take. Most of them look like scarecrows."

"It's the best pasturage we can find," assured Morgan.

"How big is the herd now?" queried Grant significantly.

"Over three thousand. We get more in every day or so.
This army's eating beef pretty fast."

Grant was silent for several moments. "We'll locate the
dismounted cavalry camp at Coggin's Point. That would
help. Sheridan's back with eight hundred men waiting for
horses."

"They've got scouts operating all through that section," said Morgan. "They know everything we do."

Grant smiled. "I'm not surprised. Every little farmer inside or near our lines is a sort of rebel spy or guerilla. Don't forget that. Mostly older men resentful of our taking over their country. They spend half their time innocently farming their godforsaken land and the rest of it finding out what we're doing and passing it on to rebel headquarters. Farmers by day and often killers by night. The scouts are another story. We've got 'em too."

Grant was stating bluntly that a second undercover front was opening behind his fortified lines at Petersburg, City Point and its chain of small bases along the south shore of the James. The wide arena between the James and Blackwater rivers, interlaced by obscure roads, blotched by weird, festering swamps, was seemingly created by nature for this bitter sort of warfare. Largest of these sickly, impenetrable quagmires was Blackwater Swamp that spread out like a putrid sore on both sides of the stream whose name it bore. From hideouts deep in its confines irregulars struck and faded out like spectres. Mysterious, deadly *petite guerre*—hit, run and vanish—infested the place. Guerillas, it seemed, lurked behind every bush, in every patch of undergrowth. They were the big X in Grant's victory formula, the unknown quantity. Unorganized, unorthodox, they followed no rules, no system, but struck when and where they could, then galloped off into the marshy nowhere. Their ranks were recruited from the bitter stay-at-homes, the conscript dodgers and even blue deserters—and sometimes women burning to take a hand in avenging the excesses of the Northern intruders.

By midsummer, couriers were being waylaid, dragged

off their horses and left dead on the roads. In the darkish, eerie hours before dawn, blue pickets were shot down mercilessly. Grant's telegraph line was sliced repeatedly. Men sent to repair it were ambushed and killed. Venturing east beyond City Point's fortified line soon grew hazardous. At Indian Point fire was twice set to huge pyramids of hay steamered up the James for Grant's transportation system—now almost 60,000 mules and horses.

Grant was no stranger to the deadly character of irregular warfare against Northern supply and picket lines. He himself had once barely escaped capture by shadowy raiders who almost made off with the newly commissioned general-in-chief of the Union armies. It was the narrowest escape of his career. The deep impression this near-capture made on Grant is recorded in his memoirs. His near-captor was rebel freelance John S. Mosby.

But there was the other group to whom Grant had referred—the scouts. There were scores of them. Hardly a handful of these patient, experienced trailers and enemy-watchers ever made the headlines. They were bold, fearless men. They had to be. Living and operating inside enemy lines, they knew every hog and bridle path, every woodlane, every little track through the swamps and forests. Lurking and prowling, hanging on the blue flanks, watching and waiting in the shadows, reconnoitering, even penetrating enemy camps, they led a life of stealth, adventure and danger. Here today, and off tomorrow on mysterious missions—often never to return. They killed without qualm and sold their lives dearly when need be rather than be captured. Many found death in the forests. To this day these men remain unsung and unburied. Dissociate them from guerillas. They were not the hit-and-runners. Their business was to hang on and find out. If driven off, their job was to come back and find out what was up and speed "home" with it. Their lives read like storybooks.

City Point itself was anything but spy and scout proof. Intelligence chief was Colonel George Sharpe, Assistant Provost Marshal. To him fell inquisition of suspected spies as well as extraction of information from prisoners taken on the Petersburg front. Stringent orders forbade passage in and out of the base save by passes issued by Sharpe. But somehow spies and scouts penetrated even into Grant's headquarters.

Told in Petersburg after the war was the story of an old Negro who one day casually sauntered through the City Point guard lines and strolled on umolested until he came to supreme headquarters. Grant was seated—as was his wont—under his tentfly fanning himself. He hurried an aide off to fetch Sharpe. While waiting he questioned the obviously frightened Negro. Realizing that the visitor was no spy Grant told him to go, but the dusky old fellow stood cogitating and then observed with a smile:

"Gen'ral," he began, "you've asked me a lot of questions this mornin'. Now I'm gwine ter ask you some, if you don't mind."

"Go right ahead," said Grant.

"Where're you gwine when you leave this place where you's at now?"

Grant smiled. "I'm going to one of four places: Richmond, Petersburg, Heaven or Hell."

But the Negro shook his head. "You can't go to Richmond because Gen'ral Lee's there; you can't go to Petersburg because Gen'ral Beauregard's there. You sho can't go to heben because Gen'ral Stonewall Jackson's there. So I don't see but one place left for you to go, gen'ral."

12

Molly Tatum Meets an Old Friend

Molly Tatum was her name. She was pretty. There is no mention of her in the massive official records. In Kautz's regimental papers there are several references to "the girl on Lawyer's Road." It is conjecturable this was Molly. She flitted across the troubled back reaches of Grant's lines at Petersburg like a jack-o'-lantern in Blackwater Swamp in whose shadows she lived.

Molly vanished leaving no trace of her whereabouts. Even the road she lived on went back to wilderness. The home of her "aunt," Katie Tatum, with whom Molly lived, apparently went the way of the road. In the Sixties it squatted on a sort of island clearing on the edge of the vast matting of the swamp.

Through this primeval tangle of live oak, cypress and wild vines, the Blackwater coiled and writhed like a huge moccasin back to its headwaters barely a mile behind the headquarters tent of General George Meade, Commanding General of the Army of the Potomac that looped around Petersburg like a great blue sickle.

Sharp-tongued folk about Blackwater Swamp a century ago whispered things about Katie Tatum. Unpleasant things of how once she lay rapturously in the arms of a young man who bore her away and how Katie came back, alone, with little Molly in her arms. Gossip stripped her of every virtue save one, intense love of the child born out of wedlock, who knew her as "aunt." But Katie faced up to whatever sin and shame there was in it, to live alone and raise the child who reached her teens as lovely as they come.

Slowly the scorn heaped on Katie seared her very soul. She regurgitated it in hate for her detractors. Then the Yankees came—to share Katie's hate with the mouthy swamp folk.

A sultry July day was ending. Dusk was falling, the evening damp rising. The little swamp singers were tuning up for their all-night chorus. In the kitchen Katie Tatum was frying a chicken for supper.

Molly and her "aunt" had up to now enjoyed miraculous immunity from the blue intruders. Only once had their chicken coop been raided. Their old cow, unmolested, was still doing business as usual. A boneyard of a horse and a rickety buggy seemed to bear charmed lives in the area where the blue had snatched everything on four legs. Once a week the ancient steed carried the two women up to City Point to sell eggs to the hated Yankees. Blue cavalrymen picketed Lawyer's Road round the clock. Sometimes endless columns of blue troopers shuttled by in a wall of dust. Occasionally a bluecoat dismounted for a cooling drink at the Tatum well or to poke a little fun at the bare-footed rebel girl in calico just to see the sparks fly from her dark eyes. Twice war had crackled nearby, blue and gray shooting it out furiously. They laid out the dead and wounded on the Tatum porch.

After setting the kitchen table and lighting candles, Molly stepped out into the dusk on the front porch for a breath of air. It was cooling off. A moon poised on the treetops; the sky was darkening. From the west came the sullen growl of Yankee siege guns opening their evening symphony. As she stood drinking in the freshness, a song came floating clear and distinct through the gloaming. Wondering, she walked to the front gate, unlatched it and peered up the road. She listened.

> *Soft o'er the fountain,*
> *Ling'ring falls the southern moon;*
> *Far o'er the mountain*
> *Breaks the day too soon.*

What she saw in the half-light was a lone rider, singing as his horse clopclopped leisurely down the road. It wasn't a blue picket. There was no jangling. Perhaps! Her heart beat faster. It seemed to say that this was the moment she had hoped for, even prayed for. She knew who it was even before he reined up and swung lightly to the ground. Handsome Jim Fisher had come back. His horse was lean, wiry. Over his saddlehorn coiled a rope. A big pistol holstered at his waist. She was a bit panicky.

"Molly!" She retreated as he took a step towards her. "Ain't you glad to see me?"

She beat back the welcome she had often told herself she would give him. "I can't say as I am. Where you been since you left here?"

"Out West, ranchin'."

"I reckon you come home to fight?" she asked sharply.

"I got a better job than fighting."

"There ain't no better job. Not nowadays."

Jim Fisher licked his lips. The two rounds of her breasts rose tantalizingly under her faded cotton dress.

"I ain't ever forgotten you, Molly." A faint smile brushed her face. "Gawd, but you're nice! Growed into a real woman since I been away."

"What're you doing round here?" she asked.

"Herdin' cattle for Grant."

"Fighting agin your own folks," she half sneered.

"I ain't fired a shot," he asserted.

"It's the same thing."

"Come on, Molly. Don't be like that. I ain't hurting nobody. Ain't you heard about the big lot of cattle Grant brought with him? We're grazing 'em on old Ruffin's place near Coggin's Point. That's what I'm doing. Making more money than soldiers, too. I been laying off to run over to see you ever since we crossed the river."

The girl said nothing.

"How's my folks, Molly?"

She hesitated. "Your Ma's dead. When you run away and never let her hear from you it kilt her jest like a bullet. Your pa got shot at Sharpsburg. He ain't been much good since. But you'd better not go to see him. He's killing Yankees on sight. That's all he lives for. He might shoot you. And I ain't saying what it done to me. You never writ me a line."

Her words were bitter. He flinched. "How's your aunt?"

"She's all right 'cept when she sees blue. Don't let her see you hanging round. Nobody ever hated Yankees like her 'cept 'tis your Pa."

He waited a bit. Then, "I ain't the only one that's gone off like I did."

"What do you mean?"

"Where's *your* Pa?"

It stunned her for the moment. She didn't answer.

"I'll tell you. He run off only he didn't come back. I run off because I didn't want to tech you till I married you. Now I'm back. That's Gawd's truth, Molly."

It sunk deep. It burned.

Then he added, "Your aunt ain't your aunt."

"She ain't?"

"She's your Ma." The words cut like a hot knife. The girl felt faint. She waited long before she spoke again. A curious light came in her eyes, but he couldn't see it in the dark.

"How long's them cattle been at old Ruffin's?"

" 'Bout three weeks, I reckon. We druv 'em over the big bridge." His eyes felt out the shapely curves of her hips. She was even more beautiful than he'd remembered.

"How long they going to stay?"

"Till the Yankees eat 'em up, I reckon. But there's a lot more where they came from." He laughed his old infectious laugh.

"How many you got there?"

"We crossed the Jeems with five thousand. We ain't got that many now. They're eating 'em awful fast. But we're getting more all the time."

She thought: *And Lee's men ain't got enough to eat to keep 'em alive.*

"Kin I come to see you again, Molly?"

She knew the answer, but held it back. "I heard you singing, Jim. Sounds like old times. You're singing better since you . . ."

"I been using it to keep cattle quiet at night," he cut in, smiling.

She wondered. "I bet you've been singing to all them women out West."

"Nope, jest to cattle. It sort of keeps them quiet."

She didn't understand. He let it pass, then tried again, "Kin I come to see you?"

"Molly! Oh, Molly! Supper's ready!" Her "aunt" was calling.

"I'm coming right now!" she replied. "I gotter go, Jim."

"What about seeing you again, Molly?" asked Jim Fisher.

Through the dusk her eyes met his and wavered. "I reckon you can. Some night next week just about this time. I'll be listening, but don't come to the house." He mounted quickly, turned his horse and melted into the gloom. His voice came lilting back.

> *When in thy dreaming*
> *Moons like these shall rise again.*

At supper Katie Tatum was inquisitive. "Who was that you was talking to at the gate?"

"One of them Yankees," she lied. "Talk you to death if you let 'em."

Supper over, they sat on the porch until bedtime watching the moon climb the sky. The western horizon glowed dull red. Grant's siege guns were rumbling. Katie rocked and rocked.

"Ain't they never going to stop bombarding Petersburg?" she whined. "I wish all the Yankees was dead. I heerd old man Fisher got another one last night. Wish he'd kill 'em all."

"Me too," added Molly.

Bedtime came with the whippoorwills and they went upstairs. Molly's room was stifling. It would cool down later. Undressing, she said goodnight, blew out the candle and stretched out on the bed, wide awake. Presently a familiar snore announced Katie's departure for the land of nod. Rising, Molly dressed quietly: old stockings, old dress she wore working the garden. A little shawl over her shoulders, a faded scarf over her hair and knotted under her pretty chin. Old shoes in her hand she tiptoed downstairs and out into the night.

The moon was milk white. The road spread out like a silver ribbon. She walked fast. Far off, over cross-swamp towards Sycamore Church, she heard a bugle. Yankees, she thought. She walked on hurriedly, keeping watch up and down the road for blue pickets. She crossed a small bridge. Just beyond it she paused to take a long look before darting into the thicket. The path was dim, but the moon splashing down through the trees laid white stepping stones for her. The swamp was an eerie place at night, but not to Molly. She'd lived beside it all her life. Festoons of moss dripping from the trees stroked her cheeks like misty fingers. An owl perched on a dead oak hooted at her, no doubt resenting her intrusion in his "ancient, solitary reign." The hooting frightened her momentarily and she pulled her shawl tighter around her shoulders. Then she laughed. How often had owls hooted around her "aunt's" at night, with their chorus of "Who! Whoo! Whooo!" A hummock gave way under her foot. With a little outcry she sank up to her knee in a black, unsuspected pool. She dragged herself out and struggled on. Swamp odors reached her nostrils—one she loved, swamp rose, deliciously sweet.

Deeper and deeper into the recesses she went as if into another world where all was solitude and loneliness. Presently a red speck, gleaming at her like a burning eye, pierced the interstices of the trees. The speck grew larger as she neared it to find what she sought, a clearing beside the Blackwater where a campfire blazed cheerily. Stepping into the firelight her heart sank. She faced a double-

barreled shotgun held by a man in blue. Yankee!
Stretched out around the fire on beds of pine branches
were a dozen sleeping blanketed forms. Speechless she
simply stared.

"What do you want?" The voice was no Yankee's.

She stammered, "I'm looking for Mr. Shadburne."

"Lady, you was taking a big chance. I heard you comin'."

As by magic a blanket roll came to life. Out of it
emerged a tall young man in blue, George Shadburne,
Iron Scout, awake instantly.

"I'm Molly Tatum," she managed to gasp. "You came
to my aunt's house one night last week."

"Sure I did." It was a good Texas drawl. His tall figure
bowed.

"I got news for you," she said nervously.

"Bill," he called to the sentinel, "rustle up a pot of coffee for the lady." Then he smiled, "Don't be scared of my
blue uniform. We wear 'em most of the time. That's how
we do business. Now set here on this log by the fire and
dry off."

"You heard about the cattle the Yankees got at Coggin's
Point?" she asked.

"We heard about 'em, but that's about all. What do you
know about 'em?"

"I know one of the boys that watches 'em."

"A herder?"

She smiled. "I reckon that's what you'd call him. He
used to live round here."

"And he's working for the Yankees? How well do you
know him?"

"Right well, I'd say. That is, I uster. He came to see me
tonight."

"I reckon we can use him, if you'll help."

Refreshed by the coffee she talked on. Perhaps there

was something in her heart she didn't reveal and George Shadburne didn't ask what it was. He was an old hand at peering into women's eyes and hearts, and behind the Yankee lines.

The moon was at the top of the sky when Shadburne rose. "It's time you was going. I'm seeing you home. I know a better way than you came. We've got horses off there in the dark, if you don't mind riding behind me." He smiled. "It' better'n walking."

The night was almost spent as she lifted the latch of her front gate. The paling moon hinted a new day was at hand. The first birds would soon be chirping, rousing up time for her aunt. She tiptoed upstairs. As she drifted off to sleep she heard a song faraway, then farther and fainter,

> *Soft o'er the fountain,*
> *Ling'ring falls the southern moon;*
> *Far o'er the mountain*
> *Breaks the day too soon.*

13

Dead Men Tell No Tales

By midsummer the somber pattern of full scale *petite guerre,* violence and death, emerged behind and actually within the Yankee lines. It could be called a rearguard action because it posed a threat to the vast Union stockpile at City Point on which the whole fiery front hinged.

If Grant studied the buildup in the hinterland of his army, he probably underestimated it though he could not have ignored it. Yet Andrew Humphreys, Meade's chief of staff, read the danger signals aright. He sputtered off a warning of "a sudden movement on the trains and rear of this army between the Blackwater and the James." Humphreys went even further to emphasize, "That approach is unguarded."

The area was well picketed. Picket lines gridironed debated Prince George County like a football field though a Union trooper going on outpost duty at dark never knew whether he'd be alive or dead by morning. Nervous ve-

dettes were firing at shadows. Something or somebody
lurked in every dark copse. Nor were troopers alone in
their apprehensions. Even General Butler in his "bottle"
at Bermuda Hundred saw things at night. He was apparently much disturbed by "three signal lights in the sky
looking like stars, one northeast, the other due east and
the other nearly west." What could they mean? asked Butler. Had Lee turned loose bands of guerillas to harry the
Union rear? Was he signaling plans for the night's dev-
iltry? Was this the prelude to a full-scale attack from the
east? Butler wanted to know.

A Union scout was found dead half a mile outside the
City Point lines with his throat cut from ear to ear. It
brought a howl for retaliation. Mistaken at first for a dead
rebel because he wore a Confederate uniform his body
was taken to Provost Headquarters at City Point where it
was identified as Henry Pennypacker, a Pennsylvania boy,
who had volunteered for scout duty. He rated high. As a
counter-scout he had managed to join a band of guerillas.
Apparently his running mates discovered what was up and
knifed him. Intelligence Chief George Sharpe saw red.
There was no official pronouncement. Word was passed
on to kill guerillas on sight. It wasn't the bloodiest side of
war, but it was the bitterest. Sporadic bursts of bullets on
backroads killed men just as dead as mortars and sharpshooters along the Petersburg front.

The day after Colonel Morgan reported the killing of
teamsters on the road near Coggin's Point, the cattle
guard was increased by several hundred dismounted horse
soldiers, but General Meade decided to take further precautions. He ordered the cattle herd moved as "near City
Point as practicable." This wasn't easy. Or practicable.
Nor, strange to say, did Meade have authority over the
herd. At Coggin's Point Negro soldiers had erected a mile

long corral engirdling the best grasslands and so arranged that grazing could be rotated. Jockeying three to five thousand head of cattle along the narrow river road was far different from driving them across open country. It was done in relays of five hundred. It took two days and an ungodly amount of blasphemy and hard riding to joggle longhorns along to the wide river bottom five miles nearer City Point, right behind the big trains parked at Jordan's Point. Anyway, the cattle were safer and GHQ was satisfied.

Two days after the herd was moved a cavalry outpost near Sycamore Church was attacked. The bluecoats blazed back only to see the intruders gallop off unscathed and vanish in the swamp like mist, leaving two dead troopers and others wounded. Sheridan (with headquarters at Windmill Point) was wrathful. He demanded quick avenging. The best way to retaliate was house-burning. His method was imparted in his request: "Can I have permission to burn a few houses in the neighborhood?" GHQ said "no" unless he was positive the houses quartered or harbored guerillas. Much miffed, Sheridan would shortly be transferred to the Valley where he would glut his ire.

On July 4, General Burnside (he of the sideburns) commanding the Ninth Corps asked by field telegraph, "Will there be any salutes of any kind fired today?" "No salutes" replied Meade, though his staff man Lyman commented, "There was no salute except in the form of cannon and mortars along our lines." Orders or not, Grant's bombardiers showered their patriotic ardor on Petersburg.

Next morning Grant opened his eyes to be greeted with news that his military telegraph running down the James to Swan's Point, en route to Washington, was cut during the night. A report from Colonel Innis, commanding Fort Powhatan, had just filtered in. Two and a half miles of wire below the fort were stripped clean. It was the worst break yet. For nine hours Grant's armies operating against Richmond and Petersburg were isolated from Washington and also from the other far-flung fronts under Grant's command. Adding insult to injury repairmen sent out at dawn were fired on and several grievously wounded.

Plans to ambush the ambushers were made but got nowhere. The 6th New York Cavalry flogged the Prince George County roads ragged. At their head rode Colonel Thomas Devin, a tough, ex-militia horse hombre, who vowed by all the gods in Ireland to catch the banshees who were making life so miserable for the men on picket duty. A bullet from a patch of scrub oak nicked his knee and thudded into his horse's heart, killing the splendid mount instantly. Devin had a cavalryman's true love for his faithful steed and said so mournfully.

The third week in July brought headache of another variety. It could be called dress rehearsal for the inevitable. Grant's cowboys had cut two hundred beeves out of the General Cattle Herd, now pastured near Jordan's Point, and driven them along the military railroad to an open field half a mile behind the V Corps sector on the Petersburg front. It was regular procedure once a fortnight, sometimes oftener. Nobody dreamed beeves would be molested under the noses of an army corps of bluecoats armed to the teeth. The cattle were delivered to Warren's provost guard on a field near the Daniels farmhouse, which, incredibly, was within shooting distance of the headquarters of the Army of the Potomac—Meade's. It was, however, hidden from the eagle-eyed rebel lookouts. Twice a week regimental butchers killed as many as were needed. Fifteen infantrymen guarded the cattle night and day. There wasn't a good cattle man in the bunch.

On this July night a cutting out party of rebels (so the

report called them) crept Indian-file out of the underbrush and crawled, unchallenged, to the very edge of the
elliptical meadow where the cattle—standing quietly or
lying down—were bedded for the night. The raiders had
apparently cased these alluring beefsteaks. There was no
moon. The roar of the siege guns deadened the noise of
their approach. The cattle guard was asleep except for
two sentinels posted at opposite ends of the field. With a
technique that might have shamed old-style western rustlers, the marauders bashed in the head of the sentinel
nearest them. He never knew what hit him. Quite calmly,
it appeared, they proceeded to filch a score of beeves and
were nudging them into the thickets when the second sentry fired his gun and gave the alarm. The guard came to
life with a furious banging, shooting all over the place.
Bullets whizzed promiscuously. When the melée was over
(and the provost guard dashed onto the scene) three
men, one with a bullet in his back, were prisoners, but
sixteen head of good Yankee beef had departed with the
raiders. The prisoners admitted they were stealing cattle.
That was all. They wore no uniforms. After several weeks
in the bullpen at City Point they were turned loose with a
warning: caught stealing again they would be summarily
shot. And George Sharpe meant it.

But apparently the moral of this episode failed to register, eclipsed no doubt by the glare of the big battle soon to
be staged on the Ninth Corps front. What mattered a few
cattle stolen when the curtain was about to rise on a blood-
red drama?

Along the ridge in rear of the rebel front facing the
Ninth Corps ran Jerusalem plank road, a highway leading
south from Petersburg since colonial days. This crest was
stripped bare except for a house or two and the roofless,
ivy-covered walls of Blandford Church amid the graves of

the town's forefathers. Here the moldering sanctuary had stood since 1735. A poem had invested it with some luster. Legend had credited the stanzas to Irish comedian, Tyrone Power, who, on visiting the town in 1841, had grieved over the gaping windows and crumbling walls and voiced his sorrowing in lines found written on the walls in a neat scholarly hand. Eight lines epitomized the plight of the old church:

> *Thou art crumbling to the dust, old pile!*
> *Thou art hastening to thy fall;*
> *And round thee in thy loneliness,*
> *Clings the ivy to thy wall;*
> *The worshippers are scattered now,*
> *Who knelt before thy shrine,*
> *And silence reigns where anthems rose*
> *In days of Auld Lang Syne.*

But now July, 1864, silence no longer reigned around the ancient kirk. Thousands of shells ripped and screeched above it. To their credit Grant's gunners had spared the mellowed remnants of its holy past. Nor had Lee's men used it as a lookout lest it draw a rain of fire.

On this high ground, a half a mile south of the old church, a rebel earthwork known as Elliott's Salient protruded towards the Federal defenses like a rhinoceros horn. Squatting on the east side of the ridge its enfilading fire killed many a bluecoat. In the hands of an enemy this impregnable position would render Petersburg untenable. Its capture could set up a chain reaction that might wrap up Petersburg and Richmond to boot.

A regiment of miners, the 48th Pennsylvania, recruited from the hard coal region, were at the moment burrowing a shaft from a deep hollow in the Yankee lines towards the strongpoint immediately opposite. Once they were directly below the "key to Petersburg," galleries would be hollowed out right and left and jampacked with powder enough to blow the rebel work sky high.

Idea man of the project was Lieutenant Colonel Henry Pleasants, accomplished engineer and practical miner, who had attained eminence in his profession by boring the 4200-foot hole through the Alleghenies for the Pennsylvania Railroad. He was fairly vociferous about his ability to exterminate "the only God-damned thing between us and Petersburg." He could, he asserted, open a breach in Lee's works big enough for assaulting columns to plow through, capture the ridge commanding the city and keep on going, if—and it was a big if—GHQ would only authorize it. In a colossal upsurge Elliott's Salient would go soaring to kingdom come.

Hopped up by Pleasants' sales talk, Ninth Corps commander Burnside in turn gave Meade a hard sell. That officer okayed it with his tongue in his cheek though his engineers urged its brushoff. Grant acceded to it unemotionally. He didn't think much of it, but he wouldn't oppose it

The digging of the mine was top secret. Nobody knew about it except the hundred thousand officers and men of the Army of the Potomac. Trench gossip created fantastic shapes of things to come. The end of the war was in sight. Even the rebels got wind of it though they failed to pinpoint its exact location or the precise hour when Pleasants' trap would be sprung. Lee's efficient artilleryman, Porter Alexander, seems to have called it to the day. At Confederate GHQ he put his finger on a calendar on Lee's field desk. Touching the date "July 30" he said, "It'll be exploded about then."

In the Yankee trenches and shelters, on the picket lines, in the signal lookouts, talk of the big blast went on unceasing. Prognostications were as numerous as Minié balls. The stalemate was about to be broken. The Army of the Potomac would be on the move again, this time to victory.

"I may come home soon," wrote a young fellow in blue to his mother. "I ain't saying what's going to happen but it's something that might end the war."

The Federal disaster at the Crater (aptly named because it resembled the mouth of a volcano) has no place in this narrative save as a landmark. The mine was sprung at 4:44 A.M., July 30. In a mushroom cloud of smoke, flame, debris and dead men, Elliott's Salient went sailing skyward. But its backfire was immediate and disastrous, a sort of volcano that turned on itself. Federal storm troops, massed by thousands to plunge through the rent in the rebel lines, were stunned for long minutes by the very awfulness of the spectacle. By the time they reached the break-through and began clambering into the smoking chasm, rebel mortars were flipping thin-skinned shells that fragmented into thousands of killing bits, slaughtering them unmercifully. With inconceivable stupidity and arrant cowardice in the higher brackets, Federal leadership went to pot while hundreds of brave men pressed into the pit to their death. The general commanding the storming division, James H. Ledlie, decided the best way to lead his troops into Petersburg was to hole up in a bombproof with a jug of rum, five hundred yards from the Crater. The big opportunity was muffed within twenty minutes.

Caught off balance, the rebels were momentarily dazed. Recovering from their first shock, grayjackets were rushed to the danger point. On the Jerusalem plank road batteries were parked hub to hub lobbing shells into the smoking abyss.

Over an hour after the explosion, when not the slightest

hope of success remained, the colored troops were ordered on stage. These men, thousands of them, were originally assigned the place of honor, first to charge into the gap opened up by the explosion. They had rehearsed their role behind the scenes for several weeks, chanting their battlesong "We looks lak men a-marchin' on, We looks lak men of war," as they went through their paces. Discipline had been drilled into their very souls. Their commander was General Edouard Ferrero, former dancing master at West Point, who apparently knew more about teaching the light fantastic than leading men into the jaws of death. Now, when the last vestige of possible victory had faded, these men were hurled like sheep to slaughter into the Crater already jammed with dead and dying white soldiers. They were massacred.

Heard in Petersburg for half a century after the fight was the story of a colored boy who kept on going as he was ordered. Inconceivably, he pushed on through death and gunfire, Rebel and Yankee, over hill and down into the town, on through the rebel lines, a single man breakthrough. By luck, the grace of God, or sheer rebel indifference to a solitary Negro soldier slogging along by himself, he plodded on until he reached Poplar Lawn, Petersburg's park on its main thoroughfare, Sycamore Street. How did he get there? He couldn't remember. Dazed by the hell of gunfire and carnage through which he had passed, his mind went blank. He'd been ordered not to stop. He hadn't. As he infiltrated Flanner's Battery on the plank road a gunner had swiped at him with a sponger, knocking him down, but he got up and kept going. Finally relieved of his musket, all he wanted was a drink of cold water from the spring that bubbled in the park.

The Crater was a dismal fiasco to be written off on the dark red side of the ledger. The death toll was less than

Cold Harbor's, but heartbreak enough for one day. Casualties for the two-hour fight ran over 4400. Grant figured,
"It cost us about four thousand men." Brunt of the losses
fell on the colored division, one third of them dead and
wounded. But the war must go on. Two days later the
death pit reeked with the stench of sulphur and human
decomposition. Cries of the wounded perishing in the ori-
fice under the broiling sun brought Meade's request for a
three-hour cessation of hostilities to bury his dead and
succor his wounded.

Yet even while dead white and black boys were being
bundled into common graves (so lightly covered that their
bones would for years protrude like pale accusing fingers)
Grant summoned his cipher operator. To young Beckwith
he handed a telegram he had just scribbled. "Send that at
once please." In fifteen minutes a wire was cleared direct
into DI (code for the War Department) at Washington,
addressed to liaison man Halleck. It was the historic message that dispatched Phil Sheridan, chief of cavalry, to the
Valley of Virginia to take command of the Army of the
Shenandoah and redeem the ignominies of Sigel and
Hunter. It said in part: "I want Sheridan put in command
of all the troops in the field, with instructions to put himself south of the enemy and follow him to the death.
Wherever the enemy goes let our troops go also."

In those words Grant sounded the doom of the loveliest
vale in the land, the breadbasket of the Confederacy. He
would give Sheridan enough horse soldiers to stretch a
screen across the Valley and sack it unmercifully. Women
would wail, old men plead, children cry, but to no avail.
Grant's orders were specific, harsh, "Make all the Valley
south of the Baltimore and Ohio Railroad a desert as high
up as possible. I do not mean that houses should be
burned but that all provisions and stock should be re-

moved and the people notified to move out." Ghenghis Khan could have done no better than Sheridan. The Valley was given the full holocaust treatment. If ever the heel of a conqueror ground itself on the neck of a people, it was Sheridan's in the Valley. Grant had said in effect, "Go forth and burn." Sheridan was just the man for the job, a raving, ranting cavalryman, who wore a queer flat hat that looked as if he had sat on it. Cocky, cussy, conceited but able, he was the best God-damner in the Union armies—and flamethrower as well. A gray watcher on the mountain top wrote his wife, "By night the Valley glows like a bed of lava, flames jetting all over it."

It was stark tragedy for a people whose forefathers had cleared the wilderness on the floor of the valley and brought forth on this continent the richest, most beautiful pastoral landscape between the two oceans.

2

Sheridan was in the Valley. He had taken thousands of Grant's cavalry with him, three crack divisions headed by Wilson, Averell and Merritt. It was a matter of vital interest to Iron Scout George Shadburne. Sheridan was a tough customer. He had tightened up the picket lines between City Point and Fort Powhatan and down through Prince George County. Now he was gone. But who had taken his place? At dusk this July evening Shadburne donned his blue uniform and set out to find the answer. He took scout Jack Shoolbred with him. Jack was a South Carolina hotshot, as fast as they come with a Colt. Mounting their horses they rode to the "exit" from their hideout. No two Yankees ever looked Yankee-er. They fished around the Stage Road, asking questions of the farmfolk. Yes, a new man was on the job, new outfits on the pick-

ets and outposts. Shadburne still didn't have the answer
when the moon rose over the pines. Tethering their
horses in a thicket they entered a farmyard and tapped out
a signal on the back door. It was answered by a knock
from the inside.

"Can we sleep on the porch?" Shadburne whispered as
the door opened.

"You sure can. Ain't you hungry?"

"We jest want to sleep several hours. We stayed out
later than we thought."

"Maybe you can use a little breakfast before you get going."

"Won't have time for breakfast, thank you."

Before day they were heading down Lawyer's Road for
the entrance to their hideaway. They were hungry. Shadburne had a suggestion, "Suppose we go by Miss Tatum's.
Maybe she's got a piece of ham or something. Her aunt's a
crosspatch, but I reckon I can handle her."

Shoolbred's eyes brightened. His stomach proclaimed
its emptiness.

The sun was well up when they rode up to the Tatum
place, dismounted and led their horses to the back of the
house. They did not see two other horses at the rack behind the small barn munching oats. Going to the kitchen
door they were startled to find two Yankee troopers, standing in the kitchen watching Molly Tatum rounding up
a breakfast. It was too late to withdraw. Shadburne had to
lead with his ace.

"Howdy, lady!" said Shadburne in his best Yankee
"talk." Not the barest sign of recognition crossed his
poker face. He didn't look at her as he spoke. "Could you
oblige us with a little breakfast? We'd be happy to pay
you, if it won't crowd you."

Molly replied mechanically. "I reckon I can. I ain't got much. Might as well cook for four as two. 'Twon't take long."

"We'd sure appreciate it, lady. We've been up all night. Rebels been chasing us since yesterday." Then to the two strangers in blue, "Howdy, pardners!"

It was all sort of jolly. Molly kept up a light flow of nervous banter. The bluecoats, one from New York, the other from Maine, seemed affable enough. That is, their conversation was. But were they telling the truth? wondered Shadburne. He dished out a cock and bull story about how he and "this boy" had escaped from the rebel clutches down on the Blackwater, stole a couple of horses and made their getaway. Both members of the 140th New York Cavalry. The numbers didn't run that high, but it sounded all right. "They grabbed us up near Richmond the day Butler butted his head at Drewry's Bluff. I could have done better than that myself." The yarn was plausible enough and apparently accepted at its face value.

Not once during these preliminaries did Molly glance at Shadburne. Nor he at her. Nor did she look at Shoolbred. The set-up called for nimble stepping. Shadburne's thoughts spun fast. Are they Federals, or Confederates in blue uniforms? These men could be Yankee deserters. Each of the four was feeling his way, watching closely. Shadburne was confident gray spies would not be sent into the area without letting him know. If they were Federals, it was kill or be killed. Somebody was going to get shot, but who? To Shadburne it looked as if the strangers were likewise on the qui vive, going through the same mental gyrations as he. He filled the wait for breakfast with small talk. The rebels are tough. They treated us rough. Grant's just the man to tame 'em. But Shadburne wanted to be

sure before he made a move. He reasoned: Molly must
know, but how could she tell him? She knew all the pickets. It seemed as if the two men kept their eyes fixed on
her. He knew instinctively that Shoolbred was watching
him for the cue.

At the cookstove the girl tinkered for time. She knew
what was up. But how could she tell him with the two
men gazing hypnotically at her. With tantalizing slowness
she spread the threadbare tablecloth. Still no glance at
Shadburne. Nor he at her. Plates, cups, saucers, spoons,
knives, forks. She dragged it out. Then she filled the
plates. Eggs, ham, cornbread. It smelled delicious.

"Breakfast's ready," she said with a smile.

"Sure does smell good," gushed Shadburne. The strangers agreed. Shoolbred likewise.

Still feeling their way the four sat down, vis-à-vis, on
opposite sides of the pine board table. Four pistols at four
belts. It was like a four-handed poker game with all four
standing pat. Molly picked up the coffee pot from the
stove. Holding it gingerly she walked behind Shadburne
and Shoolbred and filled their cups. Then, slowly—very
slowly it seemed to Shadburne—she crossed over behind
the chairs of the strangers. As she finished filling the second cup she raised her eyes. Shadburne sensed it. Now,
and not until now, did he raise his. Their gaze met for
barely an instant. Her quick warning flash was unmis-
takable. It was only a look, but enough. As she stepped
back to the stove Shadburne's hand reached for his pistol.
Shoolbred doubled. In a fraction of a second two rebel re-
volvers poked across the table. Two flashes, two sharp reports. The strangers slumped forward in a slush of blood
and coffee. Shadburne and Shoolbred leaped back to avoid
being splashed with the mixture. Shadburne's slug had

drilled a clean hole over the eye; Shoolbred's slug, evidently defective, had plowed a slit twice its length, folding its victim's forehead back on his scalp. Fired at only inches' distance, the flashes blackened the faces and singed the beards of the dead men. Gunsmoke filled the kitchen. With a scream the girl staggered out of the kitchen white as a ghost.

The two scouts worked fast. It was gruesome business. After dragging the corpses into the tall weeds behind the outhouse they went back to clean up the mess. It took half an hour to wipe out the last telltale red stain. But there was more to be done. The dead men had to be put where they'd never be found. Every house on the road would be searched. Making a crude stretcher with the dead men's belts and two saplings, they lugged them deep into the swamp. Laboriously they dug deep, watery graves, tossing the bloody tablecloth in the bottom. Before tumbling the bodies into the hole, they rifled their clothes. By this time the dead men were covered with bluebottle flies.

"New pistols," commented Shadburne. "We can use 'em."

He searched their pockets. It yielded a few greenbacks and a watch. From the dead men's saddlebags he unearthed a folded sheet of instructions for troopers on the care of horseflesh. It was signed "August V. Kautz, Brigadier General, Commanding Cavalry Division."

"New man running things round here. I thought so. My old friend Kautz."

It was an hour before they returned to the house. Molly met them at the kitchen door. She was still pale.

"Where's your aunt?" asked Shadburne.

"She went up to City Point to sell eggs. Good thing she warn't here. I reckon we'll have to move away fast."

Shadburne shook his head. "There won't be any trouble. They'd a knocked us off, if we hadn't beaten them to it. We'll be back to get the horses tonight. We hid them way out in the swamp. They won't miss these boys till tomorrow at least."

14

A "Two-Pistol and Often Three" Man

Late July had indeed brought a new overlord—August Kautz—to the picket lines that entwined Prince George County. His bailiwick was extensive, embracing the dank, mysterious Blackwater region east of Petersburg. Blackwater Swamp itself was bad enough, but the area boasted other putrescences with ominous names: Black Hole Swamp, Jones Hole Swamp, No Head Swamp. Kautz was ordered to make hot war on scouts, spies, guerillas, bushwhackers that were spreading terror behind the Yankee lines. More importantly, he was to throw a protecting screen around the big cattle herd that was being jostled nomadlike from one pasture to another along the James.

Kautz was given carte blanche. His four cavalry regiments were reenforced by four companies of the 5th Pennsylvania loaned by Provost Marshal Patrick at City Point. Still basking in the glory of killing Jeb Stuart at Yellow Tavern, Sheridan had ridden off to the Valley.

Wilson had gone with him. This was a relief to Kautz. He and the dashing young cavalryman (who had Grant's ear) had not seen eye to eye since the Reams Station affair where Lee's new cavalry chief gave them a fearful cutting up. Custer, Kilpatrick, Torbert and other fresh-out-of-the-Point boys had departed with Sheridan.

On the muster roll of Grant's forces Kautz's command was still labeled "Cavalry Division of the Army of the James." He and his men were actually "on loan" to the Army of the Potomac. An awkward set-up. The day after Kautz took over, he rode the picket circuit down country to Lee's Mill, then up and down the fanlike roads as far east as Fort Powhatan. Division headquarters were set up on the Stage Road near Prince George Courthouse. Grant's military telegraph ran along this road. It meant prompt connection with GHQ and HAUS, if trouble broke out. To the 3rd Pennsylvania Kautz gave the "bull-guard" duty, watching the herd. He stationed the 1st District Cavalry at Sycamore Church directly down Walls Road from Coggin's Point.

On his inspection tour Kautz was amazed to discover the beef herd five miles south of Coggin's Point peacefully grazing near Cooke's Mill, as if inviting gray rustlers. He immediately reported to GHQ the danger of losing the herd by a fast in and out attack. His lines were attenuated, with only fourteen hundred men to picket forty miles of roads. For that reason, he urged, "It would be safest to call the cattle in nearer for the present." He added that scouts and bushwhackers were as numerous as chiggers.

Just now GHQ (Meade's) was feuding with HAUS (Grant's) whose subsistence chief, Michael Morgan, was insisting that the General Cattle Herd be moved back to Coggin's Point where pastures were ankle deep again.

Grant shunted Morgan's request on to Meade, who disagreed because the "force of cavalry between the plank road and the James is still small. The cattle should not return to Coggin's Point."

But HAUS spoke again with finality. Send the cattle back to Coggin's Point. Meade caved in with the lame admission, "I would say that beef cattle can be safely herded and grazed near Coggin's Point," but Meade was hedging, merely saying "beef cattle." He did not specify the General Cattle Herd. Meade's clear-visioned Chief of Staff, General Humphreys, however, sensed something in the offing. He would later say, "Someone had sent the great cattle herd from which both armies (of the Potomac and of the James) drew, close to the left of the picket line near the James River where there was good grazing but no security. It was no one belonging to the Army of the Potomac." Humphreys never identified the "someone." Obviously, he pointed to a someone higher than Meade. He added, "We are not strong in cavalry, two divisions being absent with Sheridan in the Shenandoah Valley." As for Kautz, he moaned in his Journal, "My remonstrance was not heeded."

Grant's beef herd had become one of the sights shown the more venturesome visiting VIP's, who came in droves to City Point. Amply escorted by cavalry (always a headache for Kautz), politicians, ministers of the gospel, foreign diplomats, newspaper men, toured down to Coggin's Point to marvel at the beefsteaks fattening there. The New York *Tribune*'s correspondent wrote a glowing description of the "great herd of beeves" grazing contentedly behind Grant's lines awaiting their turn to sacrifice their succulent red meat for the good of the cause.

On his work sheet of plans for exterminating "scouts and guerillas" in the Blackwater realm, Kautz noted that hunting for them was like searching for needles in haystacks. "Numbers of so-called scouts are captured every day and the prisoners sent into the provost marshal. Quite a number are caught going through the lines. They are always in our uniform and representing themselves as belonging to some regiment in our army." He proposed "to ambuscade and watch for the enemy at various crossings of the Blackwater. I do not believe they have an established camp that can be surprised or broken up." He was quite mistaken.

Eight miles from his headquarters as the crow flies, deep in the recesses of Kautz's domain, lay the camp of the Iron Scouts, as reckless and wily a crew as ever prowled the flanks of an enemy or resided *within* his lines. In their swamp-girt Sherwood Forest they made themselves quite at home. At first sight one would have mistaken their abode for a Yankee outpost. They were togged out in blue. Their "barracks" was a huddle of lean-to's covered with pine boughs and vines shrewdly woven into roofs that sheltered them from the rain unless it was very heavy. One or two of them slept in puptents stencilled "US." Their horses, tethered near at hand, bore the big "US" brand on their shoulders. Around their "headquarters" they erected a high screen of closely intertwined vines and bushes that blacked out their camp fires by night. To while away their time between missions they puffed their pipes, fished in the Blackwater, cleaned their weapons, made soap and mended clothes. This was the pleasant side of life behind the Yankee lines. They lived —it seemed—on the fat of the land. For them hams came out of hiding, and chickens too. Many a farmhouse was ready to give them a meal or hide them out if they were pressed too hard. Between times they courted the pretty rebel girls famishing for attention.

Lodged almost at Grant's back door, they were a brash, industrious lot. It was dangerous living. Secret service was their business—espionage, scouting, spying out blue troop movements. For them there were no bands, no thrills, no showoffs, no parades. Finding these boys hard to catch and kill, the Yankees had nicknamed them Iron Scouts. Jeb Stuart had found their services invaluable in a thousand ways. For him they waylaid blue couriers galloping through the night with saddlebags packed with vital information. Stuart used them both as pickets and couriers. Their last service to Stuart was to inform him that Sheridan with ten thousand cavalry had wriggled round the Confederate right and was driving for Richmond—and Yellow Tavern where Stuart overtook them and where he fell. He never tired of boasting of their remarkable escapades. Wade Hampton, who inherited them from Stuart, had recruited them in South Carolina and Mississippi from coonhunters, bear trackers, deer stalkers, woodsmen, who knew the ways and wiles of the forest. Favorite weapon of their trade was a shotgun charged with buckshot. Untidy weapon. At close range it could blow a man's head off. Pistols came in handy too. Army Colts captured or snatched from dead Yankees. Fighting was not their mission except for close quarters or making a get-away. They were information-getters and they played close hands to get it. Standard scout uniform was blue. The line of distinction between scout, spy and guerilla was finely drawn. General Order Number 6, issued early in the war, prescribed hanging for rebels caught in Federal uniforms. Captors frequently wasted no time debating the fine points of whether a prisoner was a scout, spy or guerilla. They took the shortest way out with a Colt slug. A lot faster than a rope. What did it matter how you killed him, just so you did it.

Top Iron Scout was a remarkable six-footer from Texas,
Sergeant George Shadburne, a "two pistol and often
three" man, who could handle himself handsomely in any
fracas. He gave the orders. His discipline was exact but
sketchy. Shadburne himself was as elusive as a landgoing
eel. It was jested about that Shadburne "had eyes in the
back of his head and two pairs of ears." He left no memoirs, only patchwork accounts of his hairbreadth escapes.
Yankees knew him well. Twice they captured him. He
made his get-aways with a noose dangling before his eyes.
Shadburne could "talk Yankee" better than a Yankee
himself, and decked out in blue his transformation from
Confederate to Federal was a feat of sartorial ledgerde-
main.

Wade Hampton described him as "a handsome young
fellow, with large, soft, mild eyes; but as soon as a fight began he was instantly transformed into the dashing cavalryman, his whole soul seemed to be in the battle, and his
black eyes blazed like fire. Armed with at least two pistols,
and often three, he would dash against the enemy firing
with a rapidity and precision not surpassed by even
Mosby, who was very handy with his pistol."

It was Shadburne and his boys who scouted Judson Kilpatrick's raiders heading south to pillage Richmond in
March 1864. He got the information to Hampton in time
to nip the daring expedition in the bud.

While Grant was shaping his Grand Design at Culpeper before plunging into the Wilderness to attack Lee,
Shadburne spent three days loitering around the generalissimo's headquarters. Procuring a small cart and disguis-
ing himself as a countrywoman, he boldly drove into the
Yankee lines. His gastronomic come-on was a basket of
pies and cakes cooked for him by a farmer's wife down be-

low Culpeper. Shadburne set up shop not far from Supreme Headquarters. For three days he plied his game—peddling his sweet wares while snitching bits of information about troop movements.

From Wade Hampton himself came this sketch of a Shadburne exploit:

In all the excitement of a battle Shadburne was perfectly cool ready for any emergency, or to avail himself of any advantage. He proved he possessed qualities which only needed a wider field for their exercise, to make him a leader. Let me illustrate. If you remember, Wilson and Kautz with a large force made a raid against the South-Side & Danville Railroad. At Staunton river-bridge they were repulsed and returned to join Grant near Petersburg. Near Stony Creek they were met by our cavalry and defeated with loss. Retreating towards Reams' Station they were met by Fitz Lee and Mahone, when their rout became complete and final. Kautz pushed down to cross the Halifax road, so that he could get into his lines, while Wilson fled towards the Nottoway River. Shadburne was sent by General Hampton just after the fight at Reams' station to find where the enemy were.—Taking five men with him, he moved up a county road leading from Halifax to the Stage road.—On this, he had not proceeded far, when he met the advance guard of Kautz's retreating column. —He at once ordered them to surrender, when they began to deploy. Without a moment's hesitation, he gave orders in a loud voice for "two regiments to be brought up; one on the right, the other on the left." As soon as this order was given, the Yankees said they would surrender.—Placing one man on one side of the road and

occupying the other, Shadburne directed the Yankees
to advance and drop their arms. While doing this, the
main column of the enemy came in sight, and seeing the
condition of their advance guard, they charged to re-
lease them. But Shadburne was too quick for them. He
put his prisoners in motion, guarded by three men on
each flank, made them gallop, then "form fours" and all
swept down towards our command. As soon as his prisoners were closed up and *charging from their own men,*
he dispatched a man to inform General Hampton to
"look out, for the Yankees were charging down the
road he was on." The general immediately took a few
men back and soon met Shadburne, who had brought
off safely *seventy-three prisoners,* the whole advance
squadron of Kautz's command, and this too in full sight
of the enemy!

But Shadburne was not alone. With him ranged a cote-
rie of fearless, ghostlike cavalry scouts like himself, whose
exploits read like fables. They were valiant, sleepless
daredevils whose job it was to hang on to the fringes of the
enemy and keep cavalry headquarters informed of what
was "cooking"—a day in and day out task, touch and go
sometimes every hour on the hour. A colorful crew they
were. To name a few: Hugh Scott, Billy Mikler, Dan
Tanner, handsome Jack Shoolbred with a spiked chin
beard, "Snake" Harris, Dick Hogan, Jim Niblett.

These men's amazing talents had won Jeb Stuart's
heart. The mysterious missions on which he sent them
and from which they seldom returned empty-handed—
their bold at-home life inside enemy lines—had the flair
and risk in which the dashing cavalier gloried.

When Stuart fell in the gunsmoke of Yellow Tavern,

Wade Hampton took over the Iron Scouts and they served and worshipped him as they had Stuart. Now, ensconced a few miles back of Grant's headquarters at City Point, they were up to their old tricks. They knew everything, almost as soon as the Yankees planned it.

15

Tapping Grant's Telegraph Line

In mid-July 1864, Lee ordered the tapping of Grant's military telegraph line that ran down the James from City Point, worming and twisting by wood, swamp and water until it finally wriggled into DI at Washington. Vital secrets of Grant's plans on the Petersburg front were hourly filtering through this skein-like line. It veiled a thousand things Lee would like to know. The line dangled temptingly.

To his cipher operator, young Charles A. Gaston, Lee assigned the hazardous eavesdropping task. He was ordered to hook a wire onto Grant's line somewhere between Fort Powhatan and Swan's Point where it crossed the James by underwater cable, set up his instrument and go to work. Gaston's immediate job was to find out just what was going on behind Grant's lines. Grant was mining somewhere. But where? If Grant was creating a man-made volcano to blow half of the Petersburg front to kingdom come, just where would it erupt?

Reid's Rangers came forward to protect Gaston on this mission. The young man was escorted to the area by General Roger Pryor, former political hotblood, who had joined up with Reid's band of irregulars making *petite guerre* in Surry Country. This outfit had won considerable notoriety harassing Yankee outposts farther down the Blackwater and, most effective of all, cutting Grant's telegraph communication with Washington. Deep in a bog near Surry Court House, Reid's men constructed a crude hideout in a thicket of wild plums. Working fast between blue patrols that rode the line hourly Gaston spliced a fine, silk covered wire onto the Federal line. Using a special insulator to hold the two ends of the main wire Gaston ran his line under the tree bark to the ground and half a mile cross-swamp to a camouflaged hut where he set up his battery, magnet and key. Two rangers kept watch. Food was brought him daily.

In this cramped, lonely cubbyhole Gaston spent six weeks, virtually alone, while he milked the wire of hundreds of code messages passing back and forth between Grant's headquarters and Washington. Sometimes he listened for eighteen hours at a stretch. It was a nerve-racking task. Fully ninety percent of the messages he transcribed were coded. He dispatched them to Lee by special underground. The rest came through wide open—uncoded. One of the latter was to prove a boon to Lee's hungry army. This message is not to be found in the Official Records. It can only be presumed that Gaston caught it as it flitted by. The Official Records reveal something else that should be noted. Late in August blue patrols captured a "rebel operator" hooked in on the line near Cabin Point five miles from Gaston's hideaway. The

Official Records hinted the second eavesdropper had "turned turtle" as ran the current identification of a turncoat.

By 1864 wire cutting was an old Confederate custom and Grant's connection with DI was given special treatment. Estimates of line breaks over the City Point-Swan's Point sector ran as high as a hundred though only twenty odd are reported officially. Confederate wire cutters became experts. They were mostly irregulars, guerillas, scouts and citizen volunteers, anxious to help the resistance movement near their homes. One of the most accomplished was a farm woman near Lewes, Delaware, who had two sons in Lee's army. When she was caught redhanded, she was given the choice of Old Capitol Prison or of keeping her hands off the military wires.

Protection of Grant's line was hazardous, far more so in the trackless, often impenetrable area along the James than elsewhere. Cavalry performed this irksome duty. Kautz complained constantly that his forces were inadequate to guard the first relay from City Point to Fort Powhatan. Fully a dozen reports were sent in from Colonel Innis, commanding Fort Powhatan. A sample, "I think there is a considerable force of rebels between here and Swan's Point led by Roger A. Pryor. Two colored cavalrymen repairing the telegraph line were killed last night and one missing." To maintain security of the line at all times would require—he said—two regiments of horse. Line repairers led a perilous existence. After snipping the line the wire cutters would hide out near the break to pick off the repairers when they galloped up. Like firemen, these men were on call ready to leap in the saddle and dash off to mend the gaps. Operators at each relay point were required to check in every half hour. Failure to report meant a gap in the line. It also identified its general location. But wire cutting was not a one way street. Sherman said he tore down five hundred miles of telegraph wire in Georgia on his march to the sea.

The wire itself (a flexible, seven-twist, insulated cable) from City Point to Washington was literally the lifeline of Grant's drive on Lee. It was also the marvel of its day. Skirting the James by way of the Stage Road to Fort Powhatan, it cut across to Surry Court House, then looped back to Swan's Point where it dived under the river to Jamestown Island. Crossing the Peninsula to Yorktown it ducked down to Fort Monroe, master relay station, then shot up to Gloucester Point and under Chesapeake Bay by cable to Cherrystone. Running up the Eastern Shore it wound through Salisbury, Lewes and on to Wilmington. At this telegraph nerve center it was spliced onto a trunkline to double back to Washington.

This wire kept Grant in contact with the widespread fighting fronts. Sherman pinpointed it, "Hardly a day passed when Grant did not know the exact state of facts with me, more than fifteen hundred miles away as the wires ran. So on the field, a thin, insulated wire may be run on improvised stakes from tree to tree, for six or more miles in two hours, and I have seen operators so skillful that they could by cutting the wire receive messages with their tongues."

Wire-tapping—telegraphic espionage—came of age with the Civil War. It flourished from the moment the Federal high command recognized the war potential of Morse's invention. In his first campaign Grant gave military telegraphy the kickoff. His cipher operator, Samuel H. Beckwith, served him over three years. In the use of the wires the North really stole a march on the Southern military hierarchy. Grant's use of it popularized it. On the other hand in 1862 Confederate Secretary of War Randolph was censured for having telegraph wires run directly into the War Department at Richmond. To give the full picture it should be known that during four years of war over six million messages passed over the Federal military telegraph system. Nearly two million of these were dated 1864 when the North's all-out drive on the South rose to its peak.

It is significant that the Federal telegraph, signal and mail codes were never actually broken by the South. Union experts invented cipher codes the Confederates never unlocked and which the operators and translators never betrayed. The smartest code breakers in the Confederacy spent four futile years trying to unravel these well-held Union secrets. On the other hand Washington experts seemed to possess uncanny talents for disentangling Confederate codes and ciphers.

Confederate raider John Morgan was apparently the first to employ the telegraph to find out what his enemy was doing or proposed to do and to mislead him about his own movements. Generals were soon carrying their own operators with them though many of the older wardogs found it hard to adopt the new trick. Morgan's famed operator was "Lightning" Ellsworth for whose feats there is only one word—fantastic.

Ubiquitous, rollicking Jeb Stuart supplied the classic comedy touch to wartime wiretapping. Swooping out of the night on Burke's Station near Alexandria, Virginia, his men seized the Federal operator in the act of transmitting orders from General Heintzelman for catching the wily raider, who was at the moment rampaging through the countryside. Putting his own man on the wire Stuart checked the disposition of the blue forces spreading out to catch him. After learning what he needed and before cutting the wire he indulged in a historic bit of raillery with this message to Quartermaster General Meigs of the Union Armies at Washington: "The quality of the mules lately furnished me is very poor. It has interfered seriously with our moving the captured wagons."

The first week of September, 1864, two dispatches were flashed to City Point by Quartermaster General Meigs, one on the heels of the other. Both were wide open. Gaston caught them as they darted by. The first, to Grant's QMG Ingalls, announced the shipment of one thousand fresh-shod horses down the Chesapeake and up the James, in lots of about three hundred by barge. The second, to Grant's Subsistence Chief Michael R. Morgan, read, "Two thousand five hundred beeves shipped from Baltimore; three hundred a day. Will land them at wharf below Coggin's Point. Arrange to receive them." There are several reputed variations of this message which was to have significant gastronomic repercussions.

16

Shadburne Goes A-Visiting

Had August Kautz suspected the killing of two of his troopers in Molly Tatum's kitchen he would have burned her home (as Sheridan was doing in the Valley in retaliation for the surreptitious slaughter of his men). The girl herself would have been whisked off to City Point and grilled by Grant's expert inquisitor, George Sharpe. But apparently Kautz didn't smell a rat. He reported the men as captured. It was nothing unusual. Unwary pickets were being gobbled up with painful regularity.

Kautz's reports were eloquent with fusillades out of the darkness, desertions, horse-stealings, wagon-burnings, death and mayhem in a variety of forms. He ordered his men to be more vigilant, take better aim and fire at anything. Do a little bushwhacking on your own account. Fight the daredevils with their own fire. As for guerillas, he repeated Major General Daniel Butterfield's drastic prescription—"Catch and kill guerillas, *then* try them, will be a good method of treating them."

When the two troopers vanished Kautz ordered an in-
tensive search of the area. Not a clue did they find. Shadburne and Shoolbred had buried the dead cavalrymen in
a bottomless "sink" where the morass itself would suck
them down deeper. Not until Judgment Day would it
render up its secret.

A safeguard was billeted in a tent in the Tatum yard for
a week or so after the mens' disappearance, not that she
was suspected, but because of blue resentment that flared
over the mystery. But she hardly needed protection. She
was making friends with the bluebirds—for one purpose:
to help the South. Arch-guile it was, but the Confederacy
possessed her heart and soul as it did her "aunt's." Obsessed with this idea she discreetly widened her acquaint-
ance, making her pitch for orderlies, couriers, troopers
who rode the picket lines. These men had sharp ears and
generally knew what was going on or coming off.

Quietly she memorized the elaborate military network
that criss-crossed the Blackwater area. She knew the ring
of blue outposts by heart. On her mental map she tabbed
the location of regimental camps, strength of the units stationed at bridges, the beats of the pickets, where the colonels were quartered and where Kautz himself snoozed
while his patrols were making their rounds through the
long dark hours haunted by expectations of a bullet any
moment. Once in a while she watched the stocky Kautz
ride by with a guard of horse clattering with him. It may
have suggested something to her, but Kautz never toured
by night. It was probably well he didn't. All this information she relayed to George Shadburne who came for it by
night like a phantom. Nor did she forget the tidbits of
information let fall at her kitchen table, memorizing them
the moment they dropped.

Breakfast at Molly's was a delightful respite for a jaded,

sleepy picket worn to a frazzle by an all-night, lonely patrol. Her special pets were the 1st District of Columbia Cavalry whose encampment was spread out at Sycamore Church over on Walls Road several miles up from Lawyer's on which she lived. Of clear nights she could hear the bugles cross-swamp sound Taps on the quiet air for the sleepy horse soldiers. Weary blue troopers vowed they could smell her bacon and eggs all the way to Sycamore Church. Many was the tasty meal gulped down by hungry horse soldiers, sick and tired of the hectic existence war had forced on them, longing for a good, home-cooked meal and the sight of a pretty pair of eyes and a shapely waist. Molly was an appetizing morsel. Her cherry red lips and firm, young breasts made their mouths water.

Her ardent Southern proclivities were outspoken. She joshed her blue clad guests unmercifully at times. Her witty cracks at "damn Yankees" only led her guests to tease her into more of them. To the young fellows who succumbed to the tempting aromas of her culinary come-on she was just an innocent country lass making the best of a war crackling on her doorstep. Nor is it improbable that more than one—had she offered the right bargain—would have swapped blue for gray.

One mistake she was never guilty of: extending her favors from the kitchen to the bedroom. She had already done what she had vowed not to do: let her heart get entrapped again by the young man who had abandoned it only to reappear "herdin' cattle for Grant." But when Jim Fisher came back Molly had melted fast. She tried not to let him know it.

From the sutler's at City Point bluecoats kept her larder well stocked: chickens to fry, bacon and eggs to whip up, coffee, cheese, sugar and sometimes boxes of candy from those hard smitten.

Nor was Molly suspected the night a crowd of the boys rode over from Sycamore Church for an old style Tidewater fish fry in her kitchen. *Pièce de resistance* of the get-together was a mess of fat perch caught in the Blackwater. The party was a huge success. Something for the boys to write home about. Molly fried the succulent perch to a tasty brown turn. But it seems someone had invited Shadburne & Company—not to the festivities, of course. On the way back to camp shotguns had blazed from the dark undergrowth. The dampish air was heavy with gunsmoke. When it cleared several bluecoats lay sprawled in the moonlight, riddled with buckshot.

Coldblooded work at the crossroads, but Molly read her Bible plain and literally: an eye for an eye, a tooth for a tooth. To this she added: a Yankee for a Confederate.

2

A few nights later Molly sat on her porch waiting, listening. Her "aunt" had gone upstairs to bed. Presently she heard what she was hoping for: a song rising clear through the dark.

> *When the moon had climbed the mountains*
> *And the stars were shining too,*
> *Then I'd take my darling Nellie Gray . . .*

She rose and hurried to the gate to greet the rider as he loomed out of the dusk. He swung lightly to the ground.

"I love to hear you sing, Jim," she said, her eyes shining.

"Do you, Molly?" He reached out and caught her in his arms. Her struggle was brief. Then he kissed her passionately. Her body was warm and pliant.

"You're sweet, you know it," he breathed, holding her at arm's length. "It's jest like old times."

"You're right nice yourself, Jim. I missed you last week. Waited half the night, but I reckon they're keeping you right busy."

"We been getting in more cattle. Coming up the river every day." Then warily, "Is your aunt gone to bed?"

Molly smiled, "Oh, I fixed that. She says she don't mind you coming, if you don't stay too late."

Jim rambled on. "Never saw people eat so much beef. Them boys of Grant's just like a pack of wolves."

Arm in arm they walked to the porch and sat down. Presently she ventured, "You ain't going to keep on herding cattle when the war's over, is you?"

"I reckon I oughtn't," he admitted. "But the war ain't over yet. I signed for two years more, but I give 'em another name. They don't know I'm Jim Fisher. I'm saving money, Molly. Maybe when the shootin's over me and you can get a little farm round here somewhere."

"Maybe we could, Jim. How many cattle you got over there on the Point?"

" 'Bout twenty five hundred in the big herd, five hundred in the little one. We jest got in a big new lot. They're mean, onery and fat. One of these days the Confederits is going to sneak round and rustle a passel of 'em."

"Is it that bad?" she asked under her breath.

"They ain't got enough soldiers watching them cattle to stop a rabbit."

He talked on. His experiences in the west—a hair-raising cattle-thieving tale—and how he still loved her. The hour grew late. The swamp air grew damp and chilly. The stars looked shivery.

"I reckon it's time you was going, Jim."

"I reckon 'tis," he agreed. "I'll come back 'bout this time next week."

They walked slowly, silently to the gate. He kissed her

again before mounting his horse. As he merged into the
dark he began singing gaily—

> *Georgia gals are handsome,*
> *And Texas gals are sweet,*
> *But a gal in old Virginia*
> *Is the gal I long to meet.*
> *When this here war is over*
> *She's a-goin' to be my wife,*
> *And I'll settle down along the Jeems*
> *And lead a quiet life.*

A new song, she thought, as singer and song faded in the
distance. But she didn't climb the stairs to her cubbyhole
bedroom. Tipping into the dark house she lit two candles
and set them on a table by the parlor window. Tensely she
waited in dead silence. It seemed hours before off in the
swamp an owl hooted. Her heart quickened its beat. Long
minutes stretched by and then a second hoot, nearer this
time as if the wise old bird were perched on the cowshed.
Quickly snuffing the candles she returned to the porch.
There was a rustle in the yard, the thin blast of a whistle,
and a figure stole out of the murk. It was George Shadburne. Molly had news.

3

It was long after midnight when George Shadburne rode
out of his "headquarters" in Blackwater Swamp and
reined his horse southwest towards Reams Station. The
moon was down. So deep was the silence it seemed to ab-
sorb and mute the clopclop of his horse's hooves. The
blackness was impenetrable. He traveled light. Two pistols at his waist. Slung from his saddle was a sizable ham

and a bag of forage for his horse. Night-wise as an owl he hugged the side of the road.

Avoiding main highways he felt his way cautiously, stopping often to reconnoiter. Short cuts, side roads, abandoned paths were as familiar to him as if he'd been born right in the middle of the swamp. Twice he encountered blue outposts. Their white tents showed ghostlike in the pitch dark. Before one, the embers of a small fire made a faint red stain on the murk. In the other a lantern burned low. Maybe troopers having a late "bull" session or too plagued by mosquitoes to sleep. Climbing out of the saddle he led his horse on wide detours. Horses sloshing through the undergrowth made noise enough to startle an army.

In the predawn Shadburne broke cover on Rowanty Creek near Monk's Neck Bridge, two miles west of Reams Station. Fifteen miles lay behind him. The bridge was enmeshed by felled trees and hastily thrown up earthworks. Sharp fighting had crackled hereabouts. Dead horses stank horribly. He counted a score of Yankee graves with the usual crackerbox headboards.

He crossed the Weldon railroad well below Reams Station. The rails were still intact though Hancock held the road from just below Petersburg down almost to the station. Two days ago Hancock had pushed out to destroy the road farther south. Gray cavalry had pounced on him at Monk's Neck Bridge and mauled him badly. Threatened with loss of his foothold on the road he put up a bitter defense. There was a lot of blue dying and bleeding. At this point Shadburne was six miles due south of the left flange of the big blue army whose gigantic coils were slowly curling west to outflank Petersburg, cut the Boydton Road and anchor on the Appomattox.

At the bridge Shadburne paused to reconnoiter. It was

tricky business, and hazardous, getting into the gray lines at any time and much more so in a blue uniform. A watchful gray vedette spotted him at once, challenging sharply. Shadburne took a few steps towards the voice. The challenger barked again. Next time the man behind the voice would fire and these boys were pretty sure of hitting something. Identifying himself, Shadburne crossed the bridge, complimented the boy on his vigilance and struck out up Gravelly Run. Now inside the gray lines he dismounted and fed his horse. The early morning mists were lifting as he crossed Quaker Road. Pickets eyed him suspiciously.

Presently he spied a familiar scene: a long array of pup-tents (once property of the Federal government) lining both sides of the road. Camp-fires smoking, cavalry cooking breakfast. Scores of lean, lank-haired fellows in weathered gray waiting to devour it. Messpans, skillets rattling. Coffee brewing. Shadburne was hungry, and the bacon smelled good. It neutralized the dead horse stench that lingered in his nostrils.

Up ahead he drew rein before a big white tent pitched well back from the road under a live oak. A Negro was puttering about, setting a long table under the tent fly. A small two-starred flag identified the place as headquarters of the Cavalry Corps of Lee's Army. Nothing very pretentious about it, reminiscent, perhaps, of the camp of Francis Marion, another South Carolinian, who in the Revolution had harassed the flanks of the British. A row of smaller staff tents and a dozen horses hitched to saplings or tree limbs, munching forage, completed the picture. Across the road orderlies were cooking breakfast.

As Shadburne dismounted, a massive, bearded figure, buttoning up his gray tunic, emerged from the tent with a "Good morning, gentlemen" to several aides whose interest at the moment was fixed on the activities of the dusky culinary department, but who snapped out of it at once. This was the man Shadburne had come to see, Major General Wade Hampton, Chief of Cavalry, who looked at least seven feet tall. As Shadburne unslung his ham he heard a hearty, booming voice.

"Here's a damn Yankee for breakfast! Howdy, George!"

Hampton strode to meet him. Shadburne saluted respectfully, noting as he did so the second star gleaming in the wreath on Hampton's collar.

"Howdy, General!" He proferred his ham. "I brought you a little something."

"A ham!" roared Hampton. "I bet you hornswaggled it off a gal you're courting." His aides gathered round. "Gentlemen, meet the best ladies' man in the Confederacy. And the best scout, George Shadburne."

Shadburne parried. "I reckon she wouldn't mind my giving it to *you*, General."

To most of the staff Shadburne was a shadowy figure who had a habit of appearing out of the nowhere, mostly by night, bringing information. His exploits were legend.

Introductions and breakfast followed. Hampton regaled the meal with a repeat of how Shadburne and six scouts captured Kautz's entire advance guard down below Reams Station. Breakfast over, the staff withdrew to a respectful distance.

"Well, George, what's up?"

Shadburne drew out the paper he had taken from the dead man's pocket at Molly Tatum's home. Hampton ran through it quickly.

"Your old friend Kautz again. I wondered what he was doing since Sheridan went to the Valley, but I knew you'd let me know. Where'd you get this paper?"

"Off a Yankee we had to dispose of." He smiled sort of grimly. "But there's something else you ought to know, general. You know those cattle I told you about. Well, they're just waiting for somebody to come and get 'em."

Hampton's humor died instantly. His eyes flashed. "Where are they?" he cracked.

"They've been moving them all about. Right now they're on Coggin's Point eating old 'Secession' Ruffin's grass."

"How many are there?"

"It's not a small herd. Two or three thousand, maybe more. Grant came across the James with five thousand, but they're eating 'em awful fast and getting more all the time."

Hampton whistled. "Makes my mouth water. That's considerable beefsteak. The army could use it. Walk out there on the road and holler beef to my hungry boys and see what happens. They'd trample you to death in the rush." Now dead serious, "How can we get at them?"

Shadburne spread a rough, battered map on the table. He'd made it himself. The two men bent over it as Shadburne traced a possible route.

"You'd go down the Boydton Road till you got to Big Cat Tail Creek. Then you'd turn right on the Flat Foot Road, cut across to Stony Creek and work over towards Cook's Bridge. Up Lawyer's Road, up Walls Road to Sycamore Church and you'd be right on top of the cattle. You'd have a little job to do at Sycamore Church. Kautz has camped the 1st District Cavalry there. They got a log barricade around it."

"What'd the Yankees be doing all this time while we were sneaking round to the back door?"

"They won't know we're coming unless somebody tells 'em."

Hampton put his finger on Sycamore Church. "When we get there Grant's whole army'd be between us and the rest of ours." He grew silent for long seconds. Then he spoke, weighing every word. "Find out two things for me: when Grant expects to visit Sheridan in the Valley, or goes to Washington. That's first. Get me the exact locations of Kautz's outposts and picket lines. One thing more. No blabbing to anybody. Keep this one to yourself. I won't say a word to my staff until I see what General Lee thinks. If we do it, we'd have to do it fast. Meanwhile see what you can find out."

17

Portrait of a Cavalryman

Jeb Stuart was dead. His plumes trailed in the dust at Yellow Tavern. No more would the gay cavalier pound the Virginia roads under the stars at the head of his gray horsemen singing "Lorena," "Nellie Gray" and "Jine the Cavalry." The Confederacy had buried her Roland and dried her tears.

In his stead rode Major General Wade Hampton, South Carolina's grandee and *beau sabreur* and now commander of Lee's Cavalry Corps. Stuart's scarlet-lined cape had fallen on his logical heir.

In the Confederate Museum at Richmond there is a twelve-pound, double-edged, straight sword, a hefty weapon, forged for the man who wielded it prodigiously. With this blade and a small pearl-handled Colt, Hampton became as fierce a front-fighter as any who wore the gray. At hand-to-hand in-fighting he was without peer among the general officers in American history save possibly Bedford Forrest.

After the war a former trooper asked him how many Federals he had personally slain in battle. "Eleven," replied Hampton. "Two with my sword and nine with my pistol." "But how about the two at Trevilians?" interposed the veteran. "Oh," said Hampton, "I didn't count them. They were running."

In the hurlyburly cavalry butchery at Gettysburg, Hampton brought his sword down so violently on an adversary's head that it cleft the bluecoat's skull down to his chin. After the battle he wrote Senator Wignall, "I have been pretty roughly handled, have received two saber cuts on the head, one of which cut through the table of my skull, and a shrapnel shot in my body." He was three months recovering.

If Hampton had a fault it was one he shared with the dead Stuart: reckless exposure in battle. Like moth to the flame he was drawn to the thick of it. He fought in probably a hundred little cavalry fights and all the big ones.

Hampton was forty-six, fifteen years Stuart's senior, when on August 11, 1864, he became Lee's ranking cavalry commander. He was no knight errant. Gone was the hilarity that kept Stuart's camp in an uproar. Dead was minstrel Sam Sweeney, who tickled his banjo and sang ditties for the fun-loving Stuart. No midnight serenades, no impromptu balls in the wee hours enlivened Hampton's entourage. War was a deadly business in which he was a flaming leader. But he hated it. To his sister he voiced the deeper feelings of his heart: "We gain successes but after every fight there comes to me an ominous paper, marked 'Casualties,' 'killed,' and 'wounded.' Sad words which carry anguish to so many hearts. And we have scarcely time to bury the dead as we press on in the same deadly strife. I pray for peace. I would not give peace for all the military glory won by Bonaparte."

Nor could he have foreseen, when thus writing, that he would shortly include, in his casualty report of a fight along Hatcher's Run, these sad words, "In this charge, while leading the men and cheering them by his words, and example, Lieutenant William Preston Hampton, Aide-de-Camp, fell mortally wounded and Lieutenant Wade Hampton, who was acting on my staff received a severe wound." Two sons at once, one dead, the other nearly so. From here out Wade Hampton no longer prayed for peace. He would shed the last drop of his blood to avenge the killing of his son.

An observant Petersburg lady, Mrs. Betty Venable, saw him: "General Hampton came to dinner one Sunday with his adjutant, Major Reid Venable, who was my husband's cousin. A more magnificent man I never saw. I had never seen General Stuart so I can't make comparisons. Tall, erect, Hampton looked like a giant. I remember watching him mount his horse. He appeared to me the perfection of horseman and soldier."

An officer in Hampton's command left an unforgettable impression of him, whom he first saw as a colonel of cavalry:

> His figure was tall and splendidly proportioned. His forehead was broad and high, his hair black and his beard moderately long and thick, with a heavy mustache curling gracefully about the corner of his lips. His form and bearing on horseback were commanding and graceful. Taken altogether he was a military figure to arrest attention and command admiration. To hundreds of young and admiring soldiers he seemed the beau ideal of Southern grace and chivalry. Horsemen must have been timid and laggard indeed not to have felt the stimulus and inspiration of his dash and ges-

tures as he galloped forward into the smoke of the guns.
I saw him leading his division into action at Gettysburg.
No cooler man in the heat and rush of mortal combat
perhaps ever wielded a sword than Wade Hampton.

Heroic in size, iron-sinewed, nerves of cold steel, he
looked what he was, a cavalry chieftain. He never tired.
All-night rides that wore other men to frazzles found
Hampton daisy fresh in the morning, ready for whatever
the day might bring. War was not his profession. Nor was
West Point part of his background. Sportsman, horse
lover, hunter, he rode like a centaur. He was famed before
the war as a bear hunter who gave the coup de grâce with
his bare hands and a long knife.

Hampton brought changes to cavalry fighting. For long
chances against big odds he substituted heavy pressure at
the right time and place. Find a weak spot and throw on
force. From here on in gray cavalry would do more dismounted fighting, enabling them to cope better with blue
troopers armed with repeating carbines.

Captain Frank Myers, in his history of the "Comanches," explained it, "They (the men) soon discovered a
vast difference between the old and the new, for while
General Stuart would attempt his work with whatever
force he had in hand and often seemed to try to accom-
plish a given result with the smallest possible number of
men General Hampton always endeavored to carry every
available man to the point of operation and the larger his
force the better he liked it. The advantage of his style of
generalship was soon apparent, for while under Stuart
stampedes were frequent, with Hampton they were unknown and the men of his corps soon had the same un-
wavering confidence in him that the Stonewall Brigade
had in their general."

Wade Hampton, who succeeded Jeb Stuart as Chief of Lee's Cavalry Corps. (*Cook Collection, Valentine Museum, Richmond*)

Union batteries bombarding Petersburg the
night before the city fell to Grant's assaulting

columns. This massive line of circumvalla-
tion enveloped the city in a fifteen-mile arc.

Robert E. Lee

Ulysses S. Grant

August Valentine Kautz (*Photo courtesy of his daughters*)

Ulysses Grant, on a bluff overlooking Wilcox Landing, watching his vast army cross the James River on the half-mile-long pontoon bridge laid by his engineers in the amazing time of eight hours.

The famed Battle of the Crater, showing Confederates charging to retake the vast abyss blown in Lee's line by Grant's huge mine. Painted by John Elder in wartime, it now hangs in the Commonwealth Club, Richmond.

This unique drawing shows Wade Hampton's gray raiders driving off Grant's big cattle herd they had just captured. Union combat artist Albert R. Waud hurried to the scene where he made the rough sketch on which he based this large

drawing, now in the Prints Division of the Library of Congress. Note pistols pointed at the heads of Grant's "cowboys" whom the Confederates forced to help trail-drive the 2,400 beeves over sixty miles to safety within their lines.

James Dearing (*Cook Collection, Valentine Museum, Richmond*)

Thomas Lafayette Rosser (*Cook Collection, Valentine Museum, Richmond*)

W. H. F. (Rooney) Lee (*Cook Collection, Valentine Museum, Richmond*)

In August 1864 Hampton's cavalry was keeping watch on the extreme right of Lee's lines. His pickets ranged as far down as Dinwiddie Courthouse, fierily debating every foot of Grant's encroachment west towards the Southside Railroad. The Weldon road was really already lost. Hancock had straddled it incontestably from near Petersburg down to Reams Station. His efforts to destroy the road further south brought a daily small war—hot dogfights with blue and gray hacking and shooting, vicious spats that lasted only a few minutes but killed men awfully dead and then—the sudden breakoff.

2

The day after Shadburne's visit Hampton mounted his favorite bay, Butler, and rode into Petersburg. Beside him cantered an aide with a ham slung over his saddle. Passing through the shell-torn town Hampton crossed Pocahontas Bridge to the south bank of the Appomattox. Just beyond the river, a stone's throw off the turnpike, Hampton dismounted before a pleasant country house that bore the name Violet Bank. In this pastoral setting, shaded by ancient trees, Lee had opened Confederate GHQ the day he reached Petersburg in time to checkmate Grant's threatened seizure of the town. His tent was pitched under an oak. Little glamor, no fanfare of war, marked the spot. It was well within range of Grant's batteries east of town; shells sometimes splattered uncomforably near. Later when the leaves fell, Lee's headquarters would be plainly visible to Federal gunners. Yankee spies had already spotted it. Lee would then move GHQ to the western outskirts of town.

Lee greeted his cavalry chief with warmth. The gray chieftain had hesitated confirming Hampton's appoint-

ment. It was whispered that Hampton lacked the dash
and impetus exacted by the top cavalry command. At
stake were his staying powers at forty-six. A younger man,
perhaps Lee's nephew, Fitz Lee, Hampton's rival, might
do better. In Lee's mind this was a hurdle that led him to
pigeonhole the appointment, but the South Carolinian's
lightning overhaul of Sheridan's foray at Trevilian's had
dispelled Lee's waverings. Hampton's stubborn gallantry
on this occasion, with odds almost three to one, by repuls-
ing seven determined assaults by perhaps the most resourceful cavalry leader in the Federal armies, left no reason for Lee to withhold Hampton's confirmation any
longer.

Lee was still a compelling military figure, dressed in a
plain gray uniform. His knee high cavalry boots shone like
mirrors. War had whitened his hair. An unusual description of him was given by a prisoner taken on the Federal
Fifth Corps front, who said he was Joseph Fridell from
the 3rd Georgia Infantry, "Lee's head was white as snow,
but he showed a strong neck."

Inviting Hampton to sit down, Lee opened the conversation with a word of caution. Grant had moved Gregg's
cavalry to the front as if he planned an attack on the gray
right, near the Weldon railroad.

"I hope you will be prepared for this, General Hampton," said Lee. "Keep your cavalry as much together as possible, your pickets on the alert and your scouts out and
watchful. If you hear of his being in motion, strike him
with all the force you can and destroy him."

"That I will try to do, General Lee," assured Hampton.
"My pickets are active and wary."

"I note also," went on the gray leader, "your scouts say
City Point and possibly elsewhere in Grant's rear, are

open to attack. Inquire into this, please. A sudden blow there could be far reaching."

"That's what brought me here this morning, general," began Hampton. "My scout, Shadburne, came in yesterday with an interesting suggestion."

Quietly Hampton repeated Shadburne's description of the loosely guarded cattle herd at Coggin's Point and how it might be captured by a quick gray horse dash.

Lee's eyes brightened. "Three thousand beeves! Fresh meat. My men have forgotten the taste of it."

"There may be more," said the cavalryman. "They are brought up the James in quantities every week."

"If Grant's that careless, we ought to do something about it." A smile flickered along Lee's lips. "It's a strange coincidence though nothing is strange in war. Read this."

Lee handed a sheet of brownish paper to Hampton. "It came in from Gaston yesterday. He's been on Grant's telegraph line down in Surry County for a month."

Hampton's eyes widened as he read "Two thousand five hundred beeves shipped from Baltimore three hundred a day. Will land them at wharf below Coggin's Point. Arrange to receive them."

"That verifies what Shadburne says," observed the cavalryman.

Lee continued, "I see only one drawback: getting back to your lines after you get the cattle. You'd have to swing wide coming and going. You may have a fight on your hands."

Hampton grinned. "I sort of expect I would. But once we get our hands on this much beef, we wouldn't let it go without a fight."

Lee flattened out a map on his headquarters table. Together the two soldiers, in quiet tones, studied the approaches, the escape routes, sized up the risks. It was a bold venture, one after Lee's own heart. Dashing round Grant's whole army and rustling several million pounds of live beefsteak bore the Jeb Stuart stamp. For an hour they assessed the undertaking.

"Your chief object is to get the beef," warned Lee. Perhaps he was thinking back to the exuberant, impulsive Stuart who'd rather fight than eat. "Avoid a fight if you can, but be prepared for one."

Lee liked Hampton's calm assurance. "If I can get to the cattle without being discovered, I can bring them out."

"When would you plan to move?" asked Lee.

"As soon as I find that Grant's gone to Washington or to visit Sheridan in the Valley. With Grant away our chances of success would be better. I've asked Shadburne to find out what he can."

Lee eyed his cavalry leader significantly but said nothing. He might have been thinking the same thing. "Keep me fully informed of your movements. And what about this man Shadburne. Is he reliable?"

Hampton's eyes met Lee's squarely. "As reliable as the sun and the moon and the stars put together."

Rising, Hampton beckoned his aide chatting nearby with Colonel Walter Taylor, Lee's adjutant.

"I almost forgot something, General Lee," said the cavalryman. "This is for you, sir."

"Ham." Lee's eyes twinkled. "Yankee or Confederate?"

"This one's Confederate. The Yankees overlooked it, I reckon. Cured right under Grant's nose behind City Point."

"I'll take it over to Doctor Claiborne at the hospital this evening. I think the boys will appreciate it more than I."

"I think they would," said Hampton admiringly.

Saluting, he mounted and rode off.

18

"Beef! Glorious Beef!"

So wrote a Confederate private gazing back on his yesterdays. "How seldom were you seen, how welcome your presence. In the generous pot you parted with your mysterious strength and sweetness. Impaled upon the cruel ramrod you suffered slow torture over the fire. Sliced, chopped, and pounded; boiled, stewed, fried or broiled, always a trusty friend, and sweet comforter."

But for Lee's men holding the lines at Petersburg there was little beef, glorious or otherwise. This "sweet comforter" had long since departed from their bill of fare. War was far harder for a rebel private, living like a half-starved rat in ditch and cave, pinched with hunger and cold, than for his warm-clad, well-fed counterpart, just two hundred yards across the deadly swale, living as high on the hock as soldiers ever lived, with a menu that boasted warm beef stew at least twice a week.

Little wonder the low man on the gray totem pole ransacked the haversacks not only of dead Yankees but of his own comrades. Grisly business, but it brought many a windfall to boys with craving hunger in the pit of their stomachs. There's the oft told story of two gray sharpshooters who both fired at a bluecoat and saw him fall in a patch of woods. They got to him at the same time. "I seen him first," said one as he rummaged into the dead man's haversack. "I kilt him," said the other as if to assert that his bullet had staked out a prior claim.

Ersatz stories by the hundreds fleck the gastronomic records of Lee's men before Petersburg. A venturesome muskrat ventured once too often out of a bog near the lines. Caught, skinned and cleaned, he was buried for a day or two, disinterred, cooked and eaten with relish. One night the orderly sergeant of a horse artillery outfit went calling on a widow in Petersburg. On leaving he quietly picked up her gray cat in the yard and stuffed it under his jacket. Next day he treated his mess to "rabbit" smothered in wild garlic. They all knew it was cat. That made no difference. It was meat for all that.

Starving or not, the rebel-in-the-ranks humor was irrepressible. The very thought of food evoked many a choice morsel of wit. One evening about suppertime a trooper in Hampton's corps came out of the woods along Rowanty Creek where his outfit had bivouacked and knocked at a nearby farmhouse. A lady opened the door and asked what he wished.

"Madam," said the cavalryman, "could you lend me your frying pan?"

"Certainly, I'd be glad to," and forthwith came the pan. He took it, looked in it, turned it over and inspected closely as if not certain it was clean.

"Is there anything more I can do for you?" asked the lady.

Stuttered the horse soldier, "Could, could, could you lend me a piece of meat to fry in it?" He laughed in spite of himself. He got the meat.

Tragically amusing was Private William Dame's description of an imaginary Christmas dinner eaten by himself and a dozen congenial, very hungry comrades gathered around a campfire trying to keep warm. Rations were very short—only a little meal and a trifling sliver of meat. One of the "celebrants" proposed they play a game of eating Christmas dinner. They were to *suppose* they were seated around the table at Pizzini's sumptuous eating house that somehow kept going all through the war, in Richmond. Private Dame admitted it was an absurd performance that only made them hungrier. It's worth repeating:

Well—in reality, now, we were all seated around that fire and very hungry. But in imagination we were all gathered round Pizzini's with unlimited credit and free to call for just what we wished. One fellow tied a towel on him, and acted as the waiter—with pencil and paper in hand going from guest to guest taking orders—all with the utmost gravity. "Well, sir, what will you have" he said to the first man. He thought for a moment and then said (I recall that first order, it was monumental) "I will have, let me see—a four pound steak, a turkey, a jowl and turnip tops, a peck of potatoes, six dozen biscuits, plenty of butter, a large pot of coffee, a gallon of milk and six pies—three lemon and three mince—and hurry up, waiter—that will do for a start; I'll see about the rest later."

That was an order for one, mind you. The next several were like unto it. Then, one guest said, "I will take a large saddle of mountain mutton, with a gallon of crabapple jelly to eat with it, and as much as you can tote of the other things."

This, specially the crabapple jelly, quite struck the next man. He said, "I will take just the same as this gentleman." So the next and the next. All the rest of the guests took mountain mutton and jelly.

All this absurd performance was gone through with all seriousness, making us wild with good suggestions of good things to eat and plenty of it. The waiter took all the orders and carefully wrote them down and read them out to the guest to be sure he had them right. Just as we were nearly through with this Barmecide feast one of the boys, coming past from the commissary tent, called to me, "Billy, I think there's a box from home, or something, for you down at the tent."

Sure enough there was a great big box for me from home. The top was off that box in a jiffy and there, right on top, the first thing we came to—funny to tell, after what had just occurred, was the biggest saddle of mountain mutton you ever did see and a two-gallon jar of crabapple jelly to eat with it!

19

Who Stole Grant's Big Secret?

At 8 A.M. September 14, 1864, Grant summoned his cipher operator, Samuel H. Beckwith, to his tent and dictated a message to be dispatched at once to Chief of Staff Halleck at Washington. It was top secret.

> I will leave here tomorrow morning for the Shenandoah Valley to see Sheridan. Will not pass through Washington either coming or going unless it is the wish of the President or Secretary of War that I should do so. Everything is quiet here and indications are that it will remain so until I take the offensive.

Above all Grant's absence from City Point should not reach Lee. Grant went to extremes to mystify his departure.

A veil of masquerade shrouded this message from the moment it was committed to words. Beckwith coded it and put it on the wire within twenty minutes after receiving it from Grant. Halleck got it promptly, but so, apparently did somebody else for whom it was not intended. Outside of the cipher operators, who transmitted it and received it, not half a dozen knew of Grant's intention to visit Sheridan. Grant revealed it to only two of his staff.

Not until 3 P.M. that day did he notify Meade of his plans. This was playing it pretty close. It seems almost an afterthought on Grant's part. The message traveled to Meade by military telegraph in code:

> I shall leave here tomorrow morning for General Sheridan's headquarters. Will be gone five days. General Butler also leaves here today to be absent a few days. You will, therefore, assume command of all the forces operating in this field if you find it necessary.

Meade, only eight miles away, did not reply until nine o'clock that night. He may have felt miffed. One wonders. So apparently did Grant who late that afternoon wired a second message to Meade:

> I think it would be well to push our reconnaissances, both west and south from our extreme left, to ascertain if any movements are in contemplation. If you have occasion to telegraph me after I start in the morning, despatches directed to me at Harper's Ferry will reach me. I will have a cipher operator along.

The fact is Meade was delighted Grant was leaving, if only for five days. His second fiddle role was onerous and galling. He welcomed these brief respites as high man on the totem pole.

At nine that night Meade replied with reassurances that

Grant's fears of "movements" being contemplated by the rebels were groundless. At the same time he dropped a prophetic gem:

> Our cavalry is out so far to the south that any advance meets the enemy at once. I do not think the enemy will be likely to attack our immediate left or the rear of it, but may, perhaps, endeavor to threaten still farther round in the direction of Prince George Courthouse so as to try and draw us away from our intrenched lines. This would be running a great risk on their part unless they have a very large force.

He polished it off with a grand flourish, "I will be vigilant and keep a sharp lookout."

Grant's purpose in visiting the Valley was to get action in that sector. Six weeks had passed since he ordered Sheridan to get south of Early's army and follow it to the death. The enterprising cavalry leader had made a blazing start only to back off at Early's readiness to give battle. The administration, behind the scenes, was apparently pulling strings, fearful a setback to Sheridan would mean a reversal in the national election coming up in November. Meanwhile Sheridan and a perfectly good army would stagnate around Harpers Ferry. Grant put it bluntly, "I knew it was impossible for me to get orders through Washington to Sheridan to make a move because they would be stopped there and such orders as Halleck's caution (and that of the Secretary of War) would suggest, would be given instead, and would, no doubt, be contradictory to mine."

Speeding up Chesapeake Bay, Grant bypassed the capital. Boarding the B&O he hurried on to Harpers Ferry and on to Charlestown, arriving after dark shortly before

Sheridan appeared with his cavalry escort. Some idea of what transpired between Sheridan and Grant was recorded by a veteran Vermont sergeant who, from a little way off, watched the confab between the diminutive Sheridan and the slightly stooped Grant. Opined the all-knowing sergeant, "I sort of hate to see that old cuss around. When he comes there's sure a big fight on hand."

But Grant, after listening to Sheridan's ideas and smoking half a dozen cigars, summed up his instructions to his chief of cavalry in two words, "Go in."

2

Just how George Shadburne gained access to Grant's telegram to Sheridan, or the contents of it, can only be conjectured. He may have snaked it out of the telegraph tent though more likely, he employed a keen-eared operator doubling as orderly or clerk at Grant's headquarters. If Shadburne penetrated Grant's security screen—as he must have done—it rated as one of the cleverest espionage coups of the war. Like the nine words Mrs. Greenhow sent to Bull Run, it paid off. Shadburne never claimed to have captured a courier bearing the telltale despatch.

Dressed in blue he had spent the forepart of September at City Point, prowling in the shadow of Grant's GHQ. It may be recalled that, rigged up as a farm woman, he had tinkered around Grant's headquarters at Culpeper picking up scraps before the plunge into the Wilderness.

Grant's excursion to the Valley bore portentous military implications. Its end results would be the dispersal of Early's army and the destruction of the Valley as a source of supply for Lee's hungry fighters.

Shadburne sniffed out Grant's intended trip even before it was made known to the commanding general of the

Army of the Potomac, but, more amazing, at least three days ahead of Grant's actual departure. Grant must have discussed the impending trip with certain of his military family. Somewhere along the line it leaked out to Shadburne's ears.

The scout was a modest fellow, who, like Caesar, described his exploits in the third person, yet he never revealed how he tracked down this vital piece of intelligence: Grant's itinerary and the date he would leave City Point. A girl might have had a hand in it, but how? Molly Tatum? That's only a long-shot guess. It could account for Shadburne's never breaking the seal on how he did it.

It is improbable that Grant notified Kautz of his intended absence. There was no reason to. If he failed to notify his tête-d'armée (Meade) until the last moment, he certainly would not have felt it necessary to advise Kautz.

On September 5, Shadburne had addressed a scrawly, pencil-written despatch to Hampton. Dated "Near Blackwater" and signed "Your obedient scout, Shadburne," this missive, packed with troop data, ranks with the best in the undercover business. Beginning with "I have just returned from near City Point. The defenses are as follows," Shadburne proceeded with keen acumen and precision to disclose Union troop dispositions, the whereabouts of tempting supply depots, the exact distances between strategic points, and advice on the dangers of coming and going. Shadburne's word-map left nothing to the imagination. "At Coggin's Point are 3000 beeves, attended by 120 men and 30 citizens, without arms. At Sycamore Church is one regiment of cavalry (1st District of Columbia). This is the nearest point of the picket line to Coggin's Point, about two miles. The greatest danger, I think, would be

the Jerusalem plank road in returning." For good measure
Shadburne threw in a few niblets of picket line gossip.
"Colonel Spear is under arrest for drunkenness."

Shadburne entrusted the delivery of this message to
scout Dick Hogan whose career, like Shadburne's, had the
ring of fiction. Through Hogan, Hampton relayed his
previous instruction to Shadburne: Find out when Grant
leaves for the Valley. Then he sped Shadburne's report on
to Lee, who gave Hampton the discretionary go-ahead,
though again enjoining caution. "Let your movements depend on the reports of your scouts and let me know your
route." Lee would then move two brigades of infantry
down the Boydton plank road to demonstrate when Hampton and his raiders pulled out.

A week later, probably September 12, Shadburne appeared out of the dawn at Hampton's headquarters on
Gravelly Run. He had the answer. Grant would leave City
Point on September 15. Destination: Halltown near Harpers Ferry. That was all, but it was enough. Hampton
had utter confidence in the scout, who had never misled
him. Now to ride round the Union army and raid Grant's
big beef locker before he got back.

At sun-up this September morning the encampment
was startled to see a flock of orderlies galloping off in flur-
ries of dust. Hampton was a fast mover.

PART III

The Raiders

20

"To Horse! To Horse! The Sabers Gleam! High Sounds the Bugle Call!"

Presently, from their respective vigils along Lee's right flank, they came riding up to cavalry headquarters—Hampton's paladins, hard-pants, war-wise veterans. What they didn't know about horse fighting wasn't yet dreamed of. A diehard breed. They were the last gleaning of cavalry command of Lee's army. Not one of them whose body wasn't scarred by bullet, shell or saber. These men had never known what it was not to fight against odds.

Gone before them—*mort sur le champs d'honneur*—were Stuart, Ashby, Pelham, Farley and a host of those who rode to battle as if they gloried in dying that way. Gone, too, were the splendid mounts on which gray cavalry rollicked off to war in 1861. Killed off like their masters or worn down to a walk and a rattle by the fierce exactions and gruelling drive of the horse soldiers.

These "latest left of all the knights" were masters of cut and thrust warfare, white weapon fighting—great blocks of men in gray, sometimes two hundred yards broad, a quarter-mile in depth, yelling wildly, high in their stirrups, sabers glittering, horses at a pounding gallop, hurling themselves against another great block of men in blue.

"It was," glowed Captain William Blackford, Stuart's engineer officer, "like what we read of in the days of chivalry, acres and acres of horsemen sparkling with sabers . . . . flags above them, hurled against each other at full speed and meeting with a shock that made the earth tremble."

Now here they come. Look at them closely as one by one they swing out of the saddle, toss their reins to orderlies and stride up to Hampton's headquarters tent. They'll soon be gone. The South will see their like no more. Some yet to die in battle—the rest to gallop off into the sunset of the Confederacy. There's an air about them. They're cavalrymen every inch. They have an unconscious swagger, a sort of restlessness that seems to say "Where're we going and when?" You can almost see their bright guidons fluttering in the dust and thunder of battle.

First to arrive is a rugged, dark-eyed fellow with stars on his collar, Tom Rosser, 27, who'll carry the brunt of the show coming up. His grenadier mustache and short chin whiskers are becoming to him. Barely three weeks back in the saddle he's primed to go. A Yankee carbine at Trevilian's had splintered his knee. A nasty wound, his second. Virginia bred, Texas reared, he had shucked off West Point gray at the flash of the first cannon. Stuart dubbed him "the bold cavalier." In later times Douglas Freeman would call him, "The daring Lochinvar." He was made for the showy, slam-bang clash of the yellow legs. Stuart had eyed him during the Seven Days Battles before Richmond and told him to "come-arunning." He came just that way, but galloping.

He cusses like all get-out and sits his horse like a giant. A front fighter like his chief, Hampton. Give him a couple of drinks and he's liable to break out

> *Oh, there's not a trade that's going,*
> *Worth showing, or knowing,*
> *Like that from glory growing,*
> *For a bowld solger boy!*

He used to sing it at West Point with his classmates. Something in his make-up says reckless. It isn't far wrong. But that doesn't mean losing his head when perils beset him. He's as proud of his famed "Laurel Brigade" as his men are of him. An old cattle hand, he had lifted Yankee beef before but never had he thought of rustling on such a big scale. In the end Thomas Lafayette Rosser would ride off with Fitz Lee and escape Appomattox.

That's "Matt" Galbraith Butler coming up now, a South Carolinian like Hampton. He limps as he approaches the huddle in front of Hampton's tent. At Fleetwood a year ago a Yankee shell sliced off his leg below the knee as clean as a knife. But he corked it up. Now he rides and fights as well as ever. Like Rosser, he's just turned 27, a Major General, but no West Pointer. He is so handsome that a Greek god would have envied him, and oh, what a sweet fighter as Sheridan himself testified, "That damned man (Butler) has caused me more trouble than all the rest of the rebel cavalry put together." And Sheridan ought to know. Matt has an unfailing reliance when the going is tough, "Charge 'em! Show 'em the steel!" In the thick of Trevilian's when disaster loomed, Hampton ordered him to withdraw. Replied Butler, "Say to General Hampton it's hell to hold on and hell to let go." He won't go along on this show. His old wound is bothering him, but he wants to know what's up.

That tall, good-looking fresh-faced youngster, with the new star on his collar and a springy step, is the johnny-come-lately of Lee's Boy Brigadiers, Jimmy Dearing. An artilleryman who'd succumbed to the lure of the horse soldiers. At the Point he was a banjo twanger. From his classmate in blue, Morris Schaff, this memoir, "The first time I ever heard that song (*Dixie*) so consecrated to the Confederacy, it was sung by Dearing. I wonder how many campfires in Virginia he enlivened with that same banjo. But what went far beyond the crackling toned instrument to light up the wan face of the Confederacy was his cheerful and naturally buoyant voice."

Jimmy Dearing will exit before the drama closes. Amid the roar of Lee's last desperate fight at High Bridge he will take a mortal wound while giving one to a West Point friend he fails to recognize in the clangor of battle. But he isn't looking that far ahead. Today he is as merry as a troubadour with a new song, "Irish Lad from Dixie."

That clean-shaven officer strutting up now is Colonel Elijah White. A picturesque, colorful character. Sleepy-eyed, high-cheekboned, he is a rough and ready cavalryman, who can ride and shoot like a Parthian. He commands the "Comanches," famed 35th Battalion Virginia Cavalry, wild as Indians. That's why he called them that. Hard as nails is Lige White. Not very long on military maxims. Contrary fellow, he likes to fight his own way and did. Perhaps that is why they don't make him a brigadier. He rode down from Maryland at the start of the war and joined up with the dashing Ashby in the Valley. Captain of a band of partisan rangers he was a raiding terror at border warfare, waylaying Yankee wagon trains, shooting up their outposts. Twice bluecoats shot him down for dead. But he wouldn't die. Stuart took him on, tamed and taught him the fine points of horse fighting. Now he is carrying on for Hampton. Once when ammunition was running low and a whole hillside of bluecoats spilling down on him Captain Frank Myers called out to him, "Colonel, how can we fight those fellows with no ammunition?" Grimly Lige replied, "What are your sabers for? Draw your steel!" Hampton once said of Lige White he "never ordered White to clear the road of the enemy that he didn't ride over everything in sight." He will hold on to the last. In the final tragic hours before the flags were furled at Appomattox he will ride off with his Comanches—unsurrendered.

Yonder comes another of the fighting Lees, big William Henry Fitzhugh "Rooney" Lee. Don't confuse him with his fighting cousin, Fitz. Son of the gray commander in chief, he's made good. No West Pointer like his father, but a Harvard boy, who lately pulled the stroke oar on the crew. He joined Stuart early and got a division when Hampton took over. An old stager at this raid business. In 1862 he rode round McClellan with Stuart. Later he rode into Pennsylvania on Stuart's Chambersburg raid. Handsome like all the Lees, but too bulky, some said, for cavalry.

Here come others. Gallant Dunovant, just three weeks from death, but today as gay as a lark in the fine, rare September sky. Paul Barringer, fighting colonel and now a brigadier whose pride in his North Carolina boys is unquenchable. J. Lucius Davis, who wrote the Troopers Manual only to find a lot of tricks in fighting he never dreamed of when he wrote the book. Pierce Young, West Pointer, handsome, valorous, beau ideal of his men. He

has a battle motto, "Here goes for hell or promotion."
Able, hard-shooting, horse artilleryman Preston Chew.

For each Hampton had a salute and a bit of banter.
Pride gleamed in Old Wade's eyes as they roved over the
resolute band taking seats on the rustic camp benches
under the overspreading oaks. They were all there now,
including a tall figure in blue, who stood a little apart,
fidgety, awed by the ring of toprankers. He'd lots rather
be crawling up in the dark on a Yankee outpost in Blackwater Swamp or poking his way about City Point making
as if he were a good bluebelly.

Lee's Master of Horse spoke. "Sergeant Shadburne
needs no introduction, I'm sure."

Maybe not, but at the moment Sergeant Shadburne
wished the earth would open up and swallow him. He was
that uncomfortable.

For moments Hampton's fingers explored the depths of
his flaring beard. To make sure no scraps of information
got loose he ordered staff and orderlies to withdraw a trifle further. Then he began in a subdued voice, "Gentlemen, it looks like extended mounted service again."

It had a familiar ring—"extended mounted service."
It meant anything from a skirmish to a whangdang fight.

"You can blame it on Sergeant Shadburne. He's dug up
a situation that looks interesting. We're going to do something about it—quick. General Lee has approved it."

He flicked his eyes from one to another. "We're riding
directly behind Grant's army. Our chief and only object
is capture of his main cattle herd at Coggin's Point on the
James. And bring it back." He emphasized the words.
"Beefsteaks, gentlemen! Two million pounds of them!"

"Ye Gods!" slipped from a tongue.

Lige White whistled. "What wouldn't I give for a steak
about two inches thick!"

Chimed in Rosser, "I'll settle for a ten pound roast right now."

"Sounds like riding round McClellan at Richmond," averred Matt Butler, "only we weren't so goldarned hungry then."

Hampton grinned. "Shadburne says there are about three thousand steers over there waiting for us. Fat, tasty beef. Enough to feed this whole army for forty days."

Even to these hardened veterans it was breathtaking. It had the dare and flair of Stuart's stuff only this time it was Hampton's. Questioning eyes rested on Hampton. A volley of queries fired out. Confidently Hampton parried each "but what if."

"This is no scouting expediton. Shadburne and his men have done that. Done it well, too."

He continued, precise, deliberate, occasionally calling on Shadburne for embellishment. "Success will depend on three things: secrecy, surprise and implicit obedience to orders. Tell only your adjutants what's in the wind. The rest of your staffs nothing. They'll find out soon enough. The undertaking is desperate, audacious, but hunger's cutting into the gray ranks. Empty bellies have to take chances. The survival of the Confederacy itself depends on food and this army. It means riding up to Grant's back door and knocking loudly—crossing rivers, swamps where blue cavalry may be lurking, detouring on miles of narrow roads. Good ambush country. Luck and chance as always will be for us—or against us."

Hampton depicted the darker side. "We can be trapped, our retreat cut off, if we let them. One thing's sure: we'll have to fight to get the cattle and fight to get them back. Grant won't let three thousand beeves slip through his fingers without a scrap. He isn't that kind. Did you ever try to steal a bear's cubs?"

Nobody had.

"Well, I did once, down in Mississippi. What a clawing I got!"

Hampton spread his map. The group huddled over it as he traced the proposed route.

"We're taking the longest way round but we'll be out of sight of Yankee lookout stations all the way. The bridge over the Blackwater's burned. We'll build another in a hurry. If they have an outpost there, Shadburne and his boys will take care of it. Not one must get away to give the alarm. But they'll hardly expect attack from that quarter."

"How far is it from here to where we snitch the cattle?" asked Rooney Lee pointedly.

"Over sixty miles."

An audible gasp escaped the group.

"That's counting all the twists and turns in the road," added Hampton. "About one hundred and twenty-five in all."

"We'll have lots to tell the ladies when we get back," said Dearing.

"That *when* should have been an *if*," grinned Rosser.

"That's a powerful long haul," observed Rooney Lee. "What'll Gregg's cavalry be doing while we're circling round?"

"I'll come to that in a minute, general. Shadburne says we'll meet an old friend while we're getting acquainted with the cattle." He shot an amused glance round the faces. "August Kautz."

"Kautz!" The name popped from half a dozen lips.

"If he's all we've got to worry about, what are we waiting for?" commented Lige White with a shrug of his shoulders. "I can already taste beefsteak."

"But he isn't. Kautz is a hard fighter. Don't let's make

the mistake of being too sure. He'll put up a pretty sharp fight."

"How many men has he got?" asked Rosser.

"Four regiments of cavalry strung out on pickets from the plank road to Fort Powhatan. One of them is camped here." He put his finger on Sycamore Church.

"What regiment is it?"

"The 1st District of Columbia."

Lige White spoke up. "Them's the boys with the carbines that shoot all day with one loading."

Hampton nodded with a smile. "There are about one hundred and fifty cattle guards, 11th Pennsylvania. And fifty or more herders. Shadburne says they're unarmed. On that I have my doubts."

"Exactly where are these beefsteaks?" inquired Jimmy Dearing.

"Grazing on 'Secession' Ruffin's farm. That's about ten miles down the river from City Point. If we work fast, strike hard, we'll have the cattle on the way out before Kautz can get his regiments together. They're so spread out he couldn't concentrate enough to stop us. We'll hit the 1st District in force, destroy or capture it. That'll be up to you, General Rosser."

The big cavalryman grinned. "If I tell my boys they're going after beefsteaks, they'll ride those Yankees down like tumblebugs."

In crisp words Hampton laid down his exactions. "There'll be no marching orders. Destination and extent of the expedition kept strictly to yourselves." Hampton knew he'd be obeyed to the letter. His discipline was superb. Had he ordered them to charge directly into hell itself they would have spurred their horses on without quail. "We'll ride light and fast. No wagons, no ambulances. No sleeping in the saddle, no singing, no smoking.

That's absolute. Sabers strapped tight. Sound travels far.
No straggling, no looting. Three days rations cooked for
the men, two days forage taken for horses. It'll be a hard
ride. See that your horses are well shod. Watch for back-
sores."

Lige White broke in. "When do we start?"

"Squadrons will form on the Boydton road near Gravelly Run at 3 A.M. the fourteenth. That's Wednesday. Reveille without bugles. Shake your men out. No lights, no
fires. Rations must be cooked the day before."

Rooney Lee spoke up. The inquiring Lee mind asserted itself. "Is there any special reason for moving on
the fourteenth?"

Hampton's spacious beard spreadeagled into a wide
grin. "A pretty good one, I think. Shadburne says Grant's
taking off for the Valley that day. Going up to see Sheridan. With Grant away they might let down their guard
just a little. That's all we need—just a little."

Cut in Matt Butler, "When the cat's away . . ."

Hampton took it up. "But the gray mice'll have to be
mighty slick all the same. George Meade'll try powerful
hard to show how well he can handle things without
Grant peeking over his shoulder every moment."

Irrepressible Rosser popped the big question. "Who's
going on this beefsteak raid?"

Hampton had already handpicked officers and men for
the bold, circumnavigating ride. He named them. "Rosser's Laurel Brigade." That meant Lige White's "Comanches" as well as the 7th, 11th and 12th Virginia Cavalry.
"I ride with Rosser and the advance," he announced, then
continued. "Dearing's Brigade; Rooney Lee's Division."
That took in Barringer's North Carolinians and J. Lucius
Davis' Virginians. That should be enough, something
over three thousand sabers. Horse artillery, of course.

"Major Chew with four guns from Graham's and McGregor's batteries. Tell the boys to muffle their guns. Something else: an engineer detachment with axes, saws and ropes. We'll have to build a bridge, maybe two. Don't forget their pistols. Even engineers have to fight sometimes. You can't do it with axes these days. Lieutenant John F. Lanneau will command this detachment.

"Now, general,"—Hampton turned courteously to Rooney Lee—"to answer your first question. I think Gregg will stay put over this way unless somebody lets the cat out of the bag. Generals Young and Dunovant will extend their outpost lines down and take over as we move out. General Lee will cover us with an infantry demonstration down the Boydton road. That'll keep the Yankees confused in this direction. They won't know we're gone."

Hampton grew silent as if communing with himself, reconnoitering through his mind for an overlooked bit of instruction. He looked the leader. Everything about him spoke courage and endurance. Admiration for him burned bright in the eyes of the alert, restless group, who at the word of command would toss out the guidons in this last raid of the war done in the grand manner, the last of the epic, wide cavalry sweeps that struck like a rolling, gleaming thunderbolt.

"One thing more: we'd be riding blind if it wasn't for Shadburne. And let me repeat. If you must say something to your staffs, we're going to the Valley, or they're sending us north of Richmond. Tell any lie you can think of. But not a whisper about cattle."

They were gone, whisking off in swirls of dust. Hampton turned to the scout. "Sergeant, come to these headquarters at midnight the thirteenth. As I said, you ride with me."

"I was sort of aiming to get into this fight," smiled Shadburne. "General, there's a few of the boys who'd like to go along with us. Jo McCalla, Hugh Scott, Dick Hogan, Shake Harris and a couple of others. They could be a powerful help."

"We'll have to have them," said Hampton. "We couldn't move without you and your men."

Shadburne stood for a few moments as if embarrassed. "General, you said for me to come here at midnight the thirteenth. Reckon you could shave that just a little, say, about five minutes after midnight. I'd lots rather start on the fourteenth than the thirteenth."

Hampton laughed heartily. "Agreed. Anything else?"

"Yep," drawled Shadburne. "We oughter take a passel of houn' dawgs along with us."

"For what?" queried Hampton.

"To help round up them cattle after we get to them. I can get my hands on four or five pretty smart ones, if you say so."

Hampton lapsed into rumination. "Houn' dawgs. They'll remind me of the pack I had back home in South Carolina. I can hear them now baying a bear. Bring 'em along."

Dreamily—for his thoughts too were roaming afar—Shadburne spoke. "That's just what I'm going to do. When the war's over I'm going back to Texas and round up a few cattle of my own."

Hampton repeated his words, "When the war's over! I wonder when that will be."

21

Thunderbolt Through the Forest

Under the ice-white stars, at 3 A.M. September 14, Hampton's vanguard swung into the saddle and headed south along the Boydton plank road. The moon was dipping down in the sky. The night air was chilly. Banks of fog hovered like lost ghosts over Hatcher's, Gravelly and Big Cat Tail Runs that tinkled east towards the "lordly main."

Reveille came without bugle. Noncoms' rude "Git up!" cut short cavalry's dreams. No fires, no cooking. Eat your cold cornpone and like it. Half-awake troopers fumbled about in the dark saddling up their rawboned horses, strapping on their gear. Squadrons fell in line mechanically like sleepwalkers.

The secrecy Hampton had enjoined on his commanders was scrupulously observed. Even his staff groped in the dark. Likewise his son, Preston, riding as his father's aide. Rank and file knew action was afoot. Orders to cook three days rations said that plain enough. The wise old-timers had it all figured out: we're heading over the Blue Ridge for the Valley to help "Jubilee" Early lick Sheridan. Whoopee! How those pretty Valley gals do love the horse soldiers! Orderlies, with knowing winks, strutted about importantly, but they didn't know anything. Rumors ran through the cavalry camps like quack grass, but the wildest guess flew wide of the mark. Not the faintest suspicion ever whispered beef.

But the men had implicit faith in Old Wade. Wherever he was taking them was all right. Maybe into the jaws of the Union army. What of it! He'd get 'em out again.

Gunner David Cardwell of McGregor's Battery, never forgot that before-dawn start: "The command to which I belonged (horse artillery) was ordered to saddle up and move out behind the 13th Virginia Cavalry. We waited on our horses a long time—all waiting seems long—and while we waited we speculated upon where we were going and what we were going for. So little do soldiers know of the intentions of their officers that some said we were going to surprise and capture a brigade of negro troops, and we began in a spirit of humor to tell what we were going to do with our share of the negroes. We had no idea that beeves had any place in the picture at all."

For an hour under the paling stars the cavalcade trotted south. At the fork of the Flat Foot Road the gray riders, stretching out over two miles, trended southeast along Rowanty Creek. Their swift gait was putting distance between them and the gigantic blue army around Petersburg, still wrapped in sleep behind its vast fortified coil and fringes of watchful pickets.

"This ain't the way to the Valley," wailed a disappointed "Comanche." "I'd sho like to see them Valley gals again."

Noncoms shut him up fast. Talking was strictly taboo.

No quips, no jests, no horseplay. It was hard to take. Cavalry loved to jabber. About anything. Songsters were stifled in midair. The thin rosy glow of dawn tinted the east. Red bird and robin began cheeping. An occasional rooster crowed his salute to the day as the column slid by. Far off north they could hear the good morning growl of Yankee artillery. The sun drank up the mist as it cleared the tree tops. All morning they pushed on: the steady scuffle of hooves kicking up dust, the creak of leather. The thick woodlands were divinely sweet. The first faint reds and yellows—dabs from autumn's palette—were showing on the oaks and hickories. Ironweed glowed purple in the fence corners. The September sun had a balmy warmth. Noiselessly, dreamily, rapidly, they flowed along the forest track. Occasionally a horse whinnied but not loud enough to reveal three thousand lean, lanky unmilitary looking horse soldiers rattling off the miles. The route led through a dejected countryside that bore scars of Yankee visitation. Back in June Wilson's and Kautz's raiders had sacked it.

At noon they halted to feed their horses. Then back in the saddle. They splashed over a dozen little creeks called runs. One, Troublefield Run. Lordy, what a name! They whisked by an old mill, an abandoned smithy, an ancient church in the wildwood. Farm folk came out to watch them sweep past and wish them well whatever they were up to. They knew three thousand cavalry were not just riding for exercise. There was something happening up ahead. Ranks kept well closed up. Major Ryal's provost guard saw to that.

Long stretches of the road were completely screened by overarching trees, like endless, cool tunnels of green. The sun filtered through making a dappled pattern of light and shade on the gray dust. On through the languorous afternoon travelled Hampton's thunderbolt, steal-

ing deeper and deeper into the hush of the forest, a
gleaming gray rocket orbiting round toward Grant's backdoor. Subdued excitement infected the hurrying column as the day wore on. This was something bigger
than they thought. The men sensed it. But what? Tension
mounted. Riding in the ranks were men who, under Stuart, had screened Jackson's column as it uncoiled through
the Wilderness to crush Hooker's right. Now they remembered. Maybe Old Wade was trying to catch Grant napping. He was, but they didn't know why or wherefore.
The sky was red and gold, the sun slanting through the
September haze when the column reached Wilkinson's
Bridge across the Rowanty. Low-pitched orders flew down
the ranks. Bivouac here. No lights. No fires. Watch it.
They were twenty miles directly south of Petersburg. A
good day's marching. Tired, dusty, hungry, heads hanging
down, one by one the troopers slid to the ground, unsad-
dled and fell asleep at their horses' feet. Night stole over
the forest.

Said Gunner Cardwell, "We had now ceased to specu-
late where we were going. We were too sleepy and soon
most, if not all, were dozing on the ground our bridle
reins around our elbows. If we dreamed, it was of home,
not of cattle nor war's alarms. The horses, too, slept, and
showed no disposition to move or disturb their sleeping
masters."

Up front, astride his great bay, Hampton rode all day
beside the Texas scout. Fatigueless he seemed. He could
ride round the clock wearing down the best of them, men
and horses. His staff trailed at his heels. Scouting a mile or
two ahead, Shadburne's men poked into byroads, farm
lanes, foot paths, rummaged around farmhouses. They
knew their business: McCalla, Hogan, Mikler, Scott, Tanner, Shoolbred. These men could almost smell a bluecoat.

They had orders: kill any picket you flush unless he surrenders at once. A single sharp-eyed vedette could gallop off and give the alarm. All the stealth in the world would go for naught.

Hampton summoned his acting chief of staff, Major Reid Venable. He gave orders: reveille two hours before sunrise. Rouse the men without bugles. Feed the horses well. Then, spreading his oilcloth, he rolled up in a blanket and was asleep in a twinkle. Staff stood about whispering in the dark for a few minutes before they too curled up.

Presently three thousand horsemen were sleeping, soundlessly it seemed, with only the dirges of the whippoorwills to disturb them or the hoots of an owl wrathy at this invasion of his woodland domain. Pickets watched both ways. Flankers on the sides.

They got to horse before daylight. Thumping across the rickety bridge spanning the Rowanty the column bent northeast until it struck the Jerusalem plank road. The highway was undesecrated by Yankee cavalry. Horse soldiers always left signs aplenty. No hoofprints, no droppings. It assured Hampton the Federals had no suspicion he was on the loose striking for the great corral on the James, prowling perilously near the vast City Point base. Kautz had sneaked up this plank road back in June to the outskirts of Petersburg only to be thrown back on his haunches by the old men and boys and robbed of a chance to glorify his name by capturing the key to Richmond.

Before noon the command reached the dismantled Norfolk and Petersburg railroad. It couldn't be called a railroad any longer. Yankees had left only a streak of dirt. Near Ebenezer Church old Cap'n John Belsches, portly, Confederate to the marrow, stood on the roadside to offer the hospitality of his pleasant home. His mill and pond were nearby. He held out a ham to Hampton, who was appreciative but reckoned, at this juncture, he couldn't handle a ham. A cavalryman's stomach groaned aloud at Hampton's courteous refusal. Well, wouldn't the general partake of a mint julep? He had the fixins, assured the Cap'n with a wink. But there was no time for juleps either. Rosser's mouth watered. He came up just in time to hear the Cap'n suggest the delicious concoction. The Cap'n wasn't to be shaken off. Born and bred in the briar patch— as they said—he knew the swamp trails and roads better than the lines on his own hand. Couldn't he go along as guide? Excellent, agreed Hampton. The Cap'n had scores to even up with the bluecoats. They had robbed him of several fine horses, but he still had a lame sorrel mare. Fetching her he proudly joined the cavalcade.

The sun blazed directly overhead when Hampton's advance guard reined up at the ruins of Cook's Bridge over the Blackwater. A watery void faced them. Shadburne's men scouted up and downstream. Swimming their horses across they ranged miles up the road. Still no bluebellies. It looked suspicious.

Spurring to the river's bank Hampton gazed glumly at the charred pilings poking their heads above the inky waters, then sped a staffer to fetch Lieutenant Lanncau. Throwing his knee over the pommel of his saddle his head drooped while he waited. In moments he was fast asleep. Down the column troopers were already drowsing in their saddles, whole companies of them. Some snoring loudly.

Old stagers pushed their mounts to the edge of the turbid stream, took a look and shook their heads. It couldn't be done. Old Wade's in a tight spot now. The more philosophical disagreed. Old Wade'll get us across if he has to swim us. The men knew they were far behind Grant's lines. Tingles were running up many a spine. It was casting a spell of mystery over them. Nothing to do but wait and keep quiet.

Young Lanneau rode up as Hampton opened his eyes. He'd snatched exactly five minutes sleep and was fresh as a dewdrop.

"How long will it take to get us over?" asked Hampton bluntly.

The engineer officer studied the water lapping at his feet. He figured one hundred feet from bank to bank. A confident, resourceful young man, he was a deft hand at miracles.

"By night, sir," he replied.

"Good enough," said Hampton.

Out came axes, crowbars, saws, ropes. With alacrity Lanneau's brawny pioneers began hacking sycamore and cypress, cutting and shaping them into raw logs that were floated out to the stubs of the pilings. Others stripped and dropped into the dark waters to rescue half-burned, usable timbers of the old bridge that had snagged along the banks.

Hampton threw out a rear guard at distance enough to ward off surprise from that quarter. To be on the safer side he ordered Major Chew to unlimber two guns and cover the road. Then he posted his other two at the river's edge to protect the bridge builders.

Meanwhile cavalry dismounted. Some curled up to cat-nap in the warm shade, bridles slung over their arms. Others drifted onto the fields, prospecting as cavalry often did. The battery boys found a windfall, a bed of sweet potatoes. But they couldn't make a fire to roast them so they ate them raw. Many a belly was to ache before night. Horses rested, nibbling grass that fringed the road or dozing heads down, switching their tails at voracious swamp flies that attacked rider and mount with equal ferocity.

The sun was casting long shadows when Lanneau's men finished a footway stout enough to pass the column by two's and the guns. By dusk it was corduroyed. Hampton's advance guard clattered over at once. Pickets scurried up the road to wait for the main body. Deep night settled. Hampton stood at the jumpoff. He dispatched a staff officer down the ranks to break the big news. Take the wraps off. Tell the men where they're going.

The effect was electric. Only threats of condign punishment by noncoms and officers subdued outbursts of cheers. But there were no orders forbidding them to let go their glee in pantomime. They danced jigs in the dusty road, turning handsprings like frogs on a binge. The goddamn Yankees couldn't hear that. It helped relax pent up tension. Even the horses seemed to catch on and perk up.

"Beef! Fresh meat!" It exploded in animated whispers. "I said Old Wade knew what he was after. Two million pounds of it running loose. Lemme see: beefsteak, roast beef, sirloin, and don't forget good old beef stew. I'm gonna eat 'em all. Hooray! We're gonna feed Marse Robert's whole army!"

A meager supper was gulped in the dark. Even cold cornpone tasted good against the prospect of beefsteak tomorrow. Hampton sent a courier to call up his commanders. They rode up fast: Rosser, Rooney Lee, Jimmy Dearing, Lige White, Lucius Davis, Barringer and the rest. By a lightwood flare Hampton briefed them. His voice was crisp. The column moves at midnight. Have the men in the saddle promptly. The moon'll be down by then. He opened his map. The group studied it as he checked off each unit's role.

"We're right on top of them and they haven't found it out," said Hampton confidently. "Two hours slow ride will bring us here: the right angled fork where the fun begins."

Lean over Hampton's shoulder and listen in as he gives his last orders. He was a stupendous figure, bulking huge in the dim flicker of the pineknot flame. His eyes shone like great orbs. Dangling at his belt were two Colts: his small, favorite pearl-handled one and an enormous man-killer he had taken off a prisoner at Fleetwood. He clipped his words.

To Rooney Lee: move ahead and turn up Lawyer's Road till you reach the Powhatan Stage Road. Shadburne says you'll hit the first Yankee pickets just before you get there. Round them up if you can without a shot. Strad-dle the fork and cover all approaches from east and west. Then drive east on the Stage Road and join the parade at Coggin's Point. Right there you'll be squarely in rear of the Union Army, barely five miles from Meade's head-quarters. Same distance from Grant's at City Point. McGregor's two guns roll with you.

Lee's orders briefed down to moving his command between the Yankee base at City Point and the cattle, and holding the roads until Rosser had secured the beeves and driven them off.

To Jimmy Dearing: Move northeast along Hines Road to Cocke's Mill on the Stage Road. When you hear Rosser firing over at Sycamore Church drive towards it, rout any bluecoats you meet. That'll cut 'em off and keep the garrison at Fort Powhatan off us.

Hampton cautioned both: Wait till you hear Rosser firing before you go in. Then strike fast.

He turned to big, eager Rosser, "You spearhead the main attack and roust out the cattle. Move directly north and turn into Walls Road. Push on to Sycamore Church.

Shadburne and his men will guide you. That's about fifteen miles from here. Take it slowly. Get there just before light and hit 'em in the dark. The 1st District Cavalry is camped right there. The place is ringed with a pinelog barricade except for a gap where Walls Road runs through it. The gap is open. That is, it was three days ago. You may find them asleep but I hardly think so. Shadburne says there're only two hundred and fifty men there, but more likely five hundred. Destroy them as fast as God will let you. Break through, destroy the camp and keep on going. The cattle are about three miles further on near the river. I repeat: I ride with you. Shadburne with us. His scouts ahead of the advance."

Hampton drew out his watch and held it to the bleary light. "It's nine o'clock. In exactly three hours this command must be in the saddle ready to march. Tell your men to rest. They'll need it."

But Shadburne had other uses for the three hours. Taking stripling scout Shake Harris with him he rode off up dark Lawyer's Road from Cook's Bridge. They crept along cautiously, pausing often to reconnoiter. In half an hour they pulled their horses off the road into a clearing where a house stood well back in the shadows—Molly Tatum's.

"Hate to wake her up," whispered Shadburne, "but she might know something General Hampton should know. That's why I came."

Hitching their mounts to the rack behind the house they walked stealthily to the kitchen. The door stood ajar. Hanging on the knob was an old rag.

"That's what I was looking for," he said, tapping out a signal on the door. He waited, tense, alert, but there was no answer. He knocked again.

"Something's up," he breathed. "She wouldn't leave the door open. I saw her three nights ago. She told me to stop by if I could. She'd see what she could find out in the meantime. If things were all right, she'd tie a rag on the doorknob. That's it."

Drawing their pistols the two scouts tiptoed into the dark kitchen. The house smelled vacant. There was no odor of recent cooking. Shadburne called out, "Molly! Molly!" They searched the house upstairs and down. The beds were unmade, rumpled.

"Well, she's gone and her aunt with her," said Shadburne in a low voice.

"Looks to me like they left in a hurry," observed Harris. "Maybe she's gone to tell 'em we're coming after the cattle."

"She isn't that kind."

"I got a funny feeling she's gone to the Yankees," persisted Harris. "Warn't she crazy 'bout that herder?"

"But she's straight as a string."

"They ain't no tellin' what a gal'll do when she's in love," allowed the young scout. "Don't be surprised at anything she does."

Shadburne smiled to himself as he reined his horse back down the road towards Cook's Bridge.

22

All Quiet Along the James

There were portents in the air, but Union intelligence officers apparently took little stock in such whimsical things. On the contrary Ulysses Grant's "basilisk eye" discerned enough to presume hopefully to Meade "that our cavalry is so disposed that the enemy cannot come around Warren's flank and attack our rear without having timely notice."

General Meade replied on the dot: "Kautz's division of cavalry watches our rear from the Jerusalem plank road to the James. Gregg's division pickets from the plank road west, around our rear to Warren's flank."

Everything was under control though apparently Meade's Chief of Staff, Humphreys, beheld a cloud in the sky, "In the event of an attack by the enemy on our rear it is probable their cavalry would endeavor to cross the Blackwater at some points below where we hold and come upon our trains between City Point and our lines."

August Kautz was a trim, sometimes too incisive caval-ryman. Something was in the wind and he knew it. Once again he ventured to remind GHQ, "For several days all was quiet along the picket lines except an occasional at-tack on a picket post by the enemy's scouts who seemed to be very active. The activity was such that I reported the danger of the loss of the beef herd grazing near Sycamore Church between my lines and the James River."

Kautz had hit the nail on the head, but GHQ was not impressed by his fears. After all, the Confederates were not madmen, and Jeb Stuart, master of the ride-round-an-army technique, was dead. However, Kautz warned Major J. Stannard Baker, commanding the 1st District Cavalry encamped at Sycamore Church "to use every pre-caution to prevent surprise." The Major's reply brimmed with confidence. He, too, took little stock in his superior's surmises.

On September 14 Kautz dispatched to GHQ another scholarly dissertation on how to exterminate scouts and guerillas in Blackwater Swamp. He repeated his idea of setting up an ambuscade at Cook's Bridge over the Black-water. When this missive reached Meade's headquarters Hampton's column was well on the way to Cook's Bridge. Kautz had the right idea. Baker's men had already burned the bridge. That settled that. There'd be no crossing the Blackwater from that direction.

September 15. At daylight Grant boarded a fast steamer down the James. Meade's "I will be vigilant" was reassur-ing while Kautz that morning gleefully reported ambush-ing a posse of gray scouts, killing two and wounding others. He was correct except the dead men were not scouts.

Noon. Hampton had reached the charred stumps of Cook's Bridge unperceived. With beaverlike alacrity his engineers were improvising a crossover for the column. The morning reports from Kautz's colonels were reassuring, "I have the honor to report all quiet on the cavalry picket lines." They read almost the same verbatim.

Towards evening an alert signal officer in the lookout tower on the Jerusalem plank road wigwagged GHQ that he had that morning sighted a column of cavalry far off moving south. It took half an hour to cross the vision of his field glasses. Behind them, at a twenty minute interval, trudged about one thousand infantry to disappear in the same direction.

The cavalry, of course, was Hampton's; the infantry, as Lee had promised, was moving down to kick up a rumpus while Hampton promenaded off into the Wilderness. If Union intelligence officers interpreted the signalman's message, they gave it little credence, certainly not enough to warrant disturbing "I will be vigilant" Meade with such trivial things as rebel cavalry shifting positions along the Rowanty. It was preposterous: the idea of rebels sneaking round behind an army of ninety thousand men armed to the teeth.

Otherwise the day passed serenely. At dusk the cordon of Union signal stations from the Appomattox to anchor bastion, Fort Fisher, checked off one by one for the night. All was quiet as far as they could see from their vigilant posts,

> *While the stars above, with their glittering eyes*
> *Kept guard over the army while sleeping.*

Unfortunately, the stars failed to keep their eyes open.

23

Dawn Fight at the Yankee Corral

Sharp on midnight Hampton's men defiled across the makeshift bridge without mishap. It was wobbly but safe. A single misstep would send horse and rider into the swirling stream. Smudgy pineknot torches glimmered at the bridgeheads, castings eerie shadows on the black waters. Advance guard and scouts moved out quickly, warily. Save for the steady obbligato—jingle of spurs, squeak of leather, thud of hooves—the command moved silently along the stygian road. No need for noncoms to nudge men sleeping in the saddle. They were wide awake. Thoughts of beefsteak were dancing in their imaginations. Even the horses seemed to sense that something daring was in the wind—and they a part of it. Roan and bay, black and gray, tossed their heads as if to say "We know, we know."

To Hampton it seemed incredible. He had ridden in force, unchallenged, undetected, to within striking distance of Grant's great beef herd. At 3 A.M. the advance reined up at the right-angled fork. The moon was down; the night nippy; the sky cloudless foretelling a clear day. Rooney Lee rode up to Hampton's "headquarters in the saddle." His men were already swinging off northwest on Lawyer's Road.

With a salute, the big, boyish general said goodbye. "But not forever, sir. I'll see you at breakfast." His spirits were at the flood. "Maybe a beefsteak breakfast," suggested Hampton with a laugh. "God be with you till we meet again—at Coggin's Point."

Two miles more the road forked again. Here Dearing turned northeast up Hines Road. Old Cap'n Belsches ambled up in the dark on his plug horse to take a hand. He drew rein beside Dearing, pointing the way to Cocke's Mill.

"Countersign Beefsteak, sir," jested Dearing as he touched his vizor in a goodbye salute to Hampton.

"Beefsteak it is!" replied Hampton. "Seasoned with a little good luck."

In pitch dark, at a slow pace, Rosser's raiders moved north on Walls Road. There was utter stillness around them. Three times Rosser halted his column. Long waits that grated on nerves. Presently out of the murk glided scout McCalla. He had news. The Yankee camp was barely a mile off. He had crept right up to the barricade to find the gap, open three days ago, now blocked with felled trees. It was a strong position.

"They know we're coming," said Rosser in an undertone.

"Waiting for us, I reckon," said Hampton. "Go in hard and fast."

"Somebody must have told them," put in Shadburne whose thoughts flashed back to the vacant Tatum house.

Hampton gave the play to Rosser, who summoned Colonel Massie of the lead regiment, 12th Virginia. Drawing in his advance Rosser pulled back all but two of his scouts who waited in the gloom two hundred yards from the barricade. It was the darkest night he had ever seen. He said he could not even see his horse's ears. Men and steeds were dim blurs as they waited for his orders. The stars were paling though. Faint streaks were running up the eastern sky. The 12th Virginia edged up the road at a creep. The two scouts were waiting with warnings that the barricade was barely a hundred yards off. Not a light, not a sign of life showed behind it.

Rosser himself painted the scene, "The moon had set and, although the sky was cloudless, the night in the woods was very dark. My men were ordered to march in silence, but the road was hard and in the profound stillness of the night the tramp of the horses could be heard a long distance, and I knew it would be impossible to surprise the enemy so I made my arrangements to fight. I knew I would find a regiment of cavalry at Sycamore Church and I knew that every man of them would be in position and ready for me on my arrival there. I brought up the 12th Virginia and gave orders to the commander, Colonel Massie, a very gallant officer, to charge just as soon as he was challenged by the enemy."

But there was no challenge, only deep, oppressive silence as if the Yankees behind the barricade were wrapped in heavy sleep.

Again Rosser, "I was riding by the side of Colonel Massie telling him how to proceed in the event of his being able to dislodge the enemy, when as if by the flash of lightning, the front was all ablaze with musketry."

The sudden discharge momentarily staggered the 12th Virginia. "Fighting Sergeant" Seth Timberlake's horse fell dead on top of his rider. It was too dark to see anything except the blaze of the 1st District's repeaters chattering like mad. Rosser turned to Colonel Massie.

"Go in hard!" To his bugler, "Give 'em a Charge!"

With a wild ringing yell two squadrons of the 12th Virginia thundered up the dark road. It was like dashing against a black wall spouting Roman candles except that this time lead slugs were zinging through the fireworks. The 1st District was firing pointblank, but they emptied saddles. Emboldened troopers leaped to the ground, ran to the barricade and began pulling at the obstructions in the gap only to be driven off by the hot fire. In a black tangle of trampling hoofs, shouts and hissing bullets, the 12th Virginia drew back. Had there been light enough to see what they were shooting at the 1st District would have decimated the gray charge.

"Steady, men! Steady!" Rosser's big, booming voice rose above the confusion as he worked his way through the mass of men and horses prancing and rearing excitedly. He was at his best in times like these. "Colonel Massie, try it again! We've got to clear the road and clear it fast."

In went the 12th for another try. "Use your pistols, men!" shouted Rosser as the troopers pounded past him. They rode in at a straining gallop, firing at every enemy flash. Then, wheeling, they came back—but not all of them.

Dismounting the veteran 7th Virginia (Rosser's own), he ran it up as a line of skirmishers to push right up to the gap, drag away the trees blocking the road, and work round the flanks. The 7th went in on the run. There was no formation. Taking their losses—three dead, fifteen wounded, they worked fast, tugging at the blockade under the vicious rataplan of repeating rifles. Other men ran unseen to right and left, stealing round the sides to enfilade in the dark. A trooper came running back, "It's open wide enough for an elephant!"

Rosser ordered the 7th to stand fast and pour fire into the gap until he brought up the rest of his squadrons for the break-through. It took ten minutes to line them up: squadrons of the 11th and 12th Virginia and Lige White's Comanches panting to get into it—in that order.

Rosser rode along the line. "Use your sabers, men! Ride through and cut 'em down!"

The bugle cried. Suddenly through the gray dawn, high, fierce and quavering, rose the sound that once heard was never forgotten, "Yaiih! Yaaiiihhh! Yaaaiiihhh!" Through the shadows Rosser's raiders plunged ahead in splendid style, massed in a solid column, horses almost hoof to hoof. Rosser's voice roared like Wotan's above the hurly-burly of smoke, dust and gunfire.

"Give it to 'em! Give it to 'em!" He rode with them through the gap, his sword was out and swinging.

Sabering bluecoats right and left, the gray onrush crowded and floundered through the now widened gap, losing formation, but getting through, flooding over the camp on both sides of the road, flushing out men still asleep, setting fire to rows of puptents. The sheer weight of Rosser's onslaught was overwhelming.

But the 1st District was making a fight of it. Sabers clashed, pistols and carbines banged. Blue troopers might as well have tried to stop an avalanche. Gray horsemen seemed to spring out of the ground as by magic.

The 1st District's commander, Major J. Stannard Baker, dashed out of his tent in the gray light at the first crack of gunfire. He stood with his men, pistol in hand and firing, until Rosser's tide came pouring through the barricade. He was trying to rally his men when a saber struck him a

glancing blow on the head opening a gash inches long.
His legs crumpled and he sank unconcious to the ground
to be left for dead.

Resistance fast disintgrated into little hand-to-hand
fights. It had happened so fast that blue troopers were
taken half dressed, many in their night clothes. Others,
who had slept well but too soundly, were flushed out of
their puptents. Many were nabbed as they dashed for
their mounts. Rosser's men spread over the place as if
parachuted from the skies. There was no rally. A few of
those who had manned the barricade managed to hop on
horses and gallop off towards the Stage Road. A score escaped bareback in their nightshirts, their behinds as bare
as their horses'.

Caught by Rosser's men sweeping through the camp
were four sutlers' wagons. In desperation these wartime
profiteers had hitched up their mules to dash for safety
into the woods with their precious loads when the gray
fury struck them. In an ill-advised show of resistance the
sutlers were cut down on the spot; their wagons over-
turned, spilling out their contents like cornucopias. Pickles, sardines, cheese, cakes, candy, cigars were strewn in
the dawn light. Even a few bottles of champagne rolled
out to give a touch of fast revelry to the scene. Rosser s
gaunt soldiery pawed through the luxuries like ravenous
wolves, taking everything with them down to the last bit
of candy.

Hampton rode up. He had one word for Rosser, "magnificent." The fight at the barricade had taken half an
hour. Hampton's timetable allowed just that long. In the
lull, off to the west Hampton heard the rattle of musketry,
the bark of a field piece. Rooney Lee had broken cover.
Through the early morning rolled similar sounds from

the east. Jimmy Dearing was coming into action. The ring was closing.

Rosser's men ransacked the camp like human harpies. Spoils were large—horses, mules, prisoners, blankets and, to crown it all, three of the 1st District's guidons. They'd rounded up the whole regiment except for the few escapees scurrying off to alert the picket line on the Stage Road. No time to count prisoners now. Major Ryal's provosts herded them up and reckoned about three hundred. He wasn't far wrong. Over two hundred sixteen-shooters, gifts to the regiment by the "loyal women of Washington and Georgetown," strewed the road, tossed away as if they were redhot pokers or held aloft by those who were captured. Several hundred horses and mules were taken munching breakfast, unaware they had changed masters so suddenly. Company cooks were ordered to keep on cooking but double up the portions.

The scouts had their day in battle, too. Cavalry had poked fun at them too often, said they stirred up fights but seldom waited around to get in them. Hampton told them to join Rosser and the 7th Virginia in the final charge. They left good scout Jo McCalla dead at the barricade.

Hampton sent an aide to get Major Chew's guns to the front, thinking to penetrate the barricade. Just then Rosser struck. Hampton reported, "The enemy had a strong position, and the approaches to it being barricaded he had time to rally in the road around his camp where for some time he fought as stubbornly as I have ever seen him do. But the gallantry and determination of Rosser's men proved too much for him and he was completely routed, leaving his dead and wounded on the field and his camp in our hands."

It was nearing four-thirty. It was fast growing light. Rosser's Laurels had tasted blood. Now to taste beef. Leaving
a strong guard to reinforce Major Ryal's provost men
Rosser moved on. The bugles blew Forward. A leathery
sergeant called Old Hanover, unable to restrain himself,
let out a huge "Hooray! We're heading for the big round-
up!"

So they were. Fast, furious, and full of fight they slashed
through Kautz's picket line on the Stage Road as though
it were a spider web.

2

Captain Henry H. Gregg, 13th Pennsylvania Cavalry,
after a night of blissful repose, awoke earlier than usual
this morning. He emerged from his tent—so he said—
"just as light was beginning to glimmer in the east." Refreshed by his eight hour snuggle he stepped out in the
cool dawn and gazed off across the tranquil meadows of
the Harrison farm adjoining the Ruffin acreage on Coggin's Point.

The skies promised another fine day. After all, rumi-
nated the captain, except for war Virginia was a lovely
place. The heat had been stifling, but the cool September
nights were making amends for the torrid summer he had
spent on the low grounds along the James.

He was lucky, reflected the captain. His nights and days
were not haunted by shells and sharpshooters as were
those less lucky in the trenches before Petersburg. He had
a pretty safe berth. And why not? The 1st District Cavalry
was on watch at Sycamore Church. A mile away between
the church and Coggin's Point ran the Stage Road, picketed strongly by General Kautz's vigilant patrols. Then
there was the cattle guard, one hundred and fifty tough

troopers of the 13th Pennsylvania, who were at this moment finishing their brief morning ablutions and sniffing at breakfast cooking over a fire near the mess tent.

The captain's vision roved further. In the near distance, between Edmund Ruffin's Beechwood and the 13th Pennsylvania's camp, he observed his charges—over 2500 fat beeves. Inside a vast split-rail corral they were lying down, drowsing or chewing their cuds. The ground was carpeted with them. They were waiting for broad day before dipping their muzzles into the rich, low ground grass. The scene might have been transplanted from the Western plains. Certainly it had no warlike aspect. The herders on watch were nodding in their saddles after their all-night vigil.

Beyond the corral the officer of the guard could see other fields emerging as the daylight strengthened. On the wide waters of Harrison's Bar, two Federal gunboats were riding at anchor. The day before, the cattle had been driven a mile westward to the fertile Harrison pastures, sweeping down from the Harrison home, Rosewood, set on the crest of the long slope to the river. Not for protection's sake, but merely to rotate the grazing. Captain Gregg was to report, "The cattle were grazed, watered and corralled before sunset, with the usual night guards. At midnight the watch was changed. The cattle were quiet during the night and in the morning mostly lying down."

Mounting his horse, "sniffin' the morning cool," the captain made the rounds of his picket posts. It would soon be time for him to go off duty and partake of a hearty breakfast. He paused to chat with Sergeant Albert Kenyon commanding the picket line. All was quiet, reported Kenyon, though he had heard firing off to the south, heavy firing for twenty minutes or so and then quiet. More puzzling to the sergeant was firing off towards City Point and Fort Powhatan. Something was up, perhaps heavy guerilla attacks on the picket lines or the camp at Sycamore Church. Probably nothing to worry about, said the captain, as he spurred back to the 13th Pennsylvania's camp to get his breakfast. He passed the tents of the herders a little apart from the cavalry's camp. Most of them, save those on duty with the herd, were lounging about or getting breakfast. Apparently, aside from the suspicious firing, all was well with the captain and the world as dawn came shimmering up the James this morning of September 16.

He had just dismounted and tossed his reins to an orderly when a sudden burst of gunfire near at hand shattered the morning quiet. Horrified, he saw a swarm of men and horses piling over the rising ground from the direction of Sycamore Church. Yelling to his orderly to fetch Captain Richardson, Gregg dashed back to his sentry line where Sergeant Kenyon, as cool as they come, was throwing his meager force across the road running down to the big corral.

Enter, hastily now, Captain Nathaniel Richardson, Commissary of Subsistence, Armies Operating Against Richmond. He, too, had journeyed all night through peaceful dreamland. At forty-three, a volunteer from Massachusetts, he had found the cattle assignment somewhat disagreeable—but far more so when a breathless orderly galloped up to his tent to blurt out news of an attack on the corral.

Let eloquent Captain Richardson portray the fireworks that exploded in his face this tranquil morning:

At twenty minutes before 5 o'clock Friday morning I was awake. Light was just beginning to glimmer in the east, when an orderly reported to me from Captain

Gregg, saying that the picket-line had been attacked at three points. He further stated that Captain Gregg would again report to me, if it was necessary to move off the cattle. I arose and instantly called upon the chief herder to get up, informing him that the picket-line had been attacked. I then went through a large portion of the camp ordering the men to get up and saddle their horses. I then gave orders to saddle my horse, and in ten minutes from the time of receiving word from Captain Gregg, was at the corral. I ordered the watch to leave the corral, and saddle their horses. I came back to the camp, distant thirty rods, and heard shouting and sharp firing. I forthwith ordered the fence pulled down and the cattle driven out. I then turned to go to the corral again when I heard the yell of a charge, looked around and saw many hundred mounted men charging up to my camp and upon the men who were just leaving it.

The charging men, hurtling through the early morning, whooping, yelling like Indians, firing as they came, were Rosser's. He himself rode in the van. Beside him, revolver out, galloped George Shadburne, scout, guide and now Master of the Houn' Dawgs for Hampton's "Expeditionary Cattle Raiders."

As the gray deluge swept over the crest, plucky Sergeant Kenyon threw out his detachment in a skirmish line across the brow of the slope running to the Harrison meadows.

At shooting distance, Rosser's bugler blew Halt! Panting, blazing with excitement, his men reined up. Rosser ordered Private Cary Selden, 12th Virginia, to ride towards the enemy holding aloft a handkerchief on the point of his saber and demand surrender. At thirty yards

Selden drew rein and called out, "General Rosser demands your surrender!"

Kenyon replied stubbornly, "Go to hell! Tell General Rosser if you come to us again with that damned rag, I'll shoot you."

Wheeling, Selden cantered back to Rosser. Of what happened next Captain Frank Myers had vivid memories: "Rosser turned to the battalion and in his short, solid tone that always had something of the wicked ring of a Whitworth in it when he meant fight, exclaimed 'Come down on them, White!' and the Comanches did it with such splendid style that the Yankees were scattered in wild flight."

Rosser's voice always had a magic, electrifying effect on his men. It had it now as he roared. "Go get 'em, boys! Chop 'em down!"

With howls and shrieks that justified their nickname, Lige White's "Comanches" charged the bluecoats headlong. The clash was valiant but brief. The Pennsylvanians broke precipitately like a handful of chickens. Rosser's sabreurs slashed the thin line to pieces. A bullet ploughed through Sergeant Kenyon's neck. Clinging precariously to his saddle the wounded noncom whirled his horse and raced off. Half a dozen horses with empty saddles plunged about frantically. Their riders lay dead or wounded on the ground. Not so fortunate was Captain Gregg to whom the dawn had seemed so serene. He galloped up just in time to be caught in the vortex of the gray flood as it struck the picket line. Snatching out his pistol he had fired a shot or two when a saber stroke knocked the weapon from his grasp. Only a miracle saved his hand from being sliced off. Unceremoniously he was dragged from his saddle by two unshorn ragamuffins brandishing sabers that looked ten yards long.

"Come down offen that horse, you Yankee sonofabitch!"

The captain obeyed promptly, but not fast enough to suit his captors who assisted him violently.

"Now stand there! Hands up!" He had quick visions of having his head chopped off. He must have realized he had started his round-about journey to Libby Prison.

At this moment, as the Pennsylvanians broke and fled, the gray riders sighted their startled quarry. Beeves by hundreds. An almost unbelievable sight. Chains could not have held them now.

"Yonder they are! Great day in the mornin'! Beef! Beef!" It burst from hundreds of hungry throats.

"Yippee! Yoooo! Hooray! Let's get 'em."

With a rousing view-halloo the fox chase, or better, the rodeo was on. Rosser need not have uttered a word, but as he told it,

> When I came in sight of the beeves they were running rapidly in the direction of the James River. The herders had thrown down the fence of the corral and firing pistols and yelling, Indian fashion, had stampeded the cattle and they were running like mad. I ordered the 7th Virginia, which had just overtaken me, to run their horses until they got in front of the herd, then to turn up it and stop it. This order was not easily obeyed for the young steers ran like buffalo, and it was requiring too much of jaded cavalry to force it into a race like this, but after running a mile or so the steers slackened their pace and the cavalry was thus able to get in front of them, and then to round them up and quiet them, turn them about and start them to the pens of their new masters on the Dixie side of the line.

With gunfire crackling and blazing, the steers were milling about, wild-eyed, frightened, ready to break and run. The herders had seen the gray raiders pouring down the hill on them. Some leaped on their horses and fled. Others rushed to breach the split rail corral and drive the cattle out. Still others spurred towards the herd firing their pistols. A score drew their Colts, hoping perhaps to rally the fleeing troopers of the 13th Pennsylvania and remnants of the 1st District which Rosser had driven before him from Sycamore Church. Then, as by common accord, the herd stampeded. In a pandemonium of thundering hooves and fierce bellowing two thousand five hundred odd steers bolted out of their "freeze" and cavorted across the wide sweeping pasture like thoroughbreds trying out their underpinnings. The early sunlight, just peeking over the horizon, glinted on the tips of thousands of sharp horns.

Captain Richardson, now ahorse, gave a vivid picture of the inglorious scene:

The enemy came up shooting and firing with great vehemence, and driving before them numbers of the First District of Columbia Cavalry and the Thirteenth Pennsylvania Cavalry. By the time the fence was pulled down and twenty cattle out, mules and dismounted horses, mingled with retreating cavalrymen and herders, were fleeing from the enemy. The enemy were nearly around the whole herd. I saw that all was lost. With the chief herder and several remaining men I now joined in the retreat, the enemy firing at us and following closely. In half a mile we struck the middle Prince George Court-House road; I then started for General Meade's headquarters. By going to the left I had passed most of the retreating force who followed close in my rear, a few in advance. Within a mile we met another strong force of the enemy charging up to us and firing upon us. I wheeled my horse and came back a quarter of a mile; the enemy pressing up, I turned into the woods.

Not over fifteen minutes elapsed from the time I received word that the lines had been attacked, until my camp, with the cattle, were in possession of the enemy. Some of my men had not time to saddle their horses before they were prisoners. The enemy charged in wide and deep column upon the camp and herd, surrounding them on all sides. Outside of and independent of this line of attack, it held the telegraph road running to Fort Powhatan by the James River. The middle road running from the telegraph road to the stage road and the stage road leading back to the telegraph road.

Five herders lay dead, ten others wounded or captured. The fight at the corral was not a rout, but a wipe-out. Child's play for Rosser's rough and tumble boys. At pistol point the herder-prisoners were ordered to mount their horses, swing their bullwhips and lend a hand or take a bullet in the brain. Riding herd was a new, uproarious sensation for the 7th Virginia. They made the most of it. Delighted at their sudden transformation from horse soldiers into cowboys, they goaded their gaunt mounts to a last nimble-footed effort. Spreading out they described a continuous circle around the herd, flailing plump, meaty flanks with their sabers. Racing along the fringes like picadors they nipped the tough hides with the keen points as they rounded the steers towards the center of the corral.

Shadburne's houn' dawgs were having their day, too. Their baying rose above the bedlam of gunfire and bawling of maddened steers. Captain Richardson testified,

"With the enemy was a large number of hounds and herding dogs that attacked the cattle furiously and hurried them off."

Slowly the confused mass of bullocks quieted down. Cavalry ringed them while herders worked through them and caught the lead and bell steers. Industriously, fearful of their quick-triggered captors, the cowboys swung their long, stinging bullwhips. In a panting stream, reeking with sweat and flecked with foam, the steers surged up the slope and out of their corral. Flooding onto Walls Road they were headed towards Sycamore Church. Pushing south, the big bulky creatures began stringing out between hedgerows and worm fences, scuffing up swirls of dust. Riding alongside the stream of cattle came Rosser's men, even more watchful of the sharp horns that could disembowel them in an instant than ever of Yankee bullets. Soon Walls Road was for miles a moving mass of "fat, young steers" as Rosser described them. His men were in high spirits. They had rustled the entire herd except for the score or so the herders had frightened through the breach in the corral. It was enough beef to feed Lee's army for forty days.

"I could eat a whole one all by myself," avowed a 7th Virginia trooper licking his bearded lips as he fixed his eye on a particularly plump one. "Look at them beefsteaks."

"Old Grant's even got his initials on 'em," opined a ragged lumberjack. "Look at that US branded on their backsides. That's his name, Ulysses somethin'."

"Git along thar! I'm hungry," urged another whose stomach leaped with joy at the sight of red meat.

By 6 A.M. Rosser and his rustlers were withdrawing, their booty ambling along with them. It was twenty miles to the flimsy restoration of Cook's Bridge over the Blackwater. Hardly had Rosser's rear guard ridden out of the meadows before the Federal gunboats on the James came to life and began lobbing big navy shells into the empty corral. They exploded all over the place. In his report the commander of one of the vessels said he plunked a shell in the middle of the cattle and their captors with fearful results.

As the steers jostled out of the corral Shadburne and Shake Harris rode over to inspect the dead herders whose bodies had already been rifled. Spurs, hats, boots, neckerchiefs, treasures beyond worth of gold to a Confederate cavalryman, had vanished. Shadburne's eyes fixed on the face of a young fellow in his twenties. A bullet had cut his jugular, bleeding him to death where he fell.

"I think that's him," said Shadburne.

"Who?" asked Harris.

"The boy that's been calling on Molly Tatum."

"Good looking rascal," commented Harris.

Shadburne knelt down, rolled the dead man over and felt through his pockets. If he had a watch it was gone. A worn pocketbook was turned inside out. From the dead man's hip pocket he exhumed a small, soiled song book. No music, only words. Well thumbed. Flipping through the pages Shadburne paused and read—to himself,

> *When in thy dreaming*
> *Moons like these shall rise again*
> *And daylight beaming*
> *Prove thy dreams are vain.*

"You know, Shake, she was in love with this fellow."

"That's what I told you last night."

"But she didn't go to tell the Yankees we were coming for the cattle," said Shadburne flatly.

"What'd she go for?"

"To warn this boy to get out of the way—but she didn't make it."

Captain Richardson's report indicated he had suspected spies and "intercourse with the enemy" among the herders though he was unable to pin suspicion where it belonged. The records of the Federal Commissary Department lists the names of nearly a hundred herders hired to handle Grant's cattle.

Captain Richardson's report also paid an indirect compliment to George Shadburne and his co-workers in the Blackwater underground. "The attack seems to have been made on the whole line and reserve picket post at the same time, and unless led by someone very familiar with the topography of the country and the different roads could not have been so suddenly and successfully executed."

That someone was George Shadburne & Company.

But Richardson erred in reporting, "The enemy exhibited their usual barbarity by shooting down the unarmed herders, stabbing them after they lay helpless on the ground, stripping and robbing them."

The herders were armed. A score of them had stood and fought it out.

24

General Meade Has Conniptions

By 9 A.M.—September 16—City Point was panicky. It looked as if Grant's supply depot, with its immense stores of war materiel, faced capture or destruction while he was far away on Chesapeake Bay or parts unknown. Not yet had his secret mission leaked out. Orders flew about like sora over a Virginia marsh. Hampton really gave City Point the scare of its life. Anything could happen with this rough customer on the loose with a striking force that lively imaginations conjured as high as 25,000. Nerves were twanging like guitar strings.

Provost Marshal Patrick sounded the warning with a rush dispatch to Colonel Gates, commanding the Post Defenses, "The enemy has broken through our line near Sycamore Church and may dash on City Point. Place all your troops in the best possible position to defend the depot."

Meade's Chief of Staff, Humphreys, who had predicted

this desperate situation, was positive that enemy cavalry "would make a dash on City Point." Batteries were withdrawn from the Petersburg front and sped at a straining gallop for City Point. A hurry-up call for help was semaphored to the gunboats lounging down the James to steam up and stand by, guns ready. Fed by uncertain reports trickling in from the dismembered picket line, alarm mushroomed.

Provost chief Patrick took further precautions for a last ditch stand. Prisoners in the bullpen, including the hardrock cases, were alerted. They might be called on to shoulder a rifle in defense of the post. Negro stevedores on the wharves were ordered to man the east works. Most of them had never handled a gun in their lives. The walking wounded recuperating in the vast hospital overlooking the Appomattox were told to hold themselves ready to repel the audacious invaders of the sanctity of Grant's "rear." Any moment Hampton's dread horse soldiers might come prancing up the road, sweeping everything before them. Anything could happen. Had not his forces ridden daringly to within five miles of the nerve center of the drive on Lee's army?

The magnitude of Hampton's force grew precipitately, that is, in the imaginations of the City Pointers and of Meade himself. "Trusty citizens" reported an immense force, perhaps 25,000, including infantry. Meade estimated it at 6000. Kautz would presently boost it to 14,000. Guesses ran wild. Intelligence Chief Sharpe knew positively that Hampton had the entire cavalry corps of Lee's army. Lee was on the warpath in earnest and Grant absent. Conniptions attacked Meade. His "I will be vigilant" had a sad, accusing ring. Perhaps the whole rebel army was moving out to give the Federals the nutcracker treatment—Lee on one jaw, Hampton on the other. Anxious messages and queries flooded GHQ.

The hubbub at City Point and Meade's GHQ near the front lines rose in crescendo as the morning advanced. Couriers on well-blown horses cantered in every little while only to gallop off for dear life. The fevered dispatches, hot off the war griddle, composed amid a wave of fear and excitement (and still to be seen in the Official Records) betray the emotions of the hour.

By 10 A.M. the painful fact had emerged. Hampton had pilfered the best herd of cattle Federal beef contractors had ever rounded up. It was the pride of the Commissary Department. Probably the most woebegone man in the whole Union army at this moment (excepting Kautz) was Chief Commissary of Subsistence Michael R. Morgan. He just couldn't believe it, and he said as much ten years later on a return visit to the scene of Hampton's raid.

As the morning advanced Meade found himself faced with the embarrassing task of breaking the news to Grant, informing him that hardly had he departed for the Valley before Hampton swept in and despoiled him of 2500 prime, top-grade steers, the best the lads in blue had ever licked their chops over. Meade's telegram to Grant was lengthy and tortuous. A plaintive undertone ran through it. He approached the ticklish subject with matters other than Hampton's raid. He closed with clearance of his own skirts, "This raid was one which I have feared for some time, as with the limited force of cavalry under my command and the great extent of country to be watched, I have always considered Coggin's Point an unsuitable position for the cattle herd, it being liable to capture at any time by a *coup de main* of the enemy in force. Every effort will be made to recover the herd or a portion of it."

When Grant's cipher operator at Charlestown (after an unexplained delay) handed him Meade's caterwauling telegram the general in chief quietly hit the ceiling. Handing it to Sheridan with whom he was conversing, he observed sourly, "See what happens when I leave." Grant must have envisioned a beefless menu along his Petersburg lines for weeks to come. Steers did not grow on trees like red Virginia cherries—not this kind.

His reply was typical and to the point, "If the enemy makes so rich a haul as to get our cattle herd he will be likely to strike far to the south, or even to the southeast to get around with it. Our cavalry should either recover what is lost, or else, in the absence of so much of the enemy's cavalry, strike the Weldon road far to the south of where it has been destroyed." His military acumen told Grant that if Kautz and Davies really got on the ball they could overhaul the gray rustlers and recover the beefsteaks.

At 10:30 Meade sent another telegram. Grant was a facts man. So Meade dished it up: "The enemy retired as soon as they succeeded in driving the cattle from Coggin's Point. Kautz is in pursuit on the Prince George Courthouse road [here Meade was mistaken] and Davies on the Jerusalem plank road." He then iced it over with a bewhiskered, overworked stock excuse which Lincoln himself had ridiculed—"superior enemy forces." "Hampton's force is so superior to ours and he has so much time to get off I fear nothing will come of the pursuit except to harass the enemy." He closed with a bit of wisdom, "The affair was evidently the result of a deliberate plan." It most certainly was. However, he failed to add that Hampton had four times as far to go to safety as his pursuers to overtake him.

Later that day Meade shot off another wailing alibi to Grant. It was pathetic. Night found him writing his wife.

Yesterday General Grant took his departure and to-day my ill luck has brought a rebel cavalry raid in which they dashed into our lines and succeeded in driving off about two thousand head of cattle that had been, contrary to my judgment, sent down the James River for grazing to a point just inside our cavalry pickets and where they were exposed any moment to be run off, as they have been by a *coup de main*. Grant's absence and the usually friendly (?) spirit of the press will undoubtedly attribute this loss to my negligence. The cattle were not under my control, or that of my commissary, but under a commissary serving on Grant's staff, and I really had as much to do with it as you except that I had called attention to the danger of having the cattle there.

Meade was a good prophet. The Northern press excoriated him. One scribe went on record, "Meade had nothing to do with it except that, in Grant's absence, he commanded every man in the Armies Operating Against Richmond, one hundred thousand of them, from general to drummer boy—and the responsibility lay at his door."

25

Git Along Little Dogie!

Walking off with thousands of nice beefsteaks without paying for them was mighty fine, but getting them home from market was a problem which still had to be solved. Hampton had played for high stakes and won, but the man he was playing with was now drawing a pistol to recoup what he had lost.

So far Hampton's raid had been brilliantly executed. His surprise attacks had meshed like clockwork, but vigorous Federal pursuit was as certain as daylight once they pulled their disheveled regiments together. Between Hampton and Lee's army lay a solid wall of seasoned blue infantry. Not to mention sixty miles of narrow roads twisting through forest and swamp—rivers and creeks to be forded—mudholes without bottoms—seemingly every obstacle nature could devise. The Rowanty, which must be crossed before reaching comparative safety, was twenty-five miles distant. His impedimenta (as Caesar might have put it) was considerable—prisoners, troopers, oxen, captured wagons. Strung out for miles, it was an inviting, vulnerable target. He was encumbered by an enormous herd of unwieldy, fluttery cattle. The task alone of coddling thousands of unruly bullocks, while beating off Union attempts to snatch them back or disperse them, and wangling them around the wide-flung Federal left into the gray lines, was staggering.

Overwhelming forces of Union cavalry were stationed on the Jerusalem plank road near Petersburg barely twelve miles from the Rowanty crossing, half the distance Hampton had to travel. Moving down at a fast clip, riding light, the Union soldiers could snip this escape route or delay Hampton long enough for infantry to hurry down, exterminate his command and recover the loot. Points of interception where he could be hemmed in and cut to pieces were numerous. The logical cut-off was near Ebenezer Church where the plank road crossed Hampton's route back to his lines.

Last year—1863—Stuart's Chambersburg raid, in which Hampton played a major role, had encircled McClellan's army, swept twelve hundred horses off the Pennsylvania countryside and herded them safely across the Potomac. But horses traveled faster than cattle. You could get speed out of horses, but you couldn't speed up cattle.

Rooney Lee had fought his covering action over towards Prince George Courthouse in bang-up Lee style though he encountered real tartars in Colonel Ferris Jacobs' squadrons of the 3rd New York Cavalry. They fought him to a standstill at the fork of the City Point and Stage Roads. Lee cracked the New Yorkers wide open by swinging his horse artillery into action and catching them unawares with blasts of "shell, grape and canister" as their Colonel reported. At the same time he scooped up a score of prisoners. Reluctantly Lee broke off the action and drove east along the Stage Road to meet a squadron of the 11th Pennsylvania whom he scattered like a covey of quail. He toyed with the idea of dashing in and perhaps capturing General Meade and his staff and raising hell generally around City Point. Collared here was Surgeon John Stanton, who was brought to Lee at once for questioning.

"Is there any infantry between us and City Point?" asked Lee.

The surgeon demurred. Lee tried again, "How far are we from General Meade's headquarters?"

Retorted Surgeon Stanton, sensing Lee's thinking, "Why don't you try it and you'll soon find out where the infantry are," intimating Lee would encounter foot soldiers just beyond Prince George Courthouse.

Actually—as Meade's Chief of Staff admitted—there was only one regiment of cavalry and no infantry between the headquarters of the Army of the Potomac and Lee's men. Added Humphreys, "The moment I heard the firing (Lee's advance skirmishing with our cavalry pickets) I sent for a brigade of infantry to move up quickly to the courthouse with four guns. At the rate they moved we should have had no assistance from them if Lee had tried his hand at picking us up." But now Lee hurried east and turned down Walls Road to fall in as rear guard of Rosser's caravan.

Meanwhile Dearing was pulling back from Cocke's Mill where he struck a small battalion of the 1st District Cavalry holding the left of Kautz's picket line and commanded by an upstanding fighting man, Captain William Howe from Maine. Finding himself fast outflanked Howe decided to fall back to Sycamore Church. He had heard firing from that direction, but he was unaware of the fate of

the main body of the regiment. Regimental Chaplain
Merrill depicted Howe's plight, "Ignorant of what had
occurred at Sycamore Church, Howe and his men expected to join Major Baker's force and make a stand. But
in the meantime the enemy, having secured their prisoners and plundered the camp, had formed a semicircle
across the road, and dressed in our uniform, and were mistaken for our own men. Successful resistance was now
impossible and having done all that brave men could do,
like men they yielded to their fate."

At Sycamore Church Hampton waited eagerly for Rosser's cavalcade. A courier had already scurried back with
the good news, "We have the beefsteaks. We're driving
them south." Dying gunfire up towards the James, and off
to the east and west, told Hampton what required no
second guess.

Presently and suddenly, the road was clotted with cattle
as far as he could see. They were bawling for water. In a
serpentine of clicking horns, shuffling hooves and hover-
ing dust they came on, apparently amiably. Hampton
could hear the cusses of Rosser's troopers, now impromptu
cowboys, and the crack of bullwhips. The herd had so-
bered down considerably save for its mournful clamor for
water. By now Rosser's men were accomplished cowhands.
The captured herders, subdued no doubt by speculation
on what their special fate might be and the possibility of
having their brains blown out if they balked, were attend-
ing strictly to business. Cavalry was running over with
hilarity.

"Git back thar, you onery varmint!" yelped a lean scare-
crow spurring after an obstreprous critter that had spilled
out of the line, "or I'll jam my pie knife right through
your guts."

Sitting at ease on his bay Hampton watched the amusing procession heave in sight and begin passing in review. Smiles wreathed his face. He had witnessed unforgettable sights since he rode up from South Carolina in 1861. This was a trifle different. Wild cheers split the morning air as the men recognized him. Old-timers let go the ebullience that flooded their innards. Stuck in the mouths of not a few—those who got there first—were big cigars snatched from the unfortunate sutlers at Sycamore Church.

"Thar's old Wade! Hooray! We got it for you! Beef! Beef!"

A tall, lanky veteran with a greasy, faded sombrero simply exploded. "Yi-yi-yipee! We done captured the fattest bunch of cattle this side of Texas!"

Gay as a cadet with a pretty girl on Flirtation Walk at West Point, Rosser rode up to Hampton. At his heels trailed Shadburne. Congratulations bubbled out.

"Keep 'em moving, general," urged Hampton. "Don't let 'em stop. Have you counted them?"

"We cleaned out the corral," assured Rosser. "Got all but a dozen or so. How many are there, sergeant?"

Shadburne opined something around twenty-five hundred.

"But, George, you said there were three thousand," Hampton protested with a wink to Rosser.

"So I did, general. But couldn't you settle for a leetle less? And I forgot one. She's a cow. Dunno how she got there."

Sternly Hampton replied, "This is serious. Making a false statement to your commanding officer. Looks like we'll have to do some more shooting."

"Aw, general," grinned the scout, "we boys'll find the rest of them for you."

Rooney Lee, still full of fight, extolling his men's courage, rode up to remind Hampton of the promised beef-steak breakfast.

"Maybe we'd better kill one right here and eat it," suggested Lee.

Hampton had a better idea. "Suppose we change it to a steak dinner at my headquarters, say, day after tomorrow. Right now we've got to take it on the lam. They'll be on our tails like wolves."

Hampton's voice was cool, confident, but urgent. The only sign of his concern was his right hand, roaming through his beard, twisting his big mustache. He turned to Rosser. "Keep 'em moving. Don't let 'em stop or slow up this side of the Blackwater. Dearing will meet us at the Hines Road fork and take over the advance."

The procession marched on. Critters; gray flankers; herders; three hundred-odd forlorn prisoners, many clad only in undershirts and riding bareback, ridiculous pictures of dejection; a dozen wagons piled high with warm blue blankets that would come in mighty handy this winter; two wagonloads of sixteen shooters; scores of horses and mules; a complete field telegraph unit with telegraphers, teams, magnets, keys and batteries. In one of the wagons lay Major Baker, who had commanded the 1st District; now he was apparently more dead than alive. Struck by a saber as Rosser's men crashed through the barricade he had fallen on his face and lain there until Hampton ordered his "body" buried and the grave marked carefully. On turning him over he was found still breathing, but unconscious. Hampton's surgeon bandaged his head where the glancing saber blow had opened a deep gash. It had barely missed splitting his skull. Captured Yankee Surgeon Stanton was ordered to nurse the wounded officer.

To speed up the cavalcade Hampton split the herd into four smaller ones, with short intervals between. It elongated the train to nine miles, but it was safer, easier to handle, more defendable when and if the blue avengers overtook it.

2

But where was General August Kautz while his picket line was being so handily demolished from Prince George Courthouse to the Fleur de Hundred road? At 5:00 a courier on a lathered horse whipped up to Kautz's headquarters near the courthouse and leaped out of the saddle. It was barely daylight. The general and his entourage were fast asleep. The courier bore an urgent call for help from Major Franklin A. Stratton, 11th Pennsylvania Cavalry. Rooney Lee had swept up Lawyer's Road and struck in two directions—towards the courthouse where Kautz was billeted and east along the Stage Road towards Coggin's Point. The 11th was falling back, losing men and horses. The telegraph line was cut though still intact westward toward City Point.

Caught completely off guard, Kautz hopped out of his blanket and yelled for his staff. Rousing his operator he relayed the message to General Meade, adding a postscript to Stratton's appealing report, "The attack seems to be for some distance along the line." Next, he flashed an alert to General Davies, commanding the 2nd Cavalry Division, "My pickets have been driven back. The present attack I do not yet consider serious, as the reserves have not been disturbed yet. I think the attack is in retaliation for those we killed the other day."

Not a suspicion had apparently crossed his mind yet that the rebels were fleecing him of Yankee cattle right under his nose. Nor that the 1st District had been expunged and Hampton, with Grant's prize herd and nearly four hundred prisoners in tow, was making tracks for his own lines. Kautz's fluttery messages that fleck the Official Records would indicate a sudden attack of nerves. Through the early light he could hear the rattle of musketry and bang-bang of field pieces off to the east where Rooney Lee was mounting his two-way attack. Getting on his horse, Kautz cantered toward the firing, turning into the Powhatan Road, the most direct route to Sycamore Church. He little envisioned the hectic twenty-four hours that lay ahead of him.

At 7 A.M. Kautz hurried off another dispatch to General Davies. The enemy had straddled the stage road, the firing was lively. He had dispatched Colonel Ferris Jacob to "dislodge" the gray intruders. "I am fearful the 1st D. C. Cavalry may be entrapped." Still no intimation of cattle stealing.

Off went another message to General Meade's headquarters. By now Kautz began to fear dire results. A courier he had sped off to Sycamore Church had returned. He couldn't get through. Rebel cavalry was everywhere. "I believe the enemy to have planned the capture of the 1st District Cavalry, which I think was their object and I fear they have succeeded."

But GHQ had sized up Hampton's chief objective as meat. Meade was already bluing the air. The "goddamn rebels" had shot his promised "I will be vigilant" to Grant full of holes. They might even casually take a fling at City Point itself. This man Hampton was unpredictable. Off went a directive to General Davies. Move your available forces down the Jerusalem plank road and cut off Hampton's retreat as far down as the Nottoway River. And to Kautz: follow the retreating enemy down the road to Sycamore Church and attack them where you find them. You ought to be able to destroy them lumbering across the Blackwater River at Cook's Bridge.

At 8:30 the crushing truth dawned on Kautz. He spawned another missive. "The attack has developed itself as a foray on the cattle herd although nothing definite has been heard from that direction." On rolled Kautz's dispatch marathon. At 8:50 he was still hesitant about cattle. "I *suspect* the whole movement to be the capture of the cattle and the 1st District Cavalry."

At 9:15 Kautz reported again to Meade. Old Cap'n Belsches had paused at a "Mr. Rollins' " house on Walls Road to spread the fiction—though not to Kautz—that Hampton's force was 14,000, that they had swept the corral bare as an old beef bone. Kautz postscripted with "I have only about 500 men and two pieces of artillery."

By 9:15 he was moving along the Powhatan Road to Sycamore Church with squadrons of the 3rd New York and 11th Pennsylvania "to try and communicate on with the 1st District cavalry." His chances of doing this were, of course, anything but rosy. "I have no doubt the cattle guard and the 1st District Cavalry have been captured or routed."

At 12:30 Kautz and his command dusted into Sycamore Church to find that Rosser's men had left the encampment looking as if a prairie fire had given it a going-over. The only thing left unscorched was the little century-old church. Awaiting him were a number of dead: 1st District Cavalry troopers, four graybacks, and the sutlers. A profusion of dead horses lay swelling in the hot sun as if suddenly pregnant.

Requiring medical attention were several score of wounded, including ten of Hampton's men. Out of the woods emerged a few remnants of the 1st District Cavalry, who had managed to flee into the dawn shadows. They had a fearful tale to tell of the red whirlwind that struck the camp at break of day. From the scene of the 1st District Cavalry's debacle Kautz reported several hundred troopers, two majors and one captain taken prisoners. He failed to include six lieutenants. He was sanguine nevertheless. By now Kautz had recovered his poise. Legend attributed to him the remark, "Hampton has bought himself a herd of white elephants." What he actually said in his on the spot message was, "General Hampton has captured all the cattle and taken them away on the road leading south from this point. The cattle left here about sunrise. I do not think they can drive the cattle very far before they break down." He was at last convinced, "The attack was only to capture the cattle."

But entrapment of Hampton looked to Kautz like a sure thing. "I shall pursue them and endeavor to annoy them as much as possible." Annoy was hardly the word. The situation called for positive, aggressive action, not "annoying." With Davies' cavalry moving down the plank road to cut off Hampton's retreat and Kautz snapping at his tail and flanks, it looked easy, provided Kautz went at it without consulting his apprehensions too often. Kautz was faced with the opportunity of redeeming himself and recapturing the herd, but he closed his dispatch with an "out" in case he failed, "They have several hours start of me."

With this brave avowal of vengeance Kautz tore off down Walls Road. Never was the Chisholm Trail more generously splashed with cattle spoor than the road leading to Cook's Bridge over the Blackwater. Kautz had really underestimated the famished fury of desperately hungry men, or what *"coups de main"* ragtail rebels could pull off when they were inspired and prodded by bellies that had not tasted good red meat in months.

3

At ten o'clock Hampton's column crossed the rickety reconstruction of Cook's Bridge. He breathed easier. The Blackwater was behind him. He had lurking suspicions that bluecoats might somehow have sneaked down and destroyed the bridge. Fifteen miles of road had gentled the beeves somewhat. They marched along quietly between strings of troopers with captured herders ready to give expert cowhanding if needed. Shadburne's houn' dawgs tagged along contentedly.

Spurring to the south bridgehead Shadburne began counting the herd as it crawled across. The structure was shaky, wobbling uncertainly under the lumbering tread of the heavy bodies. Riding up to help keep tally came Major Reid Venable, Hampton's adjutant.

Pulling out of the road, Hampton summoned his commanders.

"General Rosser, cut loose and hurry your brigade down to the Jerusalem plank road. Don't stop till you get to Cap'n Belsches Mill. The Cap'n will ride with you. We've got to beat them to it. If we don't, we'll lose that steak dinner and I'm told Yankee prison fare isn't very palatable. Take a position across the road and hold it. Major Chew and Graham's Battery go with you. General Lee, have your men take over the rear and destroy the bridge behind you." Then to Dearing—who looked as youthful as the day he left West Point and now anxious to get back to write the big news to the sweetheart he would soon marry—"Move your men out as advance. The scouts will go ahead of you."

Drawing his troopers off the flanks of the herd, Tom Rosser sent Lige White's Comanches streaking off at a smart gait with Chew's guns rumbling after him. Dusting behind them, but not as fast, came the rest of the Laurel Brigade. Rosser remembered, "White moved off with his usual promptness and reached the point indicated just as the enemy got there; but White was able to secure the desired position which by nature was a strong one, and by dismounting his men he was able to hold it against a force much larger than his own. There was a large millpond on his left and a swamp on his right and the plank road was the only avenue by which the enemy could attack him."

Riding at Rosser's bridlehand old Cap'n Belsches was having the time of his life, happy as a boy on a picnic. His crowbait nag was putting her last best foot foremost.

"This calls for a celebration, general," opined the Cap'n. "Maybe we could stop at my place down near the mill for a julep—or two."

Rosser licked his lips, but he doubted it. He said so frankly. It looked as if he would find a fight and plenty of it instead of juleps "down near the mill." But he could almost taste them as the Cap'n expatiated on his julep-compounding skill and explained just why the mint should not be crushed and extolled the virtues of the jug of smooth, five-year-old palate-joy he had in hiding for the great day when the Confederacy won her fight.

While Rosser's men slipped ahead of Dearing's brigade Shadburne finished his count of the beeves and rode up to Hampton.

"General, there's two thousand, four hundred and eighty-five critters, not counting the cow."

"The cow! We'll eat her, too. She's beef any way you look at her."

Major Venable had a better suggestion. "Suppose we give her to General Mahone. His cow's gone dry."

"Agreed," roared Hampton.

The caravan trailed on. At the bridgehead Rooney Lee eased in his saddle until the last horseman of his rear point had slapped over the river. Then, he followed and ordered the engineers to blow up the bridge, but somebody had forgotten demolition charges. It was the expedition's only oversight. Burn it, ordered Lee, but the bridge wouldn't burn. Timbers were too green or too wet. Take it apart, urged Lee in desperation. They dismantled it fast and it was lucky they did. Downstream it swept piece by piece. Hardly had the last log floated away before Kautz's advance came pounding through the woods to dismount at shooting distance and open fire. Bullets began whipping up spurts of dust on the road. But a fight here was not on Hampton's agenda though Lee's men were already trading shots across the river. The get-away was the thing and the Blackwater balked the bluecoats.

But Lee's men couldn't resist taunting their pursuers with ribald yells and bellowings like the bullocks they had stolen. "Boo! Boo! Come on across Yanks and get your beef, if you can!"

Kautz cantered up as rifles began cracking. The best he could do was to stand on the river bank and gaze impotently at the insolent gray-backs firing random shots and hurling unprintable imprecations after them as they disappeared in a wall of dust with their four-legged swag. Through his glasses he watched Hampton's receding column. It was the last he would ever see of these fine, fat beeves—their dust. In a dispatch written as he waited on the edge of the Blackwater, Kautz despaired of the chase.

26

Fight for the Beefsteaks

Hampton's nondescript ponderous cattletrain meandered on. Five miles south of Cook's Bridge the road forked. Two routes lay before him. The prong leading to Belsches Mill was splotched with the leavings of Rosser's horse pressing towards the Jerusalem plank road. This was the way the raiders had come, but Hampton chose the second, veering south towards Hawkinsville on the plank road two miles below Belsches Mill where Rosser was no doubt by this time taking a position. It would give the blue pursuers something else to figure out, and the cattle more miles to lug their heavy bodies. But he had no other choice. It also added nearly ten more miles to the journey.

The dogies had been trekking virtually without rest since dawn when Rosser had snatched them from the luxuriant pastures on the James twenty-five miles away. They were tired. Their heads hung down; they seemed hardly able to lift their hooves, now dead-heavy; they were again moaning out their weariness and empty-bellies. Choking, powdery dust caked man and beast. The day simmered. Riders wilted. But rest was out of the question. This was no Chisholm Trail where everything halted for long siestas at midday. The bluecoats were hammering down the plank road in force and Kautz was presumably virtually breathing down their necks.

Presently the road sloped gently down to Neblitt's millstream that rippled across it like a shiny band of gold. Hampton rode ahead to let his horse dip his muzzle into the cool water. Then, spurring up the far slope, he kneed his horse off the roadside and drew rein. Shadburne rode up. As they sat there chatting a burst of gunfire from the northwest quavered through the hot afternoon.

"That's Rosser," observed Hampton, as he and Shadburne exchanged glances. "He got there first. Looks like we'll eat beefsteak after all, if he can whip them off. But he's got to whip 'em or hold 'em."

Heavier concussions throbbed to his ears.

"Graham's guns," remarked Shadburne as the pulsations pounded higher. "Sounds like that little mountain howitzer the boys took off Kautz last June ninth. It's got a music all its own."

Hampton made a quick decision. He called to Major Venable who trotted up followed by others of his staff.

Rapid fire orders sputtered. "We've got to support Rosser. The Yankees are piling it on him. It's the best hope they have of cutting us off. If they whip Rosser out of his position at Belches Mill and get to Hawkinsville ahead of us, we lose the herd. It's as simple as that. We can't take a chance. It's about two miles straight ahead to Hawkinsville and two miles up to Rosser."

Hampton was caught between two fires as he had anticipated. Kautz would soon be barking at his heels. That he expected, but it wasn't what worried him. Heaven only knew how many brigades—cavalry and infantry—Meade had sped down the Jerusalem plank road to intercept the rustlers and recover the meaty plunder. Hampton had crumpled Kautz's picket lines, captured one of his regiments and stolen the cattle he was supposed to protect. Kautz, he knew, would come on warily. He'd think twice, maybe three times, before tangling with the hungry gray wolves again.

"Captain Edelin: Order Colonel Miller to hurry ahead to Hawkinsville and up the plank road to Rosser's support. Order General Dearing to follow Miller. I'll wait for Lee's division to close up and ride with him and the herd."

The staffer whipped off in a flutter of dust. Hampton turned to his acting chief of staff.

"Major Venable: Take charge of the herd and prisoners. Major Ryals and Captain Henry will assist you. Watch your prisoners. Get more men from General Lee, if you need them. But we need the cattle more than the prisoners. We came to get beef and we're going to take it back with us. Move the column to Hawkinsville and bend south for Freeman's Ford across the Nottoway. Keep going towards Stony Creek till you reach our lines. I'll hold the plank road crossing with Lee, if necessary, until the cattle clear it. Sergeant Shadburne, ride with Major Venable. He'll need you."

The scout's face fell. He was itching for more fight. "Aw, general, can't I get into this little shooting match?"

Hampton laughed. "Haven't you had enough fighting for one day? Didn't I see you shooting everything in sight early this morning? Rosser told me you went hogwild with that big pistol. Major Venable needs you."

Hardly had Miller's and Dearing's men trotted ahead to

vanish in a pillar of dust before the herd went thirst-mad.
A fresh roadblock on the way to safety. They'd smelled
Neblitt's millstream afar. It came without warning. In a
surging, bawling roar they suddenly flooded off the road
and stampeded down the hillside towards the rivulet and
the millpond. There was no heading off the sea of horns
and hooves that careened down in a solid, lumbering, irresistible wall. Water they would have and God help man or
beast that intervened. Troopers, herders, sought to breast
the tide only to be swept aside by the torrent of panting,
sweating bodies cascading towards the cool, clear liquid.
In their fierce anxiety to get to water they spread out for
half a mile along the stream below the mill.

Hampton spurred further up the slope for a trying wait
while herders and his makeshift cowboys struggled with
the excited mass of cattle. The yihoos of the herders
echoed across the millpond and through the woods. It was
a rough and tumble affair.

"I'm going to send my houn' dawgs after them," said
Shadburne jamming spurs into his mount's bony flanks.

Hampton smiled as the scout cantered down the hill
emitting a long peculiar whistle the dogs knew well. They
came a-loping. In moments they were in full cry, baying
far down the stream, rounding up the recalcitrants. For
long minutes it had looked as if the herd would be scattered hopelessly over the countryside. Slowly—an age it
seemed to Hampton—the dogs yapped the truants back towards the road where the cowboy forced them in line.
Breathless, worn down, their muzzles dripping, they were
docile again. But priceless time that could not be recovered was lost, and sounds of battle over on the plank road
were rising. Sheets of musketry ripped the still air, apparently coming nearer. Rosser's dismounted veterans were

exchanging furious volleys with the bluecoats and giving ground.

The column resumed its trampling march and was surging up the slope when a courier on a hard-blown horse hightailed down a byroad from the north. Hampton sensed it—bad news—the moment the trooper scurried up on his breathless mount. Bluecoats were overlapping Rosser's right. They had a battery on the byroad and were plastering him. His men were down to ten rounds of ammunition apiece. He couldn't hold on too long. They'd soon be swarming all over him. Dearing and Miller had not yet reached him.

To the courier Hampton gave quick orders, "Get back the best way you can. Tell General Rosser, General Dearing and Colonel Miller are on the way. He must hold on till they get there."

Adhering to his belief in hitting his enemy with all the force he could throw in at the right time and place, Hampton hurried to apply his combat maxim—powerhouse attack. He ordered Rooney Lee to slip his division along the flanks of the herd, slide ahead and hurry over towards the fight on the plank road. One regiment was to guard the column and watch the rear. Though he had not too much to work with, Hampton had no fear of Kautz's stern chase. As Lee's men sped off, Hampton rode with them.

Where Rosser was the going was getting rougher. Henry Davies had piled down the plank road with cannon and over two thousand New York and Pennsylvania horse soldiers, tough hombres, who knew their business and were making it awfully hot for Rosser. Behind Davies came a brigade of veteran infantry. At the moment Davies' six-gun battery was dressing down the dismounted graycoats with shell and canister, pouring it onto Graham's guns on Rosser's right flank.

Lige White's Comanches, who had beaten Davies to the punch by hardly ten minutes, held a position across the road—Cap'n Belsches' millpond on their left, a swamp on their right. It looked unassailable, but Henry Davies was no ordinary foe. At twenty-seven, like Rosser, he had reached stardom the hard fighting way.

With characteristic audacity White played a fine game of bluff, shifting his men from point to point, suggesting he had strong backing. When Rosser and the rest of the Laurel Brigade came up, the dismounted 3rd New York was feeling round his right flank. Lige greeted Rosser with, "I'll hold on till hell or the millpond freezes over."

Said Rosser later, "I found White warmly engaged with the enemy, who were also dismounted and pushing through the swamp on his right and would have outflanked him and compelled him to withdraw."

Frank Myers, who was there, remembered: "White was assailed by a force of about five thousand cavalry and artillery, and after a stubborn fight, was forced to retire a mile, but by his strategy of keeping his men concealed, and by moving his flags from one point to another, he succeeded in deceiving the enemy and holding them in check until the arrival of Rosser with the remainder of the Laurel Brigade."

Across the pond graybacks were firing gibes as well as bullets.

"Hey, bluebellies!" they taunted. "Let us know when you get another bunch of fine cattle. We'll come after 'em."

"Gwan, you lanky rebel bastards!" growled back a Fed. "You'll be starved out long before then."

The sun was slanting and glistening across the millpond

when Dearing and Miller swept up the plank road to find
the bluecoats driving Rosser. They deployed in the nick
of time. Rosser's men were holding on by the skin of their
teeth. A score of dead and wounded lay on the road near
the mill. Davies was lavishing shot and shell with abandon.

Out of the growing dusk Hampton rode up with
Rooney Lee's men. It was as if the inspiring figure of another Richard Coeur de Lion had stepped out of the day
when knighthood was in flower. Hampton rose to his highest when hot action loomed. Now to settle the issue, throw
in Lee's force and crush the bluecoats before deep night
came on. His staff scurried off to Rosser, Miller, Dearing:
hold your flanks and clear the road. Rooney Lee's charging up it.

Vividly a 9th Virginia trooper recalled the scene:
"Hampton rode down in front of the line, making inquir-
ies, giving words of cheer, 'Keep cool, boys! We're going
in fast! Ride 'em down! Cut 'em down!' His moving figure
could be seen against the crimson sky from which the sun
had just disappeared. The guns (Davies) were flashing in
front of him, and behind him, and the meteor-like shells
were passing over his head. Such was the scene on which
fell the curtain of night. It was a scene typical of the picturesque Hampton who moved securely amidst the fire of
battle."

In the gathering twilight Hampton's battle orders were
carried out. Now he was ready. Piercingly shrill, his
bugler blew the Charge. Bugles down the line sang it out.
Hampton roweled his bay. With a mighty yelling that
roused horse and rider the grays hurled themselves up the
road in a dusky, clangorous tide. Sabers were raised for
the onset. Ahead of them carbines stabbed like red-hot
lances through the murk. Men and steeds went down,

but the impetuous mass of them kept going. Then they struck. Davies' troopers sagged under the onslaught, but recovered. In the black melee men cut and slashed and shouted and died. The bluecoats sagged again, wavered and wheeled. Through the night blue bugles suddenly sounded recall.

"Who that was there can ever forget the wild grandeur of the scene?" asked a participant in the raid. "The sun shedding its parting beams upon the battling hosts, the heavy plunging of shot and shell through the ranks of men and horses, the waving of battle flags, the galloping of officers, the defiant shouts of our men calling to the Yankees to 'come and get some beef for supper' . . . ?"

Davies' report of the fight was too succinct—no trimmings. He left unsaid what he should have said. Precious little credit he gave to men who had fought well and bled and died in the futile endeavor to cut off and destroy Hampton. Sullenly he withdrew in the dark. He probably realized that great opportunity had slipped from his grasp though he was to redeem himself two weeks later at the Vaughan Woods fight where he was brevetted Major General of Volunteers for gallant and distinguished conduct on the field.

2

As Hampton and Rooney Lee rode off to reenforce Rosser, Major Venable urged the weary column ahead. Crumpp! Crumpp! Chew's guns were slambanging away. Venable knew their sound by heart. He could hear them in his sleep—when he got any. It was Venable's big moment, or rather another one. Suddenly he was trail boss of a herd of nearly three thousand head of cattle. On him had devolved the duty of getting them to safety within the gray lines.

Twice before fate had tapped him at critical moments. At Chancellorsville, in the confusion and darkness after Jackson's fall, the fickle lady had led then-battery captain Reid Venable to Jeb Stuart's side for a dramatic under-fire reunion of two friends of prewar days. Stuart, cast suddenly in the understudy-to-Jackson role, tagged Venable on the spot. From that night Venable rode at Stuart's side until Yellow Tavern where again fate plucked at his sleeve. Pistol in hand he stood with Stuart and a handful of men trying vainly to stem Custer's plunging horse. When Stuart fell with a Michigan trooper's bullet in his groin, Reid Venable helped him off the field. To Venable the dying cavalier had willed one of his dearest possessions—the big gray horse the major was now riding.

Spurring alongside the column the major listened. Over on the plank road merry hell was breaking loose, but it was coming no nearer. That was a good sign. Rosser was at least holding them and Hampton was on the way. A host unto himself in any fight. The Hawkinsville bottleneck was still in gray hands. If the Yankees forced Rosser back that far, God knows what would happen to the herd of temporarily homeless cattle. But once clear of Hawkinsville the caravan could straggle southwards to Freeman's Ford over the Nottoway River and on to an area of comparative safety.

Beyond the top of the rise in the road Venable drew rein before a neat farmhouse framed amid beds of flowers and a white picket fence. At the front gate, a small bouquet of flowers in her hand, stood a slip of a girl staring in wonderment at the river of cattle plodding into the sunset. The men had already spotted her and were bubbling

over with fun. "Ain't she a darlin'?" "Hi, little miss! Got
a big sister pretty as you?" The girl was fascinated. The
strange pageant had appeared out of the twilight as by the
rub of a magic lamp. All at once the road had filled up
with cattle and armed horsemen jingling like Christmas
reindeer.

Pulling his mount over to the gate Venable doffed his
battered hat. "Good evening, little lady. Could you tell
me how far it is to Hawkinsville?"

"About a mile, sir." She gave Reid Venable as sweet a
smile as he had seen in many a moon.

"Are all these cattle yours, sir?" inquired the young
miss.

Venable smiled. "I'm not quite sure yet. If we can get
'em past Hawkinsville, they might be ours. If we can't,
they'll most likely belong to somebody else."

She looked puzzled.

"You see," he explained while his horse nibbled the
roadside grass, "these cattle belonged to the Yankees till
early this morning. Then, suddenly, they decided they
wanted to belong to the Confederates."

She caught on with a merry laugh. "Oh, you mean you
stole them?"

"Well," admitted the officer, who thought he detected a
hint of the heather in her voice, "we helped them make
up their minds about it."

"In the Hielands we'd say you lifted them," she volunteered as Venable dismounted.

"That's exactly what we did. Lifted them from the Yankees. Now we're trying to joggle them to Petersburg before the Yankees come along and take them back."

She handed him her little bouquet. "Maybe you'd like
to have my flowers. They're sweet."

"They must be sweet, if you raised them," said Venable. "Thank you. I'll take them to Petersburg." He drew in their perfume and stuck them in a buttonhole in his jacket. They brought back a garden he hadn't seen for three years. Might never see again if things kept getting worse. His eyes ran over the neatness about the house and farm buildings, the trim garden and fall flowers upstanding like late sentinels.

He started to remount. "But you haven't told me your name."

"Margaret Donnan, sir."

He repeated it. "Margaret Donnan. Straight from the Hielands, I presume."

"My father's a Hieland mon, sir."

"How old are you, Margaret?"

"Twelve, sir."

A particularly heavy burst of musketry smote the afternoon air.

"I hope you won't be fighting the Yankees near our house," she said.

"I hope we won't have to. Our men are already fighting them over on the plank road. I think we'll beat them off. If we don't, I'll ride back and see that your home is protected."

Her momentary fright vanished. "Your Confederate cattle look tired. They need a rest."

"They are tired. We're all tired but we won't get much rest till we reach Petersburg."

His foot was on the stirrup iron when a stocky, level-eyed man came round the house.

"Here's my father now," said the girl.

"Mr. Donnan, I'm Major Venable, Hampton's Corps, Lee's army."

"And pleased to meet you, sir," replied Donnan with a burr. "I see ye hae been moving some kine. I heard ye lifted them frae the Northrons early this morning."

"That's what your nice daughter says, Mr. Donnan: we lifted them."

"Aye, the lassie was athinking of the Hielands and how they did in the auld days. Mony's the kine that were lifted then and by the best o' men. Well, war is that a-way. General Lee's laddies will be needing guid red meat. They look like scarecrows."

Suddenly the young lady espied the lone cow wearily dawdling along amid the stream of bullocks.

"There's a cow, father," she exclaimed.

"One cow," said the major. "She just came along with us when we lifted the steers."

"Maybe she wants to be Confederate, too," suggested Margaret prettily.

"I reckon that was it," laughed the major.

The Scotchman smiled. "Coo meat is good meat."

"Oh, father, look!" The little girl pointed to an exhausted steer, that had straggled out of the line, spraddled his legs and refused to go a step further. A herder began plying his bullwhip on the drooping, panting animal.

"Stop it!" screamed Margaret. "You hurt him."

"That's what I'm aimin' to do, lady," said the herder. "Only way to make him move on."

The major cut in. "Lay off."

"This critter ain't got another mile in him," said the cowboy apologetically. "He'll be dead by night."

"Maybe we'd better shoot him," said the officer. "It'll keep the Yankess from getting him."

The herder was noncommittal. He didn't really give a damn. He was on his way to his funeral anyway—or so he thought.

"He ain't going to live, lady," said the herder.

"But please don't shoot him."

The major spoke. "But the Yankees are coming behind us and we don't want them to get back even a broken down steer."

"Please, please, don't."

"Margaret!" expostulated her father.

"I'm sorry, father." But tears glistened in her eyes as she apologized.

The major made up his mind in a hurry. Yankees **or** Margaret? Which?

"Would you like to have him, Margaret?"

"Oh, I would, I would. I'll take care of him."

"Well, Margaret, he's yours. But you'd better get him out of the way fast. The Yankees will be along here in an hour or two. Mr. Donnan, give him some water and a place to graze where the Yankees won't find him and you'll have some mighty good beefsteaks, if he lives."

"That I'll do," assured the Scotchman. "A fine, fat steer he is."

Major Venable turned to the herder. "Drive him into the barnyard. And see that you come back," added the major sternly. "I'll wait here."

Slowly, under the nudgings of the cowboy's horse, the big ox trundled off around the house.

The Scot eyed the major who had remounted. "It's too bad ye're fighting amang yourselves here in America. Ye'll both be sorry one of these days, but it won't bring back those that's gone. Scotland was once torn like this. Brother against brother. The clans quarreled and spilled blood all through the glens and the Hielands. Ye've got a guid countree where as Bobby Burns said, 'The honest man though e'er sae poor, Is king of men for a' that.' I've kept out of your family broil, but here it is on my doorstep.

Guid luck to you, sir. And mickle thanks for the beefsteaks."

Major Venable smiled. "I reckon you'd better thank
General Hampton."

"A great mon, and soldier, they tell me," said the
Scotchman.

"All of that, Mr. Donnan. Margaret, take good care of
your steer."

"I will, sir, I will."

"I'm afeard, sir," said the Scotchman, "she'll never let
us make beefsteak out of him."

Venable spurred his horse along the flank of the column. Once he gazed back. She was waving to him. Now
for Hawkinsville.

27

The Longhorns Are Coming to Town!

Deep night shrouded the Nottoway when the beeves floundered through Freeman's Ford. The critical stretch of the journey was behind them, but there could be no absolute sanctuary until they crossed the Weldon Railroad. Scores of troopers in the ranks were sleeping in their saddles from sheer exhaustion, horses stumbling and rolling against each other. It was after midnight when the dead beat caravan straggled into bivouac on open ground near Stony Creek. Troopers, prisoners, horses, dogs literally dropped in their tracks. The cattle, now well beyond Federal redemption, slumped down in a great cool meadow. For the last few miles they had to be bullwhipped ceaselessly. It was a long, long trail, twenty hours afoot. Under the glow of a splendid moon they sank down, too weary to protest even against gnawing hunger.

But there was no sleep for Major Reid Venable whose saddle had hardly cooled for twenty-four hours, nor for the bone-weary, watchful graybacks with drooping eyelids patrolling the road behind. With night-wise, tireless George Shadburne to guide him Venable rode ahead to the inter- section of the Flat Foot Road. Versed in the perilous art of infiltrating the gray lines in the dark Shadburne felt his way until he contacted "Matt" Butler's pickets to whom Venable gave a message for their commander. The beef- steaks are ours and just a few miles off. Send detachments out to meet them. It was the first direct word from Hamp- ton since he romped off for Grant's cattle pens by the James.

Leaving a sizable outpost near Ebenezer Church Hamp- ton moved his command up the plank road to turn off for Wilkinson's Bridge where he bivouacked. He said, "Fear- ing the enemy might throw a force around my left so as to interpose between the cattle and my command, I deter- mined not to follow the enemy who were falling back but to move to Wilkinson's Bridge where I could check any flank movement." It was a needless precaution. In the dark Davies and his bluecoats retired up the road, trailed by a heavy rearguard to keep an eye on Hampton in case he gave chase. Apparently one clash with him was enough for Davies. One would think, reading the reports, that Davies, not Hampton, was the pursued.

As for Kautz: hours long his troopers wrestled inex- pertly with bridging the Blackwater. It was late when they finished a crossable footway and pushed on after Hamp- ton. At nine o'clock his advance collided with the outpost Hampton had left on the road just east of Hawkins- ville. Kautz's soldiers, warily mincing their way toward the Jerusalem plank road, ran into a spatter of gunfire that flashed like oversized glowworms. The moon was up but the road steeped in blackness. After a fast ten-minute give and take of lead Kautz drew back two miles, threw out pickets and barricaded himself across the road for the night. His old malady had assailed him: excessive caution. The cattle were far beyond his reach now, but he didn't know it. His pull back was complicated by the assumption that Hampton's force was thousands greater than his own. "Had it not been dark," he told his diary obliquely, "it would not have been advisable as Hampton greatly outnumbered our force. My main hope was that Davies had pushed down the Jerusalem plank road to cut off the enemy's retreat. Next morning I sent to the plank road but could learn nothing of Davies' command." Nor of Hampton's either. Davies at the moment was making tracks back to his camp east of Petersburg.

Trapping Hampton should have been easy. Back in July Grant had supplied the right words for redeeming such a dilemma: "Boldness was all that is wanted." But precious little of this priceless ingredient of war characterized the pursuit of the big, bold rustler and the cattle he had pilfered.

Next morning Hampton's split column reunited at the fork of the Flat Foot Road. Major Venable hurried up.

"Congratulations, sir," said Venable, as he saluted and reported "all present and accounted for except one head of cattle."

"Congratulations to you, major," replied Hampton, his great beard wreathed in smiles. "How did you lose that one?"

"I traded him off to a young lady," said Venable, grinning as he added, "for a little bunch of flowers." He drew Margaret Donnan's tiny, drooping bouquet out of his jacket. Hampton laughed heartily. "The critter had collapsed in front of her home the other side of Hawkinsville. He couldn't stagger a step farther. I started to shoot him to keep the Yankees from getting him back, but the little lady begged me so hard not to do it I gave him to her. She's a Scotch lassie and her father very much of a man of the Hielands. He's got a burr like a file."

"The Yankees might grab him just to show something for their chase," said Hampton.

"Not from that Scotchman, general—dead or alive."

Towards noon dust clouds up ahead proclaimed cavalry coming, this time from the right direction. With their new brigadier's guidon streaming in the van, John Dunovant's South Carolina squadrons came pounding out to escort the wayfarers into the lines and assist the migration of the drove of huge beeves now sullenly bellowing out their disgust at the paltry breakfast they'd snatched as they moseyed along.

The Beefsteak Raid was over.

2

Legends still abound of the gala promenade of Grant's stolen cattle through the war-torn town. For Petersburg it was a red-letter day. The longhorns were coming to town! On September 19—the day Grant steamed up the James back to City Point—the dogies were herded onto the Boydton plank road and pointed for Petersburg and cavalry's last big show-off of the war. The cattle were sleek after two days' grazing on the thick green meadows along Hatcher's Run. Today they tromped along solemnly, orderly, unconcerned by their tumultuous greeting.

The town was agog. The sidewalks jammed. Graybeards and boys, women, girls and even tots in their mothers' arms lined the sidewalks to welcome the Beefsteak Rangers, as the Richmond Dispatch dubbed them. Flags fluttered, handkerchiefs waved. Shoals of pretty girls blew kisses from bright red lips.

Absent was the pomp and spectacle so loved by the fallen Stuart—mock charges at breakneck speed, sabers *en tierce;* horse artillery blazing furiously at mock enemies. Revived today—if only for a little hour—was the romance that once invested the gray riders. The Confederacy was holding on for dear life, but the "kill" was near at hand. Her very existence dangled on a single skein, something to eat. Here, waddling along the street, came over two million pounds of prize Yankee beef. Little wonder the sidewalks cheered.

Sabers flashed, pennons streamed out, but the old splendor had faded, lost somewhere along the Confederacy's hard, bloody road. Even so, it was a great day for the horse soldiers.

In the van, riding like the Cid, his guidon rippling out its pride, was the man who'd led the venturesome cattle-snatchers, Wade Hampton. Right beside him was the redoubtable George Shadburne, looking a bit uncomfortable with all those folks staring at him and wondering who he was.

The generals and the colonels were there, marching at the head of their men. Huge Tom Rosser, taking his bows like a finished actor—sleepy-eyed Lige White, whose "Comanches" tried to steal the show, to whom the smiles of the ladies were pure nectar—Rooney Lee, fierce as a tiger in battle but now gentle as a lamb, blowing kisses to his sweetheart in the crowds—Lanneau and his engineer boys, who'd bridged the Blackwater so handily—Preston Chew with his guns that rumbled along making as much noise as they pleased—Jimmy Dearing, idol of Petersburg since he came to her rescue on June ninth.

Loudest of all did the sidewalks hooray for the jingle-jangle boys, lean, bronzed and hilarious, whose accouterments rattled like all get-out and whose eyes turned to the pretty girls in the crowds like needles to the pole. Not much preening and grooming had they done. Blackwater mud still splattered their boots and horses' bellies. Unshorn, a little red-eyed from loss of sleep, they were nevertheless as bright as new Yankee dollars and quippy as the end-man in a minstrel. Riding alongside the herd they seemed particularly anxious to display their skill as two-day-old cowhands.

Least happy of the paraders were the captured herders. Not yet did they know that their willing, though enforced, cooperation would win them reprieve from a prison camp.

Yonder at Rosser's side rode old Cap'n Belsches on his beat-up nag. Pride literally ran out of his eyes. Riding through Petersburg with General Rosser was a legacy he'd pass on to his grandchildren. As cheers split the air he turned to Rosser, "General, we ain't had the julep yet. Don't you reckon we could find time for just one. I brung along the fixins." He patted a small jug strapped to his saddle.

Rosser's eyes brightened. "Cap'n, that's a capital suggestion. We'll find the time all right."

Nor were the houn' dawgs forgotten in the general jubilation. Perched precariously on Chew's caissons they got a big hand. Had they realized what they were sitting on, their canine aplomb might not have been so perfect.

And the horses: a little gaunter perhaps, a little less light of foot, but today stepping along as if they too had something to be proud of. Here and there strutted a mount with a wreath of flowers round his neck reminiscent of the old days when every day was show day for the cavalry.

Had the beeves been princes of the realm their reception could hardly have been more royal. But the pageant must have its splash of color. The patient, indispensable lead steers came into their own. Rainbowed and festooned with bright ribbons of torn up petticoats supplied by the ladies of the town, they plodded along, little aware that the commissary's butchers and skinners would soon welcome them with sharpened knives.

A weather-beaten foot soldier, with a day off from the lines, growled out his disgust at Hampton's boys running off with the laurels, "The cavalry has all the fun. Wish old Billy Mahone'd turn us loose. We'd clean Grant out of everything 'cept his skin."

As the column turned west on Washington Street the mounted band of the 7th Virginia struck up cavalry's own rollicking refrain:

> *If you want to have a good time*
> *Jine the cav-al-ree!*

Down the ranks the song broke lustily from over two thousand throats. They meant it. They'd had a good time. And profitable one, too.

> *If you want to catch hell*
> *Jine the cav-al-ree!*

Then a pause, and a voice raised words dear to Southern hearts—

> *A hundred months have passed, Lorena,*
> *Since last I held that hand in mine,*
> *And felt the pulse beat fast, Lorena,*
> *Though mine beat faster far than thine.*

The ranks picked up the strain. Hats off, boys! It was dead Jeb Stuart's favorite. Could Jeb be riding unseen in the column on a ghostly charger sharing in the fun and the glory? He wouldn't have missed it for the world.

But the electrifying word "Beef! Beef!" had already sped on to every emaciated Johnny Reb in the thirty miles of bitterly held trenches, from Lee's right wing poised beyond Hatcher's Run and curving round Petersburg like a lover's arm, running northwards to Drewry's Bluff and up to the gray outpost keeping watch near White Oak Swamp east of Richmond.

3

Ulysses Grant returned from his visit to Sheridan in the Valley to find his desk showered with glum reports. Explanations blossomed like the goldenrod then gilding Virginia's fields and roadsides. The big Federal base was still jumpy. Meade was positive imaginary gray legions were marshaling for all-out assault on the war center. Nerves were to be racked for weeks to come. Kautz's pickets heard strange noises at night down Blackwater Swamp way. They sham-battled with phantom horsemen tearing through the dark. Telltale, jittery dispatches of aftermath dot the pages of the Official Records. "Rebel cavalry are massing on the Blackwater." The river and swamp became even more sinister than they were. The commander of the new outpost at Sycamore Church (where Rosser had demolished the 1st District) sounded a grave alarm— gray cavalry was moving in heavy force, had reached the Blackwater and was no doubt planning a descent on City Point.

Meade welcomed Grant "home" with a telegram, "I am glad to hear of your return." He most certainly was. Hardly had the loss of the herd hit the headlines before Northern newspapers excoriated him. Investigation got nowhere. Cover-up seemed to have been the first thought. Speculation as to who was responsible for the exposed position of the herd never broke into the open. The name of a high officer involved is still unrevealed. General Humphreys even hinted at something in the nature of treason.

Kautz had one consolation. His men rounded up about fifteen beeves that had strayed or broken down on the way. But he failed to find the worn-out ox Major Venable presented to bright, smiling Margaret Donnan.

In his diary Kautz blasted the herders, laying on them the blame for not opening the corral the moment Rosser's men attacked the cattle guard. "Had they turned the cattle out and stampeded them the enemy would have had some trouble." But it doesn't explain the listless, unspirited pursuit of Hampton. As for the herders: they were no cowards. Six of them died of Confederate bullets to be buried, incidentally, in nameless graves on the spot. Even the records have forgotten them. They rendered Grant much needed service.

Kautz exonerated himself: "Fortunately no blame could be attached to my command. I was holding a line at the time fifteen miles in length with about fourteen hundred men. I had only a few days previous represented the danger of the capture of the herd as also the weakness of my line and the misuse of cavalry and that we were doing virtually duty that could have been done better by infantry and properly belonged to that branch of the service. Such a line as I held was a mere web against the force Hampton brought against it which was estimated by the enemy at 6000 men."

There was no such estimate by the "enemy." Hampton's force was about half of Kautz's figure, 3000 to be precise!

Hampton's report had a modest glow though it failed

utterly to reveal his own audacity. Nor did it convey a whisper of the staggering physical facts of the raid. Brilliant as was Stuart's Chambersburg Raid the year before, it netted no such welcome boon for the stomachs of Lee's thousands of hungry soldiers as did Hampton's swoop on Grant's big corral. In the inflated currency of the Confederacy, Hampton's capture represented millions of dollars, since first grade beef, if available at all, brought fabulous prices per pound.

Said Hampton: "My command returned to their old quarters after an absence of three days, during which they had marched upward of 100 miles, defeating the enemy in two fights and bringing from his lines in safety a large amount of captured property, together with 304 prisoners. Of the 2486 cattle captured 2468 have been brought in and I hope to get the remaining ones. Three guidons were taken and eleven wagons brought in safely, several others having been destroyed. Three camps of the enemy were burned, after securing from them some very valuable stores, including quite a number of blankets. My loss was 10 killed, 47 wounded and 4 missing."

After paying due tribute to the conduct of his officers and men Hampton added, "I cannot close my report without notice of the conduct of the scouts who were with me. Sergeant Shadburne, who gave me the information about the cattle, acted as guide to General Rosser, accompanied the leading regiment in its charge, kept his party always in the front and acted with conspicuous gallantry. Sergeant Hogan, also displayed great activity, intelligence and boldness. Of the scouts Sergeant McCalla, First South Carolina Regiment, a most valuable man, was killed and three others wounded."

In a letter to Hampton, General Lee conferred the accolade on the beefsteak raiders: "You will please convey to the officers and men of your command my thanks for the courage and energy with which they executed your orders, by which they had added another to the list of important services rendered by the cavalry during the present campaign."

From the statistics-minded Richmond *Dispatch* came "The Federal commissaries buy beeves of the largest size for the use of their armies in Virginia. The beeves taken in Hampton's late expedition are judged, by a London grazier, to weigh 800 pounds net. 2,486 beeves at 800 pounds would make an aggregate of 1,988,800 pounds, or within a fraction of 2,000,000 pounds. This, distributed in daily rations of a pound each, would feed 1000 men for nearly 2,000 days, 10,000 men for 200 days, 50,000 for 40 days, and so forth." It should be remembered that the raiders—the first comers—had topped off their beefsteaks with sardines and pickles and other gastronomic delights looted from the Yankee sutlers at Sycamore Church.

Comically enough, the City Point correspondent of a New York paper—he who had journeyed to Coggin's Point and marveled at the vast herd grazing so peacefully —informed his editor that Kautz by a lightning pursuit had recaptured the cattle within twelve hours after Hampton's snatch.

But the Washington *Star* disagreed and dished out the bitter truth:

"The correspondent of the New York *Tribune* wires from the front at Petersburg claiming that all our cattle captured by the enemy from the James River corral were recaptured by our cavalry. We regret to say that the *Tribune* correspondent is not well informed. We have recaptured at last account precisely one bullock, an unfortunate animal with a broken leg

whose fearful bellowings in a piece of woods attracted
our cavalry to the place, and the woods having been
carefully reconnoitered, surrounded and penetrated,
the recapture above mentioned was successfully made.
The cattle account therefore stands: Captured by the
enemy 2487; recaptured, 1; missing, the whole herd.
It seems that the rebels kept up a pother by way
of a feint in front of the raid while their cavalry were
making a 100 mile circuit by the Blackwater Swamp
and so around to the James River, in our rear. As a
piece of raiding rascality it was perfect."

Nor could Grant himself refrain from bestowing well-
earned laurels. He recognized Hampton's feat as a deed at
arms which cavalry could well be proud of. In reporting
his loss, he recorded, "The enemy's cavalry under General
Hampton got in behind us, and drove off a large number
of beef cattle. It was a fair capture, much needed by the
Confederates." This from Grant was praise indeed.

After the furor of the raid had died down Grant invited several high officers, including General Kautz, to
dine with him at his headquarters. Following a beefless
meal, segars were handed around. Smoke curled upwards
in clouds that filled the mess tent. Presently a guest ventured a leading question, "General, how long will it take
you to starve out Lee and capture Richmond?" Grant
flicked the ashes from his Havana, then replied quietly,
"Forever, general, if you keep feeding Lee's army with
beef."

Cheeks reddened. Whose? Nobody ever said. Taciturn
Grant kept on puffing.

But from President Lincoln came the aptest description
of Hampton's beefsteak raid: "It was the slickest piece of
cattle stealing I ever heard of."

NOTES AND ACKNOWLEDGMENTS

1. The humorous set-to between General Grant and the old lady whose cow had vanished that opens this book was still a lively topic in the countryside when this writer was a boy at a farm-school near Hanover Junction, now Doswell, Virginia. This rail intersection, twenty miles north of Richmond, enjoyed fame and strategic importance hardly less than the Confederate capital itself during the massive Lee-Grant battles of May and June 1864. Quarles Mill, scene of the lady's whimsical encounter with the Union supreme commander, was barely five miles from the Junction. In time, legend invested the lady with a halo and the episode itself with a variety of versions.

2. Raids—bold cavalry dashes behind and around enemy armies; deep, quick thrusts into hostile country to slash railroad and telegraph lines; stabs at supply trains and bases, and then the get-away fights—quickly assumed a major role in the grim business of civil war. By the end of the war, raid technique had been developed almost to a fine art. Chief ingredients of raiding success were speed and audacity. Fully a score of well-known raiders, blue and gray, chalked up daring, dramatic adventures. Several of them seemingly possessed the sinister attributes of phantoms—so speedily, so mysteriously did they strike and vanish from the scene of their "crimes." To their resourceful, take-any-chance leaders these daring forays brought wide renown.

Jeb Stuart set the raid pattern in June, 1862, on his spectacular ride entirely around McClellan's huge army crouched at Richmond's doorstep. His chief object was information: exact location of the Federal right wing. On Stuart's findings Lee based the strategy that drove McClellan back in disaster and brought fame to Stuart.

Grierson's Raid through Mississippi and Louisiana in 1863 (basis of a recent motion picture), destructive as it was of railbed and rolling stock, served the far larger purpose of, in Grant's own words, "attracting the attention of the enemy from the main movement against Vicksburg." This one exploit placed Grierson in the company of the best of the successful raiders.

Dahlgren's Raid, west prong of Judson Kilpatrick's abortive in-and-out plan to liberate hundreds of Federal prisoners on Belle Isle at Richmond, penetrate the city and perhaps capture the executive heads of the Confederacy, fizzled out miserably. This operation, touted as the possible "greatest feat of the war," ended disastrously in a flow of blood and the death of the daring young soldier who led it.

Sheridan's bruising raid on Richmond in May, 1864, came in sight of the city, heard church bells tolling ominously for his approach. He failed to capture the city though he killed the master raider himself, Jeb Stuart, at Yellow Tavern. Stuart's death alone was well-nigh a mortal hurt for the Confederacy. What more could the blue raider have accomplished?

Wilson's Raid through Alabama in 1865 was more of a destructive march-through than a raid. By then the South was virtually gutted, her manpower shattered. Highlight of Wilson's Raid was capture of the fleeing chief executive of the prostrate Confederacy.

In the West, gray raider John Hunt Morgan walked in glory for a time though his most spectacular dash across the Ohio into Indiana and Ohio, but accomplished little beyond frightening the countryside out of its wits and establishing the Confederacy's farthest-north penetration.

Jeb Stuart's Chambersburg Raid into Pennsylvania netted important results: intelligence, capture of prominent citizens to be used as hostages, and 1200 head of horseflesh, plus President Lincoln's celebrated wisecrack: "When I was a boy we used to play a game—three times 'round, and out. Stuart has been around McClellan twice. If he goes 'round him once more, gentlemen, McClellan will be out."

Big raids, little raids, middle-sized raids, and even a locomotive raid, adorn Civil War annals. Yet the raid that perhaps met the most acute, pressing need of the moment was Wade Hampton's cattle raid that rustled almost three thousand fat beeves from Grant's big corral on the James directly behind his blue army 100,000 strong. Broad statement, that, in light of so many dazzling exploits to compete with it. Yet Hampton and his raiders brought back millions of pounds of red beef for Lee's half-starved veterans manning the trenches before Richmond and Petersburg, men whose stomachs, shriveled up like empty pouches, were filled only with hope of something to eat—and little of that.

Up to now Hampton's cattle raid has received little attention. It is told here in detail for the first time. The author has purposely highlighted this operation against a backdrop of the thunderous battles around Petersburg.

3. New or little-known figures come onstage in this book. General August Valentine Kautz plays a far larger role in this episode than history has accorded him. He commanded Grant's cattle guards, the cavalry that kept watch over the huge corral at Coggin's Point on the James when Wade Hampton came a-knocking with his lean, lanky troopers hungry for even the sight of beefsteak on the hoof—or off. And there's George Shadburne, gray scout extraordinaire, whose story has only been nibbled at. Then, Molly Tatum, the swamp girl, who played a strange role only to vanish, leaving no trail beyond a few entries in the regimental files buried in the National Archives. And the extras: Grant's cowboys whom the Quartermaster and Commissary records call herders. They, too, were part of this show though up to now little credit has been given them.

4. I am indebted to many who have given freely of their time and suggestion, but to none more than my lifelong friend, Walter T. McCandlish of Petersburg, Virginia. An ardent student of the Civil War, he is perhaps without a peer in his intimate knowledge of the Petersburg battlefields. He knows this military area by heart, by regiments, by commanders, and by scores of sidelights overlooked by historians of the larger aspects. Without his help and advice I could not have written this book. With him as my guide I spent a fascinating day riding the roads taken by Hampton and his raiding squadrons. Many of the landmarks of that parlous era still stand. Black-

water Swamp is just as forbidding now as when it echoed with gunfire of the *petite guerre* that blazed behind Grant's lines. Even the little white house where the Scotch lassie, Margaret Donnan, lived still gazes up the dusty road. But Molly Tatum's abode and the road she lived on have been claimed by the inexorable swamp waters.

To the daughters of General Kautz, Mrs. Alvan Read and Mrs. John Beall of New York, and to his daughter-in-law, Mrs. Austin Kautz of Washington, I make a special bow. These ladies not only helped me find their father's unpublished war diary, but supplied me with many intimate facts about him. I am most grateful to them.

My appreciation goes, too late I am grieved to say, to Major Joseph Mills Hanson, former Historian of the Petersburg National Military Park. Mourned by all who knew him, Major Hanson passed away during the writing of this book. Yet he generously gave me permission to use his research on Hampton's cattle raid and the map he made twenty years ago to illustrate a newspaper article on the subject.

I am grateful likewise to my son, Samuel V. Boykin, of Arlington, Virginia, for invaluable assistance in checking the voluminous regimental records at the Archives and for research at the War College, Washington.

My thanks are due also to Mrs. Elizabeth Tyler Miles, of Charlottesville, for her descriptions, passed down in the family to her, of Grant's dusty veterans as they swung past the home of her grandfather, President John Tyler, en route to the great pontoon bridge across the James nearby.

I owe a further debt to my friends, Mary and Mortimer Price of Charlottesville, for their interest in this project and their suggestions thereon. With these ardent Civil War *aficionados* I first discussed the idea of the Beefsteak Raid.

My research pilgrimage has led to many places where I have received unfailing, courteous assistance. Among them are the National Archives, War College, and Library of Congress at Washington; the Alderman Library, University, Virginia; Confederate Museum and Virginia Historical Society at Richmond. Nor should I forget the long-distance aid given me by the Washington State Historical Society at Tacoma.

For many favors cheerfully rendered I am again indebted to Mrs. Virginia Corey and Mrs. Robert Hoskins, of the Alderman Library's Photostatic Department; and lastly, to my amanuensis, Lois De Bell, of Charlottesville, this being the fifth book she has typed so excellently for me.

EDWARD BOYKIN

Charlottesville, Virginia
April, 1960

BIBLIOGRAPHY

BOOKS

Alexander, E. Porter, *Military Memoirs of a Confederate*, 1907.
Badeau, Adam, *Military History of General U. S. Grant*, 1885.
Battles and Leaders of the Civil War, 4 vols., Century Company, 1887-1888.
Beale, G. W., *A Lieutenant of Cavalry in Lee's Army*, 1918.
Bernard, George S., *War Talks of Confederate Veterans*, 1892.
Blackford, W. W., *War Years with Jeb Stuart*.
Bradford, Gamaliel, *Confederate Portraits*, 1917.
Bradlee, Francis, B. C., *Blockade Running During the Civil War*, 1925.
Brooks, U. R., *Butler and His Cavalry*, 1909.
Catton, Bruce, *A Stillness at Appomattox*, 1953.
Coffin, Charles C., *Redeeming the Republic*, 1890.
Collis, Septima M., *A Woman's War Record*, 1889.
Cooke, John Esten, *Mohun*, 1893.
———, *Wearing of the Grey*, 1867.
Dame, William Meade, *From the Rapidan to Richmond*, 1924.
Davis, Burke, *Jeb Stuart, The Last Cavalier*, 1958.
Dolph, Edward Arthur, *Sound Off—Soldier Songs*, 1929.
Douglas, H. Kyd, *I Rode With Stonewall*, 1940.
Freeman, Douglas Southall, *R. E. Lee*, 4 vols., 1934.
———, *Lee's Lieutenants*, 3 vols., 1942-1944.
Gilmor, Colonel Harry, *Four Years in the Saddle*, 1866.
Harrison, M. Clifford, *Home to the Cockade City*, 1942.
Humphreys, Henry H., *Andrew Atkinson Humphreys*, 1924.
Jones, J. B., *A Rebel War Clerk's Diary*, 1866.
Jones, V. C., *Eight Hours Before Richmond*, 1957.
———, *Gray Ghosts and Rebel Raiders*, 1955.
Livermore, Thomas L., *Days and Events*, 1920.
McCabe, Captain W. Gordon, *Venables of Virginia*, "Obituary of Andrew Reid Venable," n.d.
McCarthy, Carlton, *Minutiae of Soldier Life*, 1884.
Macartney, C. E., *Grant and His Generals*, 1953.
McClellan, Henry B., *Campaigns of Stuart's Cavalry*, 1885.
McDonald, Captain Wm. N., *A History of the Laurel Brigade*, 1907.
Meade, Captain George G., *Life and Letters of George Gordon Meade*, 1913.

Meade's Headquarters—1863-1865, *Letters of Colonel Theodore Lyman,* 1922.

Merrill, Samuel Hill, *Campaigns of the 1st. Maine and 1st. D. C. Cavalry,* 1866.

Michie, Peter S., *Life and Letters of Emory Upton,* 1885.

Myers, Frank M., *The Comanches,* 1911.

Neese, George M., *Three Years in the Confederate Horse Artillery,* 1911.

Opie, John N., *A Rebel Cavalryman,* 1899.

Page, Charles A., *Letters of a War Correspondent,* 1899.

Personal Memoirs of U. S. Grant, 2 vols.

Photographic History of the Civil War, 10 vols., 1911.

Plum, W. R., *Military Telegraph During the Civil War.*

Porter, Horace, *Campaigning with Grant,* 1906.

Rauscher, Frank, *Music on the March,* 1892.

Schaff, Morris, *Spirit of Old West Point,* 1907.

Sinclair, Harold, *The Horse Soldiers,* 1956.

Thomason, John W., Jr., *Jeb Stuart,* 1930.

Wellman, Manly Wade, *Giant in Gray,* 1949.

———, *Ride Rebels,* 1959.

Wilson, James H., *Under the Old Flag,* 1912.

PAPERS, MAGAZINES, RECORDS

Andrew Reid Venable Papers, Virginia Historical Society, Richmond.

Cavalry Journal, 1934.

Century Magazine.

Confederate Veterans Magazine, various volumes.

Confederate Columns, Richmond *Times-Dispatch* and other newspapers in the South.

Contemporary newspapers, Richmond, Petersburg, and Washington.

Diary of August Valentine Kautz.

"Grant Before Appomattox—Notes of a Confederate Bishop," *Atlantic Monthly,* 1932.

Harper's Pictorial History of the Great Rebellion, 1868.

Harper's Weekly.

Henry B. McClellan Papers, Virginia Historical Society, Richmond.

Land We Love, 1866-1869.

Leslie's Weekly.

Official Records of the Union and Confederate Armies.

Regimental, Commissary and Quartermaster Records, National Archives, Washington.

Register of Graduates of the U.S.M.A., West Point Alumni Foundation.

Scribner's Magazine.

Southern Historical Society Papers, 49 vols., 1876-1944.

Thomas Lafayette Rosser Papers, Alderman Library, University of Virginia.

Virginia Cavalcade, Virginia State Library.

Washington Historian, Washington State Historical Society, Tacoma.

Index

MA